CALIFORNIA
GARDENS:
CREATING A
NEW EDEN

CALIFORNIA GARDENS: CREATING A NEW EDEN

 David C. Streatfield

ABBEVILLE PRESS   PUBLISHERS
New York   London   Paris

CONTENTS

Introduction

∽—∽

From the very beginning California has been seen as a place of great, almost mythical possibilities. The name California first appears in *The Exploits of Esplandián,* a novel written by Garci Ordóñez de Montalvo and published in Seville, Spain, in 1510. It recounts the fictional adventures of Esplandián, who visits a place "on the right hand of the Indies . . . an island called California, very near to the Terrestrial Paradise, which was peopled with black women . . . accustomed to live after the fashion of the Amazons. . . . Their arms were full of gold."[1] This fanciful description introduced themes that have been associated with California ever since, particularly the proximity to paradise.

The drama of California's landscape, the pleasures of its climate, and the plenitude of its resources encouraged early explorers to believe that an arcadian society could be created in this benign and beautiful place. During the two and one-third centuries covered in this book this pastoral haven has become the premier industrial state in the United States of America, with an economy that is the largest in the country and with a plethora of contemporary problems. Its gardens provide important clues to the transformation of the landscape from its edenic to its current state. Garden designers have responded to the remarkable opportunities presented by California's landscape with boldness, inventiveness, modesty, arrogance, ignorance, rowdiness, humor, integrity, poetic introspection, and virtually every other human attitude. In that sense, California gardens can be seen as a microcosm of universal attributes, yet understanding their regional meaning has perhaps even more importance. Stimulating a greater awareness of how regional garden design has evolved from a mixture of universal and local traditions is one of the purposes of this book.

California's architectural traditions have been analyzed with considerable insight and thoroughness, but its garden traditions remain largely unknown even within the state, having been studied only in Victoria Padilla's excellent book, *Southern California Gardens: An Illustrated History* (1961).[2] More recently the literature has increased with the publication of isolated articles in scholarly journals and of monographs on the landscape architects A. E. Hanson and Florence Yoch.[3]

∽—∽
**Casa del Herrero,
Montecito, 1925.
Garden designed by
Ralph Stevens and
Lockwood de Forest
for George and
Carrie Steedman.**
Photo: Robert M. Fletcher
& Associates, 1985

California Gardens: Creating a New Eden documents and analyzes notable gardens made from 1769 (when Alta California, or Upper California—the territory that became the state of California in 1850—became the last component of the immense Spanish empire on the North American continent) to the present. Most of these gardens were created by professional designers for affluent owners—the conspicuous exception being the gardens of the Spanish missions. The fact that this book concentrates on gardens professionally designed for the well-to-do does not in any way imply that vernacular gardens are inherently less interesting. Popular gardens (those created by individuals whose principal occupation is not the design of gardens) such as the Underground Garden in Fresno, Romano Gabriel's Wooden Garden in Eureka, and the Watts Towers in Los Angeles, as well as less ambitious examples, merit their own detailed treatment.

The profession of landscape architecture was introduced to this country during the second half of the nineteenth century, and it is probable that between 1856 and 1900 no more than eleven landscape architects were working nationwide. William Hammond Hall, the first superintendent and designer of Golden Gate Park, was the only member of this initial group to practice in California. Consequently, until this century most gardens in the state were designed and planted by nurserymen, who also provided the plants for gardens designed and supervised by landscape architects. The differences between the two professions can be demonstrated in a comparison between Hall and James R. Lowe. In 1864 Lowe, an Englishman who had a large nursery in San Jose, charged David Belden, also of San Jose, $1,302 for 434 "forest trees"; the cost of the design was only $25.[4] Ten years later Hall proposed to provide a design for James Flood's estate in Menlo Park "to improve your grounds just for the sake of showing Californians how such things should be done." Unfortunately, he was not more explicit about his innovative ideas, but he did describe the services he would provide:

> The subject of improving grounds is so little understood here that I hope you will excuse my offering a brief explanation.
> The practice of this art of creating landscapes—improving grounds necessitates a knowledge of engineering, construction, architectural design, and gardening manipulation, as well as with the peculiarities of the soil, climate, etc. of the particular locality where each work is to be executed, the whole to be brought together by and under the rules of artistic design and good taste.[5]

Hall agreed to provide two drawings and a report for $200. Working drawings would cost another $200; supervision and staking, $150. It would be necessary for him to be on site for an entire day four to six times a month during the grading and construction. Once the heavy work was finished, this would be reduced to three days a month.

Nurserymen still provide design services, even though landscape architects have deplored that practice ever since the formal foundation of their profession in 1899. They believe that the design of a landscape should be entrusted only to a professionally trained designer.

After 1900 most landscape architects were trained at schools of landscape architecture such as Harvard and the University of Illinois; the first department in California was founded at Berkeley in 1913. Their training included instruction in soil science, geology, ecology, and botany, as well as landscape construction and planting design. This combination was intended to produce designers who were artists but also knowledgeable about the practical aspects of construction and horticulture.

Several successful California designers in the 1920s, such as Paul Howard and A. E. Hanson, acquired their expertise in nurseries. There were a few gifted gentlemen amateurs, including Francis T. Underhill and Lockwood de Forest in Santa Barbara. And before the advent of professionally trained landscape architects, many architects designed their own gardens, since they had no respect either for garden designers or for nurserymen. For example, Myron Hunt, Robert Farquhar, Mark Daniels, Willis Polk, and others designed the gardens for houses they had created. In order to satisfy their clients' desires for gardens in a number of different styles, most garden designers maintained extensive libraries of books about architectural and garden history. Some designers traveled extensively in Europe. Florence Yoch and her partner, Lucille Council, went to Europe every other year, making copious photographic records of the gardens they visited. These photographs were mounted in albums and frequently used as the inspiration for designs of fountains, urns, gates, and other decorative features. Yoch and Council also purchased pots on their trips, which they used in gardens and sometimes had duplicated by ceramic manufacturers.[6]

The lack of landscape contractors in California meant that most landscape architects kept their own construction crews—an atypical practice elsewhere in the country. One advantage of this system was that the members of these crews became thoroughly familiar with their employers' preferences; that experience reduced the need for elaborate specifications and guaranteed a more reliable level of craftsmanship.[7]

Skilled gardeners were essential to the survival of estate gardens. From the 1850s until the Depression, head gardeners invariably came from England, Scotland, France, Belgium, or Germany, where they had been very well trained. To ensure that their designs were properly maintained, many garden designers were retained by the owners either to make annual maintenance reports or to provide maintenance manuals for the garden staff.[8] The close involvement by landscape architects in not only the design but also the long-term maintenance of California gardens is unusual in the history of American gardens, and it accounts to a considerable extent for the remarkable quality of the gardens created in the state during the first three decades of this century. By the end of World War II, gardens were still being designed either by landscape architects or by nurseries, but landscape contracting firms assumed responsibility for grading and for installing structural features and plants. Long-term supervision of maintenance was done only by the few older designers still in practice.

As a result of the social and economic changes in this century California gardens have diminished from estates of several hundred acres to plots of three or four acres, and in denser cities such as San Francisco, to very small backyard gardens. This ongoing reduction in size has established a tradition of *villeggiature* (small rural retreats) rather than one of great estates.

Whether designed by nurserymen or professional designers, and whatever their size or cost, gardens are artificial places. In them, nature is transformed through a process that reflects the values of the client, the designer, and their society. The history of gardens in California reveals the successes and failures of a heterogeneous society in settling into one of the most memorably beautiful, and varied, landscapes on the North American continent. Except in the Hispanic period these developments cannot be ordered into a simple linear pattern, and since 1850 the contradictory elements of a pluralistic society have been clearly revealed in California's gardens.

The bewildering complexities of California's garden history can be understood as having evolved through three stages—colonial re-creation, imported eclecticism, and regional appropriateness—and this cultural model might also be used to interpret garden history in other parts of the world. Ever since the Spanish conquered California in 1769, the residents of California have generally come from elsewhere and have brought with them previously developed ideals about the landscape.

During the first stage of this model, discussed in chapter 1, the Spanish settlers developed architectural and garden traditions that re-created patterns familiar to them from back home. They established their presence in the landscape by laying down boundaries for public and private territories and military, religious, and civilian settlements. In first Spanish and then Mexican California, Spain's Laws of the Indies provided a set of planning principles that had already been used successfully in transforming the landscape of Central and South America. Gardens in California were remarkably similar to those of Spain and Mexico, albeit on the simplest, humblest scale. Their simplicity reflected the fact that Spanish and Mexican California remained a colonial frontier.

The second stage of the model—discussed in chapters 2, 4, and 5—occurred with the displacement of Hispanic gardens by new, eclectic approaches to garden design that had originated in the eastern states and in Europe, where the climate was temperate and water plentiful. Re-creating gardens from back home was possible, but only with the lavish use of imported water. Even in Southern California, where most of the settled regions do not have particularly rich soils, the addition of water yielded almost ideal conditions for cultivating a vast range of plants from the temperate, subtropical, and tropical regions of the world. (The widespread importation of semitropical and tropical plants into Southern California is an extreme example of the European penchant for the exotic.)

This tradition of plant introduction has continued to the present decade, and the technologies for supplying unseasonal water have become ever more sophisticated, making it possible for Californians to create virtually any kind of garden imaginable. Despite the dominance of modernist ideas that began in the state during the 1930s, eclecticism continued with varying levels of popularity through the 1960s. The exuberant response to the multitude of choices has been central to garden design in California, and it will undoubtedly continue as long as imported water remains a cheap commodity.

The third stage of the model—described in chapters 3, 6, 7, and 8—evolved as attempts were made to fashion garden traditions that would be responsive to the local landscape rather than to the vagaries of national or international taste. This first occurred at the turn of this century in reaction to the disappearance of some natural landscapes and to the excesses of Victorian gardening. Initially, garden traditions were adapted from other cultures that had landscapes and climates similar to those of California, with the gardens of Italy and Spain invoked as especially suitable models. Later, the careful selection of native and drought-tolerant plants was used to create regionally appropriate gardens. The rise of modernism in California during the 1930s (one of the earliest manifestations of the style in this country) led to the use of gardens as outdoor rooms for a variety of social functions, including entertaining, dining, and recreation. This intensive use of garden space was a clear recognition of the potential pleasures of outdoor living in California.

Running parallel to the second stage rather than replacing it, this alternative tradition has been advocated by some of the same designers who have created gardens using imported plants and water. Such apparent inconsistency may reflect the practical necessities of satisfying clients rather than any philosophical ambivalence.

Native Plants

❦

Left, top. Live oak (*Quercus agrifolia*). This species of oak is found throughout the central California coastal region. Long appreciated for its highly picturesque form, it has often been incorporated into domestic gardens. Proximity to other plants can lead to problems, however, for watering will result in a fatal root fungus.

Photo: Saxon Holt

❦

Left, bottom. Monterey cypress (*Cupressus macrocarpa*). In its native habitat—the coastal region of Monterey Bay—this cypress twists into highly contorted shapes. In areas away from the coast, where it is protected from wind and salt spray, it will develop a magnificent symmetrical form and can be used as a solidly upright hedge.

Photo: Saxon Holt

Left. Monterey pine (*Pinus radiata*). Like the Monterey cypress, this tree is native to the coastal region of California. Its rapid growth made it favored for windbreaks during the second half of the nineteenth century.

Photo: Saxon Holt

Below. Ceanothus arboreus "Ray Hartman." This large genus of shrubs contains a number of attractive species with vivid blooms. Highly drought-tolerant, it is particularly well adapted to gardens where water is scarce.

Photo: Saxon Holt

Opposite, bottom right. Desert fan palm (*Washingtonia filifera,* also known as California fan palm). The only palm native to California, this species occurs naturally around streams and deserts in the southern part of the state. The densely thatched petticoat of old leaf fronds is highly characteristic.

Photo: Saxon Holt

Imported Plants

~~~

Right, top. Mexican fan palm (*Washingtonia robusta*).
This palm, native to the arid areas of Sonora and
Baja California in Mexico, was introduced into California by the Franciscans. Taller and more slender
than the native palm, it has a shaggy petticoat of old
leaf fronds. The Mexican fan palm remained popular
throughout the nineteenth century, but its popularity
has declined in this century.

Photo: Saxon Holt

~~~

Right, bottom. Eucalyptus (*Eucalyptus globulus*). This
fast-growing species of eucalyptus was introduced in
California during the 1850s. Despite its troublesome
tendency to shed its silvery green leaves and nutlike
fruit, it quickly became popular as a decorative
element in gardens and as a windbreak on farms
and along roadways.

Photo: Saxon Holt

Left. *Acacia baileyana*. A large genus of trees and shrubs, the acacia comes from warm, tropical regions—particularly Australia. Fast growing (though unfortunately short lived), it has been popular in California since the middle of the nineteenth century.

Photo: Saxon Holt

Below, left. Peppertree (*Schinus molle*). Its drought tolerance and its voluminous shade made the peppertree a highly valued addition to the California landscape. The specimen seen here, at Mission San Luis Rey, was grown from a seed brought from Peru and planted at the mission in 1825.

Photo: Saxon Holt

Below, right. Olive tree (*Olea europea*). The olive, introduced to California by the Franciscans, had been cultivated in Europe since antiquity, both for its oil-yielding fruit and for the highly picturesque appearance of mature specimens.

Photo: Saxon Holt

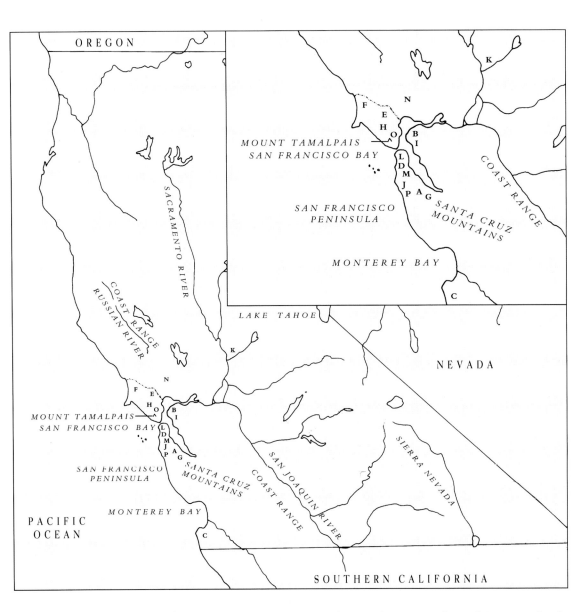

The dualistic nature of California as both a physical place and a state of mind is very clearly expressed in its finest gardens. To be properly understood this cultural phenomenon has to be placed in its physical context. Contrary to the beliefs of many non-Californians, the landscape of California is neither physically nor socially homogeneous; instead, it possesses an almost bewildering diversity.

California's landscape is defined by a series of mountain ranges. The Sierra Nevada and the Coast Ranges parallel each other on a north-south axis for several hundred miles,

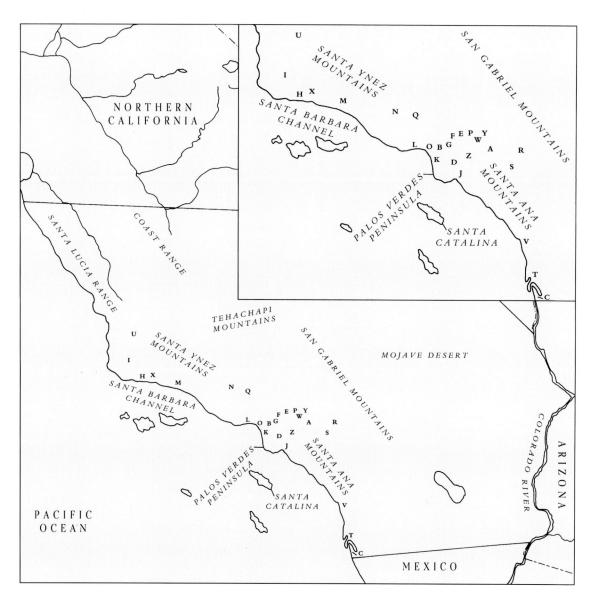

enclosing between them the Central Valley, an immense flatland with highly fertile soil. In California the coastal mountains rise directly from the Pacific Ocean and run for several hundred miles, from the Oregon border south to the Tehachapi Mountains. The northern range terminates at the Golden Gate strait at the entrance to San Francisco Bay, the first major break in this continuous wall of mountains. Below the Golden Gate the central range continues as the Santa Cruz Mountains, which terminate at the crescent-shaped Monterey Bay, formed by the delta of the Pajaro River. To the south the mountains continue as the Santa Lucia Range, which meets the Tehachapi Mountains just north of Santa Barbara. This east-west trending mountain range links the Coast Range to the Sierra Nevada and defines the northern edge of Southern California—known colloquially as "the Southland" since the turn of the century. Below and roughly parallel to the Tehachapi Mountains is the Transverse Range, which includes the Santa Ynez Mountains in Santa Barbara County, the San Gabriel Mountains, and the San Bernardino Mountains. To the south of them is a lower plateau known as the Peninsular Range, which includes the Santa Ana Mountains. To the north and east of the San Bernardino Mountains and to the east of the Tehachapi Mountains is the extensive Mojave Desert. A narrow pass at its western end links the desert to the Los Angeles Basin, a roughly triangular plain lying between the Transverse Range and the Santa Ana Mountains.

From Santa Barbara the coast traces a broad crescent shape southward to Los Angeles and the Palos Verdes peninsula. From this promontory the coast then follows another gentle arc south to the Mexican border. The narrow plain of Santa Barbara County is the only part of the California coast that faces due south. The San Miguel, Santa Rosa, Santa Cruz, and Anacapa islands form the Santa Barbara Channel and provide protection to Santa Barbara County; the Santa Barbara, San Nicholas, San Clemente, and Santa Catalina islands shelter the remaining part of the Southern California coast.

The rugged and dramatic land masses of California are geologically very young and still in the process of being formed—with the most notorious evidence of this process being frequent and potentially devastating earthquakes. The state is also subject to fierce natural wildfires, to which the native vegetation, at least, is adapted. These physical hazards were largely ignored by early settlers, who were greatly attracted by the state's benign climate and cheerfully oblivious to its perils.

California's climate resembles that of the Mediterranean Basin, with mild, wet winters from December to February; hot, dry summers; and warm springs and autumns. The climate of the state and its extremely long growing season create almost ideal conditions for cultivating a wide range of plants, provided there is sufficient water. During the second half of the nineteenth century, when settlers were being lured to Southern California, the climate was proudly touted. Every county history contained lengthy tables of climatic data to prove that it had the finest weather in the state. Major Ben Truman, promoting California for the Southern Pacific Railroad Company, called the Southland's climate "semi-tropical."[9] In fact, the Southland is really a desert facing the ocean. The harsh, white desert light is transmuted by moisture from the ocean into a lovely softness that has been celebrated by many painters. Since the average difference in temperature between winter and summer is only ten degrees, it is the presence or absence of precipitation that most clearly defines the seasons. In turn, geography determines precipitation levels. There is a marked decrease in rainfall from north to south and from seashore to desert. At Crescent City, close to the Oregon border, the average annual rainfall is just over 65 inches (165.1 centimeters); in San Diego, adjacent to Mexico, it is just under 10 inches (25.4 centimeters). Death Valley has an average rainfall of 2 inches (5.1 centimeters) a year, while Santa Barbara has 17 inches (43.2 centimeters). The San Francisco Bay region also follows the pattern of decreasing rainfall from west to east. At the summit of the Santa Cruz Mountains the average rainfall is 55 inches (139.7 centimeters), while in Oakland, on the east side of the bay, it is only 17 inches (43.2 centimeters).

There is a striking variety of climates in the most heavily settled coastal regions, especially in the Southland. Snow falls on mountaintops in sight of arid deserts. The entire coast experiences morning fog during the summer months. This is caused by a large mass of moisture-laden air moving landward over an extremely deep and cold mass of water lying just offshore. Enough condensation occurs to produce fog, which provides a form of natural air conditioning that reduces the temperature at the shore. Away from this marine influence, in the inland areas, temperatures are very high in the summer months, especially in the southern part of the state.

Despite the state's claims of climatic perfection, California's weather can be treacherous, with frequent, and frequently violent, fluctuations. Riverbeds that are normally dry in the summer can become lethal torrents of water. In October hot Santa Ana winds originating in the deserts of southern Utah can sweep through the valleys of the Southland, driving temperatures up to 100 degrees Fahrenheit (38 degrees Celsius) or higher, lowering the humidity, and creating ideal conditions for the spontaneous ignition of vegetation. The winter of 1861–62 witnessed the heaviest rainfall in California's recorded history: over 49 inches (124.5 centimeters) of rain fell in San Francisco, and it rained continuously in Los Angeles for twenty-eight days. This inundation was followed in 1864 by a devastating drought, and droughts have continued to occur with cyclical regularity.

Most of the gardens in this book are located in different regions of the coastal area, each with its own physical and social character. All are (or were) in areas associated with urban centers, but this does not mean that the gardens themselves have always been in cities—indeed, many were constructed as conscious reactions against urban life. The following chapters demonstrate how these diverse landscapes variously did or did not determine the look of California's gardens. The characters of these gardens have also been shaped by cultural tradition, by the availability of native and imported plants, by technologies such as irrigation and the transplanting of large trees, and by the designers' and clients' reactions to the sublime beauty of the regional landscape.

1
HISPANIC GARDENS

The transformations of the California landscape during the Spanish and Mexican occupation of Alta California have become part of the romantic mythology of a proud, aristocratic society that lived on the land with elegant grace. This view of the period has become so firmly rooted in California's perception of its past that it is unlikely ever to be dispelled, despite the careful work of revisionist historians.

The Spanish conquest of Alta California yielded both temporary and permanent institutions: the civilian pueblo was meant to be permanent; the mission and military presidio, or garrison town, were intended to survive only until the native Indian people had been converted and "civilized." Once that had been accomplished the presidios and missions were to be dismantled, and the land redistributed to the new civilian population in the pueblos and on outlying ranches.

Whatever their subsequent failings as managers, the Spanish followed principles for living in a semiarid climate that were appropriate and that, with few exceptions, were totally ignored by later American settlers. Spanish traditions of water usage—rooted in Islamic respect for water's scarcity and for its life-giving qualities—governed the design of pueblos, missions, houses, and gardens. Spaniards had developed highly skilled engineering methods to produce efficient, elegant aqueducts and *zanjas* (irrigation ditches) in the older towns of Spain and in Hispanic South and Central America. However, in the poorer rural sections of Mexico, such as Sinaloa and Sonora, where most of the settlers of Alta California came from, these skills had been reduced to the most rudimentary level. Yet even if California had been settled by Spanish or Mexican aristocrats and graced by lavish settlements, it is doubtful that the later American settlements would have followed them as models. The colonial history of California confirms the theory that settlers in a new place will immediately try to re-create the familiar.

Protestant visitors from Europe and the eastern United States were not impressed by the unfamiliar landscape of California or by Mexican society. Sir George Simpson, of Hudson's Bay Company, remarked in 1841: "California was a splendid country wasted on men who do not avail themselves of their natural advantages to a much higher degree than the savages whom they displaced, and who are lucky to become less and less energetic from generation to generation and year to year."[1] But even though Hispanic society did not impress Sir George, on his visits to California in 1830 and 1841 he marveled at the flowers grown in the mission at Santa Barbara. During his second trip he walked alone in the garden, recording the presence of marigolds, wallflowers, jonquils, lilies, hollyhocks, and violets.[2]

The garden was at the center of the Islamic and Hispanic tradition of settlement. The Islamic garden had evolved as a haven from the harsh desert environment, serving not only as a physical oasis but also a symbolic re-creation of the Garden of Eden and a foreshadowing of everlasting heaven. In Persia, Mogul India, and southern Spain the Islamic tradition produced some of the most beautiful gardens ever made. By contrast, the gardens of California were extremely simple, even crude, variations of these exquisite places, lacking their profound symbolism. Nevertheless, European visitors delighted in the aesthetic qualities of early California gardens, even those in an advanced state of decline. The French captain and sea-trader Auguste Duhaut-Cilly visited Mission Santa Barbara in 1827 and admired the large, well-cultivated garden. "The paths, laid out methodically, were shaded by fine olive trees, and we saw there at the same time the fruits of temperate climes and of the torrid zones."[3]

In 1846 Edwin Bryant visited Mission San Fernando, in the middle of the Southern California valley of the same name, when its two extensive walled gardens were in decrepitude. He wrote: "A stroll through them afforded a most delightful contrast from the usually uncultivated landscape we have been traveling through for so long a time. Here were brought together most of the fruits and many of the plants of the temperate and tropical climates."[4] Bryant also described a visit to the garden of Don Antonio Suñol in San Jose. "Apples, pears, peaches, figs, oranges, and grapes, with other fruits which I do not now recollect, were growing and ripening. The grape-vines were bowed to the ground with the luxuriance and weight of the yield; and more delicious fruit I have never tasted." He also noted that the gardens of Los Angeles produced "a great variety of tropical fruits and plants."[5]

In Hispanic California's early days questions of shelter and survival took precedence. Since the pueblos provided food for the nearby presidios, their inhabitants would have had little time for cultivating pleasure gardens. Information about the civilian gardens in the pueblos is limited, and no systematic archaeological excavation of them has been carried out. What evidence there is, at best circumstantial, suggests that they were simple, purely productive gardens with few ornamental plants. Herbal gardens contained plants such as mint, fennel, lavender, rue, thyme, rosemary, pennyroyal, sage, spearmint, and oregano. Fruit trees, such as orange, lime, and guava, were grown alongside peppertrees, catalpa, and myrtle trees.[6]

By contrast, the mission gardens were larger and contained a wide variety of plants, most of which were used for cooking, medicine, and church decorations. More is known about their design and plantings because numerous descriptions by travelers survive and some scientific analysis of the material remains has been done.[7] The mission garden was the central element in a complex of buildings that superficially resembled medieval European monasteries. Each mission was comprised of a church, a dwelling place for the padres, quarters for soldiers, storehouses, workshops, and shelter for the Indians. The mission buildings faced an open plaza in front of the church. Adjoining the church was the *convento* (the private quarters of the padres), which contained guest rooms, reception areas, a library, and in the larger missions, a chapel. In some missions an additional building provided housing for guards and guests. Behind the *convento* was an enclosed patio, used only by the padres. The two remaining sides of the enclosure held storage and a variety of other rooms, such as the *monjerías* (quarters for unmarried women and small boys), the infirmary, and servants' rooms. In addition there were places for weaving, pottery, and other crafts and for the storage of grain, tallow, hides, fruits, and meat, plus stalls for cattle and horses.

The visual impact of the missions in the landscape varied. Duhaut-Cilly spoke admiringly of the prospect of the Santa Barbara and San Luis Rey missions, comparing the former to a fortress and the latter to a palace. But however impressive the architecture of these structures might have been, strikingly little attention was paid to landscaping them. The only mission that planted an avenue of trees outside the buildings was the one at Santa Clara. Edwin Bryant was impressed by its "broad *alameda,* shaded by several rows of stately trees (elms and willows) planted by the *padres,* [which] extends nearly the entire distance, forming a most beautiful drive or walk for equestrians or pedestrians."[8] Duhaut-Cilly praised the mission at Santa Barbara:

> No situation is prettier than that of this mission. From the shore the ground rises so regularly by steps, that they might be said to be the symmetrical terraces of a fortification. I know not even if the grassy covering of an artificial work could ever equal the beauty of green sward clothing them like the carpet of green velvet spread out over the steps of a throne. The buildings are placed upon the third sward fronting the sea, and backed against a thick forest of large fir trees, which lend a new brilliance to the whiteness of their walls.[9]

The square in front of a mission was sometimes enlivened by a fountain. Duhaut-Cilly was especially impressed by the one in front of the Santa Barbara mission, which:

> surprised us the more, the less we expected to find in this country, so far from European refinement, that kind of luxury reserved with us for the dwellings of the wealthiest. After rising to a height of more than eight feet [2.4 meters] above the ground, the clear and sparkling water of this fountain fell again in broad sheets upon a descending series of stone basins forming altogether an octagonal pyramid; it filled a reservoir of the same shape to the brim, whence, issuing from the jaws of a bear, also in stone, it fell into a fine layer in stucco, around which some Indian women and Californian girls were busy washing.[10]

None of the mission gardens survived intact, and the flower-filled patios that today delight visitors to the restored missions convey a false sense of their original character and purpose. The garden at Mission La Purísima Concepción, near Lompoc, which was restored in the 1930s, provides a good idea of how simple these gardens actually were. The patios resembled medieval cloisters but were purely functional places in which a well or fountain served domestic needs; there may not have been any plants in them at all. No patio is known to have been planted as a pleasure garden prior to secularization, in 1834. Peppertrees (*Schinus molle*), grown from seeds brought from Peru in 1825, were first planted at San Luis Rey, but one visitor's description of that mission in 1829 makes clear that it was no garden paradise: "The building occupies a large square, of at least eighty or ninety yards [seventy-five or eighty meters] each side, forming an extensive area, in the centre of which a fountain supplies the establishment with pure water. . . . In the interior of the square might be seen the various trades at work, presenting a scene not dissimilar to some of the working departments of our state prisons."[11]

The productive gardens, in separate enclosures that adjoined the mission buildings, were known as *huertas*. Usually rectangular and divided into quadrants, with a fountain in the center, they were enclosed either by high walls or by hedges of prickly pear cacti (*Opuntia* sp.). The largest known garden, at Mission San Gabriel Arcángel, had a slightly different layout.

Mission La Purísima Concepción, Lompoc, 1812–23. The mission was founded in 1787 on a nearby site, then moved to what is now Lompoc in 1812; the mission's garden was restored in 1936–41. This fountain, which dates to 1823, sits in the main garden under the shade of old olive trees.
Photo: Robert M. Fletcher & Associates, 1981

There the usual place of the fountain was taken by a circular basin, two hundred feet (sixty-one meters) in diameter, built of carved stones. Water was let into the pool through well-maintained stone-lined ditches. The pool was used for breeding and raising rare species of fish as well as for irrigation. The mission gardens—usually encompassing a *huerta,* an orchard, and a vineyard—were irrigated by periodic flooding from the nearest stream or river.

The Franciscan padres brought seeds from Mexico for all the trees and other plants they thought could be grown in California. On his long journey by foot from Mexico City to San Diego in 1769, Father Junípero Serra carried seeds of the castor-oil plant (*Ricinus communis*), wheat, and dates, to establish new food and medical supplies, and of Mediterranean grapes to produce sacramental wine and fruit.[12] These were the first nonnative plants to be cultivated in California. The introduction of these productive and ornamental plants exemplifies the desire of the Spanish settlers to impose a pattern of order on the California landscape.

In 1784 the *padre principal* of Mission San Gabriel Arcángel sponsored an expedition to Sinaloa, Mexico, to obtain seeds, cuttings, and grafts of fruit trees that had been introduced there from Spain. The vines and trees that were brought back—including oranges, lemons, limes, olives, figs, and several others—became the foundation of California's grape, olive, and citrus industries.[13] Fifteen years later the French government arranged a scientific expedition to Mission San Carlos Borromeo, near Monterey. A glass-walled hothouse was built on the deck of the ship to protect plants on the frigid and hazardous journey around Cape Horn. Apples, plums, cherries, quinces, mulberries, and other fruits from France and Portugal, as well as beets, beans, peas, chard, garlic, and the highly prized Castilian rose (*Rosa damascena trigonapetala*), were thus introduced to California. The French took home grass seeds.[14]

A calf-bound book in the Mission Santa Barbara library, published in 1767 in Madrid and edited by Alonso de Herrera, was evidently circulated to all of the missions. Addressing every aspect of farming and gardening, it was apparently used by the padres as a guide and indicates some of the flowers that may have been grown in the gardens. The "Sixth Discourse" discusses various plants and trees, mentioning the pistachio, dogwood, cypress, laurel, jujube, carrot, buckthorn, juniper, and oak. Bulbous plants such as lilies, hyacinths, daffodils, and jonquils are listed together with old-fashioned flowers such as cornflower, larkspur, peony, marigold, sweet william, gilly flower, violet, carnation, marguerite, honeysuckle, jasmine, and rose.[15]

Although not intended as gardens of earthly delight, the mission gardens still warranted admiration, as is evident from descriptions in travelers' diaries. In 1793 Captain George Vancouver, exploring the entire North American Pacific coast on behalf of the British government, visited the gardens at Mission San Juan Buenaventura (near present-day Ventura). He noted:

These have principally consisted of apples, pears, plums, figs, oranges, grapes, peaches, and pomegranates, together with the plantain, banana, coconut, sugar cane, indigo, and a great variety of the necessary and useful kitchen herbs, plants and roots. All these were flourishing in the greatest health and perfection though separated from the seaside only by two or three fields of corn that were cultivated within a few yards of the surf.[16]

Hugo Reid, who purchased a rancho close to the Mission San Gabriel Arcángel, wrote admiringly of Padre José Salvidea, who was in charge of the mission after 1805. "He it was who planted the large vineyards, intersected with fine walks, shaded by fruit trees of every description and rendered still more lovely by shrubs interspersed between, who laid out the orange garden, fruit and olive orchards, built the mill and dam."[17] At Mission San Fernando, Edwin Bryant noted that even though it was not the flowering season (it was January), the roses were nonetheless in bloom. "Oranges, lemons, figs and olives hung up on the trees, and the blood red tuna or prickly pear looked very tempting. Among the plants I noted, the American aloe [*Agave americana*, more commonly called century plant] which is otherwise called maguey."[18]

Other plants grown in mission gardens included calla and Madonna lilies, the Castilian rose, musk rose, jasmine, lavender, pennyroyal, tamarind, anise, hollyhock, oleander, nasturtium, four-o'clock, sweet pea, portulaca, and the Matilija poppy (*Romneya coulteri*). Every mission had a peppertree, and wild cherries (*Prunus illicifolia*) were frequently grown around the buildings (they later became popular with American settlers).

The castor-oil plant and the tree tobacco plant (*Nicotiana glauca*) were widely cultivated. The European giant reed (*Arundo donax*) was grown as a windbreak and for making mats, and several palms were planted. The date palm (*Phoenix dactylifera*) was brought as a seed in Serra's original expedition from San Diego. It was not expected to produce fruit but was planted for its leaves, which were mentioned in the New Testament as being used to celebrate Christ's entry into Jerusalem.[19] The Canary Island palm (*Phoenix canariensis*), the Mexican fan palm (*Washingtonia robusta*), and the native desert fan palm (*W. filifera*) were also grown. In addition, the presence at Mission San Gabriel Arcángel of old specimens of the Chilean wine palm (*Jubaea chilensis*) suggests that this was also a Franciscan introduction. The huisache (*Acacia farnesiana*), a purely ornamental tree, had been taken to Mexico by the Franciscans, along with two prickly pear cacti, *Opuntia ficus-indica* and *O. megacantha*.

One of the most complete descriptions of a mission garden was written in 1890 by Guadalupe Vallejo, the niece of General Mariano Vallejo:

Before the Year 1800, the orchards at the Missions contained apples, pears, peaches, apricots, plums, cherries, figs, olives, oranges, pomegranates. . . . I remember that at the Mission of San José, we had many varieties of seedling fruits which have now been lost to cultivation. Of the pears, we had four sorts; one ripening in early summer, one in late summer and two in autumn and in winter. The Spanish names of these pears were *Presidentia,* the *Bergamota,* the *Pana,* and the *Lechera.* One of them was as large as a Bartlett, but there are no trees left of it now. The apples, grown from seed, ripened at different seasons, and there were seedling peaches, both early and late. An interesting fruit was that of the *Nopal,* or prickly pear. This fruit, called *tuna,* grew on the great hedges which protected part of the Mission orchards and were 20 feet high [6.1 meters] and 10 to 12 feet [3 to 3.6 meters] thick. Those who know how to cut a *tuna,* pealing it so as to escape the tiny thorns of the skin, find it delicious. . . . The old orchards were pruned and cultivated with much care, and the plants were swept by the Indians, but after the sequestration of the Mission property [in 1834], they were neglected and ran wild. The olive-mills and wine presses were destroyed, the cattle were pastured in the more fruitful groves.

The flower gardens were gay with roses, chiefly a pink and very fragrant sort from Mexico, called by us the Castilian rose, and still seen in a few old gardens. Besides roses, we had pinks, sweet-peas, hollyhocks, nasturtiums which had been brought from Mexico, and white lilies. The vegetable garden contained pease, beans, beets, lentils, onions, carrots, red peppers, corn, potatoes, squashes, cucumbers and melons.[20]

MISSION SAN
LUIS REY

Mission garden designs were usually of the greatest simplicity. The one exception was the garden in front of Mission San Luis Rey, which particularly impressed Captain Duhaut-Cilly:

Two well-planted gardens furnish abundance of vegetables and fruits of all kinds. The large, comfortable stairway by which one descends into the one to the south-east, reminded me of those of the orangery at Versailles: not that their material was as valuable, or the architecture as splendid; but there was some relation in the arrangement, number, and dimensions of the steps. At the bottom of the stairs are two fine lavers in stucco; one of them is a pond where the Indian women bathe every morning; the other is used every Saturday for washing clothes. Some of this water is afterward distributed into the garden, where many channels maintain a permanent moisture and coolness. The second garden, situated in a higher place, can be watered only by artificial aid: a chain-pump, worked by two men, is used twice a day to accomplish this object. These gardens produce the best olives and the best wine in all California.[21]

Rancho Santa Anita, Arcadia, 1831. Created by Lucky Baldwin in 1875 and restored in about 1952, this garden is now part of the Los Angeles State and County Arboretum. Cooking was done in the courtyard beneath the two large palms (*Washingtonia filifera*).

Photo: Saxon Holt, 1993

Mission San Luis Rey, 1811. When Captain Duhaut-Cilly visited the mission in 1827–28, he compared this staircase leading into the main garden to that of the orangerie at Versailles. The planting at the mission has not been restored to its original state.

Photo: Saxon Holt, 1993

Mexico's attainment of full independence from Spain in 1822 led to the secularization of the extensive mission farm estates, which made thousands of acres of the richest land in the state available for private settlement. So liberal was the new homesteading policy that at least five hundred grants of rancho land were made to private individuals, or rancheros, between 1822 and 1849.

The life of the rancheros has been so romanticized that there is an immense gap between that mythic past and the reality that can be documented. The earliest ranch houses were simple structures built of adobe blocks or of wooden posts covered with plaster, with floors of beaten earth and flat roofs covered with asphalt. Door and window openings were protected against rain and animals by rawhide hangings. There was a conspicuous lack of elaborate gardening. Edwin Bryant commented in 1846: "It is a peculiarity of the Mexicans that they allow no shade or ornamental trees to grow near their houses. In none of the streets or the towns or missions through which I have passed has there been a solitary tree standing."[22]

Many ranch houses were secondary residences, since the owner's primary residence was in a pueblo. In view of this, it is not surprising that most ranch houses were modest. The earliest in a series of houses built by Luis María Peralta on Rancho San Antonio in Alameda County was a rectangular adobe structure 42 feet (12.8 meters) long by 18 feet (5.5 meters) wide. It and three other houses occupied the center of a two-and-a-half-acre (one-hectare) garden surrounded by walls six to eight feet (1.8 to 2.4 meters) tall. The restored garden of Elias J. "Lucky" Baldwin's house at Rancho Santa Anita in Arcadia (now part of the Los Angeles State and County Arboretum) typifies the simple utilitarian character of a Mexican ranch garden. A rammed-earth courtyard is enclosed by a single-story L-shaped house and high walls. Within this enclosure is a *ramada* (arbor), a place for cooking, and a few rectangular beds for herbs and flowers. Fruit and vegetables were grown in irrigated areas outside the walls.

The later romanticizing of such crude establishments can be largely attributed to Helen Hunt Jackson's evocative but anachronistic novel *Ramona* (1884), in which she described the "half barbaric, half elegant, wholly generous, and free-handed life" of a typical rancho. Jackson's description of an idyllic nineteenth-century past was based on her own visits to Rancho Camulos, near Piru in the San Fernando Valley, and to Rancho Guajome, near Vista, northeast of San Diego. Both of these ranch buildings and their gardens had been altered and elaborated over several decades. According to one authority, Camulos was not even started until 1853.[23] In *Ramona,* Jackson lovingly depicted the U-shaped house and its setting as it was at the time of her visit in 1882. The original building was at the south end of the courtyard. A wing at right angles had been added ten years later, with a detached kitchen building parallel to the original house. Each of these three wings had a veranda facing the garden.

Rancho Camulos, Piru, c. 1853. This house
and garden helped inspire Helen Hunt
Jackson's romantic novel *Ramona* (1884).
Visible here are the main garden and the
northwestern corner of the house.
Photo: *Gardens of Colony and State,* 1934

The garden at Camulos, which still survives in good condition, functioned both as a place for growing plants of practical value and as an outdoor living room. It has a simple rectangular layout, recalling the Islamic "paradise" garden. A large circular space, defined by cypress hedges at the center of intersecting paths, contains a circular basin with a cast-iron fountain. The four corner beds are filled with flowers. According to Jackson, "great red water jars, hand-made by the Indians of San Luis Obispo, stood in close rows against the walls, and in them were always growing fine geraniums, carnations and yellow-flowered musk."[24] In addition, vines climbed the veranda posts, "some growing in great bowls, swung by cords from the roof of the veranda, or set on shelves against the walls. These bowls were of gray stone, hollowed and polished, shining smooth inside and out."[25]

Between the veranda on the south side of the house "and the river meadows, out on which it looked":

> all was garden, orange grove, and almond orchard; the orange grove always green, never without snowy bloom or golden fruit; the garden never without flowers, summer or winter; and the almond orchard in early spring a fluttering canopy of pink and white petals, which seen from the hills on the opposite side of the river, looked as if rosy sunlight clouds had fallen and become tangled in the trees and the clouds. On either hand stretched away other orchards, peach, apricot, apple, pear, pomegranate, and beyond these, vineyards. Nothing was to be seen but verdure or bloom, or fruit.[26]

A broad, straight path covered by a trellis supporting grapevines led from the veranda through the garden to a little river.

After *Ramona* was published, writers viewed the U-shaped house around a patio as the prototypical Mexican ranch house. But Camulos did not typify Mexican ranch houses at all. It was, instead, an example of a Spanish-Mexican house so thoroughly Americanized that all that remained to indicate its Mexican origins were its building materials. Such houses were not built until the last decade of Mexican rule and in the decades immediately following, when American influence was considerable. Many Yankee traders married Mexican heiresses and built houses that fused the Mexican adobe tradition with early nineteenth-century building traditions from back East.[27] Similarly, the garden at Camulos, like the gardens at Rancho Guajome and Don Juan Temple's garden at Rancho Los Cerritos, in Long Beach, confirms the Yankee settlers' practice of fusing the Hispanic courtyard with the design traditions of New England gardens.[28]

Jackson's evocative depiction of Mexican life was not a deliberate attempt to mythologize the past. She simply assumed without question that the descendants of Mexican families had always lived as they did at the time of her visit. But by then, many authentic adobe structures were either so decayed or so changed that they no longer bore any resemblance to their original appearance. The qualities of quiet contentment, simplicity, and harmony with nature that she lauded were, in fact, less characteristic of the rancheros than of a very small group of American settlers, mainly Yankees, who had synthesized local and eastern traditions into an alternative to Victorian excesses. The formal simplicity of these gardens was venerated at the turn of the nineteenth century by writers such as Charles Fletcher Lummis and George Wharton James as the quintessential Old California, despite their essentially American origins. Their relaxed, unpretentious, and leisurely way of life attracted visitors like author and editor Charles Dudley Warner, who felt "that this land might offer for thousands at least a winter of content."[29]

2

VICTORIAN
EDEN

The Hispanic tradition held no attraction for the American settlers who swarmed into California after the discovery of gold. In seeking to create a new Eden in this place of sublime scale and apparently limitless possibilities, the new settlers depended on their preconceptions of landscape imported from the eastern states and Europe. Yet even though the gardens created in California during the second half of the nineteenth century were derived from those far-distant precedents, by the end of the century Californians had transformed them into landscapes of unparalleled diversity, having taken advantage of the benign climate, imported water, and an exceptionally broad range of temperate and semitropical plants.[1] Unfortunately, these gardens can now be glimpsed only in written descriptions and old photographs. With the exception of Lachryma Montis and Keil Cove, none of the gardens described in this chapter survives—all that remains are a few scattered trees that grace the grounds of office buildings or small gardens in subdivisions.

American garden design in the nineteenth century was dominated by European ideas. This reflected the supposed superiority of European culture as well as the continuing influx of European settlers. Garden design and theory in Europe had earlier been unified by the aristocratic veneration of classical ideals, but in America the increasingly pluralistic character of nineteenth-century society encouraged a proliferation of styles designed to cater to individual tastes, including the picturesque, the gardenesque, and the revival of historical modes—a diversity reinforced by an influx of new plants from all over the world.

The picturesque mode of landscape design—associated with the English designer Humphry Repton and characterized by irregular areas of parkland or lawn defined by continuous belts of trees and broken up by individual trees and tree clumps—came to represent an idealized nature.[2] The gardenesque style, initiated by the British designer John Claudius Loudon, disdained visual compositions of plants to celebrate individual plants.[3] Both of these modes of design were practiced in this country, alongside American styles defined by Andrew Jackson Downing.[4] Much of Downing's work was derived from Loudon's scientific and scholarly books, but Downing also gave new meaning to the terms *beautiful* and *picturesque*. He associated *beautiful* with round-headed, unpruned deciduous trees planted in open groves enhanced by gently flowing paths and classical edifices. Downing used *picturesque* to define a style characterized by broken silhouettes of both buildings and vegetation, rough surfaces, and a rather wild, bold growth in the plants. In practice, this meant a preference for coniferous trees and Gothic buildings. This approach differed markedly from Repton's stated preference for contrasting the character of the vegetation with that of the architecture.

Loudon's and Downing's styles were unthinkingly adopted in California, as elsewhere, because they were fashionable. Indeed, western garden makers were offered no other model to follow, since it was not until 1879 that Charles H. Shinn published *The Pacific Rural Handbook,* the first book to address specifically California's planting conditions.[5] What distinguished the Californian interpretation of the different imported styles was the use of an extraordinarily wide range of plants. The state's first nursery was established in 1849 in Sacramento, and the rapid growth of it and other nurseries offering a multitude of nonnative plants in what was still a frontier region was a remarkable phenomenon. From the late 1840s through the 1920s nurseries dictated garden character in various ways, but it was the nurseries founded in San Francisco, Oakland, and San Jose in the 1850s and 1860s that became the most important in the state, patronized both by urban gardeners and by owners of rural estates. These enterprising nurserymen had easy access to materials coming in through the port of San Francisco, and they obtained new plants from a variety of sources. Seeds were acquired by mail from major nurseries in New York, Pennsylvania, Massachusetts, France, Germany, and England as well as from private estates in England. As early as the mid-1850s seed was being imported from Australia, and the ubiquitous eucalyptus and acacia had already appeared.[6]

Just as remarkable as the early development of the nurseries was the rapid appearance of country estates, which flourished almost immediately after California's incorporation into the United States in 1850. Located principally in the chain of communities on the Peninsula south of San Francisco, this was the largest constellation of estates west of the Mississippi. Their presence there reflects San Francisco's early economic dominance in the state as the service center for the gold rush. The great port, the large number of newly rich patrons, and the rapid appearance of nurseries combined to create an ideal opportunity for ambitious garden making on the Peninsula. Not until the last decades of the century were gardens comparable in scale created in Santa Barbara and the Los Angeles Basin.

LACHRYMA MONTIS

One of the first of these estates, Lachryma Montis (Tear of the Mountain), was built by General Mariano Vallejo near Sonoma, in 1850–51. It symbolized the complete capitulation to the new American landscape order by one of the major figures of Mexican California. In 1836 Vallejo had built the largest adobe house in the state, near Petaluma, and he had laid out Sonoma on the classic Hispanic pattern. But Lachryma Montis is a modest two-story clapboard house with Gothic details and a broken silhouette of steep gables and chimney stacks; it had been prefabricated in the East and shipped around the Horn. Vallejo undoubtedly designed his own garden and almost certainly had access to Downing's books. A typical small example of Downing's picturesque mode, it had as its principal spatial element an irregular lawn that was certainly Downingesque, though it was not surrounded by coniferous trees. Instead, it was defined by ornamental trees and decorated with a cast-iron gravity-fed fountain and a small Gothic summerhouse festooned, like the main house, with vines.

Lachryma Montis, Sonoma, 1850–51. Garden designed by General Mariano Vallejo.
Ornamental trees, such as magnolias, shade the lawn and cool the summerhouse
in the background. Photo: David C. Streatfield, 1968

Lachryma Montis. The summerhouse provided a
shady haven on hot afternoons.
Photo: David C. Streatfield, 1968

The lawn became a dominant element in California gardens. This is not surprising since Downing had described the lawn as the "ground-work of a landscape garden."[7] He hoped that "every day, as the better class of country residences increases, to see this indispensable feature in tasteful grounds becoming better understood and more universal."[8] The gardens at Lachryma Montis represent the quintessence of the rural elegance advocated by Downing— except for their exclusion of any distant landscape prospect, unlike Downing's other gardens in which the view was incorporated to expand the sense of space.

The creation of country estates on the Peninsula continued unabated from the 1860s to the end of the century. Until 1864, when a railroad was built linking San Francisco and San Jose, residents were limited by the distance that a horse could travel. Consequently, the more southerly parts of the Peninsula were not developed until the railroad had been completed. Developed by rich San Franciscan families as retreats from the cold fogs of the summer months, these estates were larger than the later summer "cottages" in Newport, Rhode Island, and the winter homes in Montecito, farther down the California coast. At least five hundred acres (two hundred hectares) in size and completely self-sufficient, they comprised stables, greenhouses, and conservatories, vegetable gardens, pleasure gardens, dairy farms, grazing grounds, paddocks, and sometimes racecourses. The area beyond the pleasure grounds and outbuildings was invariably screened by thick plantations of trees, usually quick-growing Monterey pines (*Pinus radiata*), cypress, and eucalyptus. This practice was so pervasive that it probably indicates a repugnance for the arid nature of the outer landscape, though there is no documentary evidence to confirm this.

VALPARAISO
PARK

Most gardens had personal meanings for their owners, and some gardens were clearly representations of familiar places. Faxon Dean Atherton's garden, Valparaiso Park, begun in 1860 on a site that is now in the center of the modern city of Atherton, conflates various asso-

ciations. The T-shaped two-story wooden house united the severe simplicity and symmetry of the New England houses that Atherton would have known as a boy with the wooden-shuttered houses that he had encountered as a trader in Chile in 1833–60. The formal boxwood garden was similar to formal New England gardens in towns such as Newburyport, Massachusetts, while the more pastoral qualities of the New England region were recalled by blue hound's-tongue, shooting stars, baby blue-eyes, buttercups, summer larkspurs, mariposa lilies, mallows, pennyroyal, honeysuckle, and snowberry, planted beneath extensive oak groves. Coquitos palms (*Jubaea spectabilis*), the caracalla vine, and the Chilean monkey-puzzle tree (*Araucaria araucana*) recalled South American landscapes.[9]

ANTOINE BOREL
GARDEN

Antoine Borel's garden demonstrated, even more clearly than Valparaiso Park, the desire to recapture and almost literally re-create the familiar. Borel moved to San Francisco from Switzerland in 1861 and rapidly became one of the city's most prominent bankers. At his country estate in San Mateo he faithfully used the colorful and decorative elements of contemporary French garden design, including long ribbon beds of flowering annuals and "mosaiculture." (The creation of elaborate geometric, mosaiclike patterns with annuals and succulents, mosaiculture was extremely popular in France and Germany but less so in the United States.)[10] To evoke Swiss landscapes Borel transformed the property, originally devoid of trees, with

Antoine Borel garden, San Mateo, 1864. Designed by Antoine Borel. The combination
of the cast-iron fountain with the formal mosaiculture beds demonstrates Borel's
familiarity with contemporary European fashions in garden design.

Photo: Carleton E. Watkins, 1880s

thick plantations of redwood, larch, birch, pepper, and cypress trees that simulated Swiss forests and excluded views of the nearby treeless mountains, which had recently been logged. Close to the low single-story house and defined by this forest were extensive lawns with curving paths and drives lined by beds of annual plants. Cast-iron fountains in mosaiculture beds were the principal decorative feature. The pleasure grounds surrounding the house were used by the Borels and their guests; cattle grazed in a parklike area beyond. The entire estate encompassed about five hundred acres (two hundred hectares).

The brightly colored beds, the gentle sprays of the fountains, and the chiaroscuro and delicate textures of the forest were evocatively European. But Borel's guests also encountered a more rugged image of nature. Within the birch groves an elaborate system of narrow, winding canals linked a series of trout-stocked ponds with a horseshoe-shaped defile designed as a miniature alpine pass. Catching fish in the ponds before dinner and moving through this

Antoine Borel garden, Swiss defile. Designed to represent a narrow alpine pass, this rather tropical-looking section of Borel's garden requires an imaginative leap of faith in order to grasp its intended meaning.
Photo: Carleton E. Watkins, 1880s

miniaturized alpine landscape created a set of idyllic references to Switzerland that heightened the contrast with the landscape outside the estate.

Since owners and their gardening staff came either from Europe or the eastern states it is not at all surprising that the gardening practices of those areas were used in California. The San Jose nurseryman James R. Lowe, Sr.—who was born in Chesterfield, England, and had worked in Massachusetts—used the gardenesque style frequently. With its Monterey cypresses (*Cupressus macrocarpa*) arching over the entrance drive to form a dense, evergreen tunnel, his design for the San Jose garden of General Henry Naglee, a retired Civil War veteran, reminded one visitor of an English nobleman's park: "Here I found evergreens from every clime, the Deodar cedar from the Himalaya Mountains; Cedar of Lebanon from Palestine; Chinese, Japanese, and Oregon cypress; the *Sequoia gigantea;* every conceivable variety of arbor vitae and seventeen varieties of acacias. . . . The great palms were there in all their majesty. Enormous dracenas, laurustinus, and all the plants from New Holland [Australia] flourish there in the open."[11]

Before Shinn's *Pacific Rural Handbook* (1879) there was no published guide to what to grow in California or how to grow it. Henry Winthrop Sargent acknowledged this in his supplementary essay to the sixth edition of Andrew Jackson Downing's *Treatise on the Theory and Practice of Landscape Gardening, Adapted to North America,* published in 1859: "We must grope in the dark until many more years of experience in different parts of the United States, enables us to know what we can and cannot grow."[12] W. B. West, a nurseryman, expressed the frustration of gardeners who understood the potential of the arid landscape. In 1861 he deplored the lack of cultivation of evergreens and claimed that arborvitae, pines, and cypresses would do particularly well in the hot, dry climate, growing more rapidly and with less water "than any ornamental tree."[13]

During this period the sole recognition of the need to develop design solutions appropriate to the peculiar conditions of California came from the landscape architect Frederick Law Olmsted in his designs for Mountain View Cemetery (1866) and Stanford University (1888) and from William Hammond Hall, the engineer who became the designer and first superintendent of Golden Gate Park in San Francisco. Hall's design displayed an understanding of ecological processes that is also hinted at in his letters about his residential projects, none of which were executed.[14] Olmsted was searching for a local alternative to irrigated lawns and florid Queen Anne architecture, but only the crumbling adobe mission ruins offered him any inspiration. Since nothing remained of the mission gardens, he sought sources in older landscapes with a similar climate. At Stanford University the buildings he designed were inspired by a desire to revive the tradition of California mission architecture, but the courtyards, paved and planted with drought-tolerant plants, were derived from precedents in the Mediterranean Basin, especially North Africa.

Olmsted's and Hall's approaches did not appeal to clients eager to create flamboyant gardens. The designer best suited to that approach was Rudolf Ulrich, who created exuberant, almost outrageous horticultural extravagances for three of the state's major resort hotels: Hotel del Monte, Monterey; Rafael Hotel, San Rafael; and the Raymond Hotel, South Pasadena. Ulrich had been trained as a gardener in Germany and Italy, and he was an extremely competent horticulturist, capable of orchestrating complex arrangements of shrubs and trees that had bright flowers and highly varied textures. His most unusual private garden was for Senator Milton Lathom's Thurlow Lodge (1874) in Menlo Park. The flat 150-acre (60.7-hectare) site was studded with large groves of oaks, retained to provide round masses that contrasted well with the new French Empire mansion attributed to David Farquharson. The relatively restrained garden design was notable for the absence of elaborate shrub plantings and for the

Thurlow Lodge, Menlo Park, 1874. Garden designed by Rudolf Ulrich for Senator Milton Lathom. Unusually simple for a design by the flamboyant Ulrich, this garden consisted of an expansive lawn punctuated by carefully pruned oak trees, cast-iron sculpture, a tent, and redwood-burl garden furniture.

Photo: Carleton E. Watkins, 1874

presence of numerous cast-iron statues and fountains. Mown lawns extended beneath the oak trees, which had been carefully pruned and cleared of undergrowth. This unusual, almost austere treatment intensified the visual contrasts of the flat ground plane, the rounded foliage mass of the oaks, and the long shadows they cast on the ground. It is conceivable that the restraint and the chaste sculpture should be credited to Senator Lathom, a discriminating art collector, rather than to Ulrich, who may simply have supervised the garden's execution.

The principal axes of the house were extended out into the spaces facing the two principal facades, thus connecting a series of plants and pieces of sculpture. For example, the view from the drawing room was centered on an axis that linked, in succession: a low circular mound flanked by two palm trees, a small circular planting bed, and finally, a magnificent cast-iron fountain purchased from the J.-J. Ducel et Fils foundry in Paris. This treatment was quite unlike the tradition of earlier formal gardens, in which axes had been used to organize formal spaces rather than objects in space.

The garden also contained a small rockery planted with cacti, an early example of the Arizona garden—i.e., collections of cacti brought from the Arizona desert—which Ulrich popularized. (Ulrich later gathered a large collection of such plants for Governor Leland Stanford's ranch at Palo Alto, in 1887.) This garden was another example of the nineteenth-century fascination with the exotic. Nineteenth-century gardens became collections of curiosities much like the earlier curiosity cabinets, in which scholars had displayed rocks, shells, gems, and other such finds.

Thurlow Lodge, cast-iron fountain made by the J.-J. Ducel et Fils foundry in Paris. Victorian taste favored sculpture and other garden ornaments in cast iron, which could be modeled into intricately detailed forms and was impervious to corrosion.
Photo: Carleton E. Watkins, 1874

If Thurlow Lodge was an elegant aberration in Ulrich's career, Linden Towers antici-pated his flamboyant resort hotels. It was built in Menlo Park in 1876 by James Flood, who had amassed an immense fortune using financial tips he overheard while bartending in a saloon. Ulrich surrounded the elaborate Eastlake- and Queen Anne–style mansion (designed in stages by William Curlett, Augustus Laver, and Jacob Lenzen) with gardens of diverse moods. The major living rooms overlooked a large formal garden, defined by vine-covered walls punctuated with gaslights and graced by square and circular beds filled with annuals and a huge multitiered fountain. Beyond this and forming the principal background for the entire garden were oak groves with a lavish understory of cream- and gold-flowered shrubs. Large, flowing lawns were planted with exotic trees such as Norfolk Island pine (*Araucaria hetero-phylla*). Passage from one lawn to another was enlivened by mosaiculture beds bordering the paths through the trees.

Ulrich's richly textured and colorful gardens brought together disparate flora in an obviously unnatural manner. One of Ulrich's chief rivals, John McLaren, advocated a "natural" quality that was equally unnatural. McLaren had been trained as a gardener at the Royal Botanic Garden in Edinburgh, where he assimilated William Sawrey Gilpin's principles of pic-

Opposite. Engraving of Linden Towers, Menlo Park, 1876. Designed by Rudolf Ulrich for James Flood. This view by Britton and Ray shows, at left, the formal garden that adjoined the living-room terrace, as well as the garden in front of the main entrance.

Right, top. Linden Towers. The terrace and lawn of the main garden (in the foreground) were planted with a palm and a monkey-puzzle tree (*Araucaria araucana*), plus numerous species of pine—all juxtaposed with a preexisting grove of oak trees.

Photo: Bradley and Rulofson, c. 1883

Right, bottom. Linden Towers. Succulents were the main elements in the elaborate formal patterns of the mosaiculture beds on either side of this path.

Photo: Bradley and Rulofson, c. 1883

turesque gardening.[15] McLaren advised his clients to follow the principles of nature, but the nature to which his designs referred were representations of scenery that he liked. At Golden Gate Park in San Francisco, where he succeeded the ecologically minded Hall, he attempted to replicate Sierran landscapes, a small desert, and a Scottish rhododendron glen, using a range of native and exotic species. At Keil Cove, in Tiburon in Marin County, at the turn of the century he helped the Keil family evoke the picturesque qualities of an English woodland by using a diversity of plants. These included trees such as the native buckeye (*Aesculus californica*), strawberry tree (*Arbutus unedo*), European beech (*Fagus sylvatica*), camphor tree (*Cinnamomum camphore*), melaleuca (now known as bottlebrush, *Melaleuca leucadendra*), and the umbrella tree (now known as chinaberry, *Melia azedarach*), as well as shrubs such as cassia, *Coprosma baueri,* and the Judas tree (*Cercis canadensis*).

The most elaborate gardens in Victorian California were created in the Southland during the last three decades of the century. This region had remained isolated and undeveloped until two new lines of the Southern Pacific Railroad linked it to the north in 1876 and 1888. Charles Nordhoff, Major Ben Truman, and others aggressively promoted settlement in the Southland on behalf of the railroad.[16] Initially, Los Angeles appealed mainly to consumptives seeking a dry climate and prosperous easterners seeking a warm place to spend the winter. Santa Barbara and adjacent Montecito attracted rich families who established estates on the "California Riviera." With its southern orientation and unusually gentle climate, the Santa Barbara area was an ideal setting for gardens, and the tradition of fine gardening continues there to this day.

Santa Barbara nurseries were the first to cater to an emerging fascination with semitropical landscapes. A writer in the *Pacific Rural Press* in 1874 proposed the "tropical" as an appropriate idiom for California gardens, while Major Truman trumpeted that "the sun shines upon no region, of equal extent, which offers so many and such varied inducements to one in search of homes and health, as does the region which is entitled to the appellation of 'Semi-Tropical California.'"[17] These terms implied exotic colors, textures, and forms. In practice "semitropical" was achieved with a mixture of palm trees, acacias, cypresses, Norfolk Island pine, dracaenas, pines, and araucarias.

❧⸺ঞ

Keil Cove, Tiburon, c. 1900. Garden designed by John McLaren for the Keil family.
Using a carefully chosen mixture of native and exotic trees, McLaren created the effect
of naturalistic scenery rather than of a cultivated garden.

Photo: David C. Streatfield, 1978

The Santa Barbara nurseries of Ellwood Cooper, Joseph Sexton, and Kinton Stevens led the way. Cooper is credited with having introduced more species of eucalyptus into the Southland than anyone else, as well as a wide variety of fruit trees. The eucalyptus was first imported to California from Australia in the 1850s. Popular because of its rapid growth, it was used by many farmers in windbreaks and by garden designers as an ornamental tree. Many species of this large genus are extremely messy, shedding both their pungent leaves and seedpods, but that seems not to have been considered a serious fault—at least in the beginning. Sexton concentrated on cultivating exotic flowering shrubs and trees, and Stevens was the first nurseryman to introduce tropical and semitropical plants into the Southland.[18] Soon plants such as *copa de oro* or cup of gold (*Solandra maxima*), bird of paradise, frangipani, the dragon tree (*Dracaena draco*), bulbs from South Africa, and the wonga-wonga vine (*Pandorea pandorana*) were all used frequently. These plants were introduced on a rather ad hoc basis, and it was not until Francesco Franceschi's organization of the Southern Acclimatizing Association in 1892 that plants were evaluated scientifically as they were introduced.

OZRO CHILDS
GARDEN

That the arrival of this greatly expanded plant vocabulary did not result in the adoption of new styles is exemplified by the approach taken by Ozro Childs. Born in Vermont, Childs moved to California in 1850 for his health after a brief sojourn in Ohio. He settled in

Ozro Childs garden, Los Angeles, 1890.
Designed by Childs for himself. This garden
was a collection of evergreens in which more
distinctive trees such as Italian cypresses
(*Cupressus sempervirens*), Norfolk Island pines
(*Araucaria heterophylla*), and yews were
placed in conspicuous positions against
a grove of conifers.

Photo: Thompson and West, *History of
Los Angeles County,* 1887

Los Angeles and, in 1857, established the nursery trade in the Southland with the opening of his important nursery (on Main Street between Eleventh and Twelfth streets), where he introduced a wide range of fruit and ornamental trees and shrubs. Most of his 50 acres (20.2 hectares) were devoted to the nursery plantations, but about 5 acres (2 hectares) surrounding Childs's Italianate house (built in the 1870s) were devoted to a lavishly planted garden. The thick plantations of Monterey pines and cypresses, cedars, acacias, India rubber trees (*Ficus elastica*), and golden arborvitae (*Thuja occidentalis aurea*) exemplified Downing's picturesque style; the planting of specimen palms, a Norfolk Island pine, and pyramidal cypress trees evoked the gardenesque. It was an introverted garden, surrounded by high hedges of Monterey cypress along the street and with a curving hedge with cutout windows separating the lawn from the nursery. From a distance this hedge looked almost like a wall covered with vines and may have been a reference to older English gardens. It inserted, or at least implied, an old-fashioned element in a garden that was in all other aspects typically Downingesque.

Childs's garden was one of the earliest examples in the Southland of the use of conifers, which later were widely employed, probably because of their rapid growth. Charles H. Shinn, expressing Bay Area preferences, had criticized the dense shade and gloom they created.[19] But in the arid, treeless landscape of Southern California their dark greens and dense shade were a welcome relief, and in 1888 a writer in Riverside observed that "the want of them is sorely missed."[20] Trees were planted lavishly in the new cities and private gardens. Riverside was the first city in the country to implement a city-wide tree-planting program, in 1890, and its elaborate tree-lined boulevards stretched for miles. One of the finest was Magnolia Avenue, bordered by large orchards of citrus trees and enclosed gardens.

JOHNSON GARDEN

The gardens along this boulevard, like Childs's garden in Los Angeles, were turned inward. The Johnson garden, created in Riverside in the early 1890s, was a typical, medium-sized example. It was enclosed by tall hedges of clipped Monterey cypress, broken only by an elaborate arched entrance. All that could be seen of the garden from the outside were the tops of the trees. A short, straight drive led to a circular turnaround in front of the Eastlake-style house. Scattered across the lawns was a diverse collection of eucalyptus, cedars, acacias, araucarias, and other trees; smaller and more decorative shrubs; and flowering plants in geometric beds. Such gardens represented the inevitable consequence of the widespread use of gardenesque ideas. The desire to accommodate as many different species as possible within the modest confines of such a garden overwhelmed both scientific and aesthetic clarity. This floral abundance became a new regional characteristic, encouraged by the long growing season, the increasing horticultural expertise of local gardeners and nurserymen, and the seemingly unlimited supply of water for irrigation.

CANON CREST

The apogee of this abundance in the desert was Cañon Crest (1880s), in Redlands, where lush gardens stood out against the spectacular backdrop of the snow-covered San Bernardino Mountains. Two hundred acres (81 hectares) of rocky ridge commanded panoramic views of the mountains to the north and San Timoteo Canyon to the south. Franz Hosp, an extremely talented German nurseryman and landscape gardener, transformed this barren, waterless hilltop into a lush paradise for the private enjoyment of the twin brothers Alfred H. and Albert K. Smiley. It was such a success that they generously opened their grounds to the public, and Santa Fe Railroad trains stopped in Redlands to provide tours of the garden.

Two large reservoirs were constructed, and water was pumped up to them from the valley more than 200 feet (61 meters) below. This water sustained a landscape of great diversity: more than one thousand species of trees and shrubs were planted in thick groves along several miles of drives that opened onto a chain of small ponds and lawns. Lavishly planted with lotus and water lilies, the ponds were overlooked by thatched huts and lined with wide ribbons of marguerite daisies. In front of the brothers' houses were parklike open lawns planted with specimen trees. At the edge of the ridge the vegetation opened up to views of the mountains, with the large citrus orchards in the middle ground organized by avenues of palm and eucalyptus trees. These views integrated a carefully contrived foreground of rich

Cañon Crest, Redlands, 1880s. Garden designed by Franz Hosp for Alfred H. and
Albert K. Smiley. A 200-acre (81-hectare) park was developed around the two brothers'
houses, which were approached by an elaborate network of drives lavishly planted
with ornamental shrubs and trees, including palms.

Huntington Gardens, San Marino,
1892–1927. Designed by William
Hertrich for Henry Huntington.
The Palm Garden was created with
mature specimens, all of types
known to thrive in Southern California, which were transplanted
from other gardens in the region.

Photo: David C. Streatfield, 1991

color and texture, a geometric middle ground of glossy dark greens and vibrantly colored fruit, and a sublime background of stark, snow-capped mountains. These juxtapositions, which defied many visitors' expectations, were frequently cited in articles and used in advertising images to attract potential settlers. To easterners suffering the intense cold and heavy snow of a typical winter, such images offered potent temptation.

Cañon Crest represents the zenith of flamboyance in nineteenth-century California garden design and horticultural achievement. Like Victorian gardens in England and other European countries, it was an overflowing cornucopia of plants from different ecological zones placed side by side and representing a triumph over nature. The creation of this floral paradise in such an intimidating and unlikely site also proclaimed the hidden triumph of hydrological engineering. Without heavy irrigation nothing at Cañon Crest, with the exception of desert plants, would have survived for more than one season. The desire to transform the California landscape from its natural, usually arid condition to that of a lush Eden was deeply entrenched throughout the state.

HUNTINGTON
GARDENS

An expansive example of that ambition was Henry Huntington's ranch, San Marino, located a few miles east of Los Angeles.[21] Rancho San Marino, which Huntington acquired in 1892, had gardens and surrounding citrus orchards that occupied 180 acres (72.9 hectares); the remainder of the ranch was subdivided by Huntington and became the city of San Marino. Several years before Huntington died, he had indicated his desire to open his library to scholars and his art collections and gardens to the public. This occurred in 1929, and although subsequent directors have made numerous changes to them, the gardens have been run ever since as an ensemble of botanical collections open to the public.

Huntington's gardens, created by his head gardener, William Hertrich, embodied the nineteenth-century obsession with exotica and were intended to provide a mature setting for the mansion, which was to be constructed later. Since few trees grew on the site, apart from a scattering of oaks that were carefully retained, this goal required transplanting a prodigious number of mature trees from nurseries and private gardens throughout the Southland. Tree moving on this scale had never before been attempted in this country,[22] and the success of this venture inspired the landscaping of the two expositions held in San Francisco and San Diego in 1915.

The transplanted trees supplemented the redwoods, peppertrees, pines, and Canary Island date and other palms grown in the estate's nursery. San Marino's Palm Garden was planted in 1905 on a four-and-a-half-acre (1.8-hectare) area to the east of the house. Containing 450 trees of about 150 species, it anticipated the eventual character of the entire garden as a series of scientific collections—unlike most Victorian gardens, which had indiscriminately mixed species from different families and genera.

The Desert Garden, also started in 1905, was intended as an assemblage of cacti from American deserts. Hertrich's conception was far more ambitious than Rudolf Ulrich's earlier Arizona gardens, and the San Marino Desert Garden remains the world's largest accumulation of desert plants outside a desert. At first most of the plants came from California deserts, where Hertrich often competed with other plant collectors. The garden grew rapidly, with cacti collected from Arizona deserts as early as 1908 and later from central Mexico.

In its early years the Desert Garden was laid out as a typical botanical collection, in straight rows. In the 1940s the San Marino Botanic Garden staff rearranged the plants to create striking patterns of form, color, and texture.[23] There have been several subsequent remodelings, one of which introduced trees and shrubs from desert areas and drylands, such as acacias, cercidiums, and cassias, as well as tree aloes, such as *Aloe bainesii*. This continuing infusion of new desert plants has produced great variety, and this extraordinary garden now has a fantastical quality, particularly when the plants are in bloom.

The North Vista Garden was created to focus the northward view from the mansion and to provide an appropriately formal setting for Huntington's extensive sculpture collection. The broad grass allée—in the center of an open oak woodland underplanted with Sasanqua camellias—was defined by rows of *Cocos plumosa* palms (now known under the genus *Arecastrum*), alternating with statues of Roman guards and women. A focal point was established by an elaborate Renaissance fountain set in a basin designed by Hertrich. The simplicity and impressive scale of the North Vista Garden contrasts strikingly with the formality of the Italian Renaissance and French Baroque gardens from which it was derived. The marble statues and the dark glistening green of the camellia leaves provide as strong a visual contrast to each other as the white marble urns and clipped hedges at Versailles. Here, however, the absence of hedges and the soft forms of the oak canopies produce a gentler setting in which sculpture plays a greatly reduced visual role, reflecting Huntington's preference for natural effects.

Hertrich laid out a formal Rose Garden west of the site of the proposed mansion in 1907. This involved extensive grading and the filling of a small ravine. A long pergola of concrete columns curves around to define the northern and western sides of the garden, which was laid out with two intersecting paths lined with rose-covered wire hoops. Like most of the

❧

Huntington Gardens, Desert Garden. A clump of *Dyckia rariflora* (a South American bromeliad) forms the foreground to flower stalks of *Yucca whipplei* (sometimes called Our Lord's candle); golden barrel cactus (*Echinocactus grusonii*) can be seen in the background. Photo: Bob Schlosser, 1984

Opposite. Huntington Gardens, North Vista Garden. The viewer's gaze is directed toward the San Gabriel Mountains by two rows of seventeenth-century figures, alternating with *Cocos plumosa* palms (*Arecastrum roman-zoffianum*), that terminate in an Italian stone fountain from the late sixteenth century.

Photo: Bob Schlosser, 1984

Right. Huntington Gardens, Rose Garden. A large array of old-fashioned roses—such as gallicas, centifolia, bourbons, hybrid musks, and teas—twines around wire hoops arching over one of the paths through the garden.

Photo: Robert M. Fletcher & Associates, 1991

estate's other gardens, it was designed to peak during the winter months, when the Huntingtons were in residence (they lived in France the rest of the year). Roses had long been popular in Victorian gardens, where they were frequently mixed with other plants in borders; cultivating roses in separate gardens became more popular after the turn of the century. Growing them in formal beds, usually edged with box or myrtle hedges, gave their unruly growth a tidier appearance and sustained visual interest after blooming ceased. The Huntington's Rose Garden has been substantially reduced in recent years, but the pergolas are unchanged—welcome providers of shade and reminders of the care taken early in this century to provide transitional elements between buildings and plants.

A canyon to the west of the Rose Garden was transformed in 1912 from a reservoir into the Japanese Garden, using plants and structures from a failed commercial Japanese tea garden. Additional lanterns, pagodas, and statuary were later brought directly from Asia. The garden fills a steep valley, which is entered from the top, a perspective that focuses attention on the lake at the bottom with its red bridge. Despite the authenticity of its artifacts, this garden was, and remains, highly artificial in character. Yet in 1915 a group of visiting managers of private estates in America considered it to be the finest example of the style they had ever seen.[24]

At the time the Huntington estate was being created, rare and exotic plants were symbols of wealth and social status valued almost as highly as fine art collections. Huntington and Hertrich hotly competed with other plant collectors, such as Arthur Letts and Edward Doheny, Sr., to surpass each other in the quantity and rarity of their collections. Hertrich, for example, outbid Doheny by paying eight thousand dollars for an important cycad collection owned by a Mr. Bradbury of Duarte, California. He relocated these cycads to a skillfully composed rock garden surrounding the large loggia at the east end of the mansion, which the Huntingtons used as an outdoor room. The dark, finely textured cycads made a living green wall that masked views to the north and formed an attractive foreground to the Palm Garden beyond.

With its Japanese Garden and carefully arranged collections of desert plants, palms, camellias, roses, cycads, water lilies, and statuary, Rancho San Marino exemplifies the nineteenth-century tradition, initiated by Repton, of the garden as a collection of specialized

❧

Huntington Gardens, Japanese Garden. The heart of the Japanese Garden is the vermilion moon bridge. Irises encircle a miniature shrine for the spirit of the lake, and koi carp provide flashes of color beneath the water.

Photo: Bob Schlosser, 1984

❧⁓⁓⁓❧

Huntington Gardens. A collection of rare cycads surrounds a bacchante by Frederick

MacMonnies, atop a modern marble basin on a sixteenth-century Italian base.

Photo: David C. Streatfield, 1991

places. Like Huntington's carefully acquired collections of English furniture, paintings, books, and silver, the gardens embody a detached and scientific approach to collecting. Yet this series of gardens is curiously disjointed, lacking a coherent circulation system from garden to garden.

Nineteenth-century gardeners exulted in such horticultural conquests. John McLaren's pride in the diversity of plants in Golden Gate Park was typical: "There is a tree from every hemisphere growing in Golden Gate park as well as our native varieties. A temperate climate makes it possible to grow out of doors plant material indigenous to many countries which elsewhere must be under glass. Plants from Australia, New Zealand, South Africa, the Mediterranean, Japanese, Chinese and Himalayan regions are well represented."[25]

Whatever one may think about the ecological appropriateness of importing large numbers of plants from different regions, their presence in California at the end of the nineteenth century did much to establish the state's identity as an exotic place. Few questioned such practices, with two notable exceptions being Olmsted and Hall. The popular English writer A. T. Johnson added his voice to theirs. In 1913 he wrote about gardens in Pasadena filled with exotic plants whose

> existence was equally dependent upon supplied moisture and the gardener's care. Look beyond the confines of these cities into the valleys and plains of California and you will find that they are for three seasons of the year sunburned deserts. But they respond spontaneously to the application of water. It is the liberal use of the hose pipe and the garden sprinkler which are turned on with such lavish generosity in the gardens and parks that has been the main factor in making the wilderness blossom as the rose. Indeed, the quantity of water which is used upon the ornamental gardens, not to mention the streets of Pasadena, would appear to be more than that consumed for all other purposes.[26]

Despite the beauty of Pasadena's gardens, Johnson questioned whether, in a landscape where water was not plentiful, "waste should be committed on such an appalling scale."[27]

By the end of the nineteenth century the highly skilled gardeners of California were able to re-create any type of landscape, especially of an exotic character. They established a flamboyant tradition of gardening that frequently bordered on excess. Many European garden designers had similar objectives, but what distinguished the results in California were the exceptionally long growing season and the unusually broad range of cultivatable plants from around the world, which enabled gardeners to achieve their desired effects with an unmatched prodigality.

3
ARTS AND CRAFTS GARDENS

T he Arts and Crafts movement originated in England, where its intellectual fathers, John Ruskin and William Morris, passionately advocated an alternative to the dominant industrial economy. Believing that the tyranny of the machine reduced the individual worker to little more than a cog, they advocated a return to the manual labor of the medieval period, when artisan-craftsmen had been free to express themselves. This aspect of the Arts and Crafts movement failed as an economic model, since its beautifully crafted products could be afforded only by the rich. But the movement proposed two important ideas that had important consequences for California gardens: first, that the design of both house and garden should take its inspiration from the genius loci (spirit of the place) and from vernacular traditions, and second, that the garden should become an outdoor living room.

These ideas were communicated in this country through articles in journals such as the *Craftsman, Country Life in America, House and Garden,* and to a lesser extent *House Beautiful.* California's remarkable climate permitted the second ideal to be realized more perfectly there than anywhere else in the country. The first ideal, however, was far harder to achieve. The concept of regionalism in garden design emphasizes sensitivity to the character of the local landscape and its history, but the California landscape was often so sublime and the scattered and ruined remnants of the Hispanic tradition so incomplete that capturing their essence in garden design was difficult. Such sensitivity could be achieved by using materials indigenous to the region, such as local stone and locally produced brick, as well as native plants (or imported plants similar to native ones in their horticultural requirements). It could also be achieved by referring to the design traditions of analogous regions elsewhere.[1]

Since the Arts and Crafts movement was a philosophy rather than a unified style, its designers resorted to several design traditions, including those of the Mediterranean Basin, Japan, and North Africa. Acknowledging the presence of Hispanic and Japanese citizens in the state, Charles Augustus Keeler, a Berkeley poet, advocated a fusion of Mediterranean and Japanese gardens. The architect Myron Hunt believed that the desert landscape of much of California suggested that the ideal garden was a "welled garden." Alfred D. Robinson, a prominent nurseryman and the editor-publisher of *California Garden* (a journal developed specifically for the San Diego region), called for a garden style unique to California. He disliked borrowing garden traditions from other countries and believed that the real California garden "will be born of California's sunbathed earth; [the designer] will be free from the weight of traditions—Italian, French, English, or Japanese—so that his design will not be a patchwork quilt." The ideal garden, according to Robinson, should be treated as an oasis "in our desert of too-much-everything."[2]

Theodore Payne, an English-born nurseryman, was another ardent advocate of the use of native plants, and his Los Angeles nursery was among the first to specialize in them. He designed a display garden at the Los Angeles County Natural History Museum in 1915, and a number of native-plant collections for rich clients, such as Gwethalyn Jones in Montecito.[3] But it should be emphasized that these were always elements of much larger gardens that contained other plant collections.

EL ALISAL

Arts and Crafts designers developed several garden types, including meadow gardens, hillside gardens, patio gardens, and open-landscape gardens—each of which attempted to address specific regions of the state. The unpretentious naturalness advocated by Arts and Crafts theorists was achieved by Charles Fletcher Lummis in his own house, El Alisal, at Highland Park in Southern California. The flamboyant Lummis was a scholar of California Indian and Spanish cultures and of the local landscape. His house, built by Indian laborers of boulders from the local arroyo, expressed a rooted sense of place. Next to the grove of sycamore trees from which the house took its name was a meadow of one and a half acres (.6 hectare). Lummis wrote of it: "On my own little place there are, today, at least forty million wild blossoms by calculation. Short of the wandering and unconventional foot-paths, which are almost choked with the urgent plant life beside them, you cannot step anywhere without trampling flowers—maybe ten to a step, as a minimum. One bred to climes where God counts flowers as Easterners do their copper cents, may not prefer to walk on them, but out here God and we can afford the carpet."[4]

El Alisal, wildflower meadow. Kaleidoscopic color was provided by the mix of California wildflowers, which lasted from six to ten weeks in the spring: California poppies (*Eschscholzia californica*), silver tips (*Potentilla anserina*), California wild oats (*Avena fatua*), Spanish lily (*Brodiaea capitata*), owl clover (*Orthocarpus purpurascens*), tidytips (*Layia platyglossa*), and more.
Photo: 1901, from Charles Fletcher Lummis, "The Carpet of God's Country," *Out West*, 1905

The house at El Alisal survives in excellent condition. By the 1920s Lummis's garden had been remade as a desert garden, and in the 1980s it was transformed into a garden demonstrating techniques of water conservation (see chapter 8).

Lummis's meadow garden was essentially a preserved fragment of nature, but meadowlike spaces could also be created from scratch. Kate O. Sessions, a San Diego horticulturist, designed a small garden at Coronado for a Mrs. Robert that demonstrated a drought-tolerant alternative to a lawn. An enthusiastic six-page description of this small garden appeared in *Pages from a Garden Note-Book,* by the popular writer Mrs. Francis King (Louisa Yeomans King). "Standing at the street end of the concrete walk leading from the street to the entrance porch, this picture in flowers must be the envy of many a Californian whose eyes are set toward sub-tropical beauty."[5] Sessions used plants growing up to two feet tall that had gray and green foliage and flowers of yellow and orange hues. The path was lined with streptosolen (*Streptosolen jamesonii*) and gladioli (*Gladiolus primulinus*). Behind on the right were several large and small aloes. Low plants such as *Centaurea maritima,* white alyssum, santolinas, sedums, crassulas, and *Convolvulus mauritanicus* contrasted with *Portulacaria,* a small tree. On the other side of the path the ground was covered like a carpet with *Verbena venosa* (also known as *V. rigida*), beach strawberry (formerly *Mesembryanthemum aequilaterale,* now *Carpobrotus chilensis*), three varieties of dasylirion, masses of eschscholzias, agaves, and sedums. They were carefully placed to contrast with boldly textured plants including the New Zealand flax (*Phormium tenax*), *Yucca baccata,* dragon trees, *Grevillea thelemanniana,* the fernlike tree Catalina ironwood (*Lyonothamnus floribundus*), groups of acacia, and several kinds of cactus. The ocher-colored walls of the house were clothed with trumpet vine (*Campsis radicans*) and streptosolen. The soft forms of the low plants, the dramatic textures, and the vibrant colors celebrated the Mediterranean landscape of San Diego.

Robert garden, Coronado, 1918. Designed by Kate O. Sessions. Several varieties of mesembryanthemum form the foreground, with *Yucca baccata* and several agaves rising above eschscholzias and a *Grevillea thelemanniana* in the back.

Photo: Mrs. Francis King, *Pages from a Garden Note-Book,* 1921

Edwin O. Libbey garden, Ojai, 1906. Garden
and house designed by Myron Hunt and Elmer
Grey. The native stone path, the Shasta daisies
(*Chrysanthemum maximum*), and the careful
siting of the house in relation to the preexisting oak trees all help create an effect of
regional appropriateness characteristic of the
Arts and Crafts movement.

Photo: *American Architect,* February 10, 1915

EDWIN O. LIBBEY
GARDEN

Apart from meadow gardening, which was practiced infrequently, the Arts and Crafts
ideal of designing gardens to be in harmony with the landscape was often achieved most successfully on more rural sites, where the desire for easy maintenance may have been more compelling than on urban or suburban sites. The retention of trees or other natural features on
such sites often suggested a particular design solution. At the Edwin O. Libbey bungalow
(1906) in the Ojai Valley, Myron Hunt and Elmer Grey used the abundant local stone to build
paths and a low wall along the road, visually tying the house and its garden space into the
broader landscape. An irregular paved path behind the wall led to the shacklike wooden house,
which had been carefully sited beneath a spreading oak tree.[6] The garden was a simple statement of accommodation, incorporating boulders of the wild landscape within its boundaries.
Embellishment consisted of vines on the house, liberal plantings of Shasta daisies (*Chrysanthemum maximum,* which require little water), and a small orchard of fruit trees.

Hillside gardening was developed in the Bay Area and in San Diego in totally different ways that expressed the regions' social as well as climatic differences. The Hillside Club, an improvement society founded in 1898 by Charles Augustus Keeler and the architect Bernard Maybeck, developed a set of principles for the design of private gardens and the entire landscape of the northern Berkeley hills. Under the guidance of this organization, its members, many of whom were associated with the University of California, completely transformed the existing landscape of softly contoured, grass-covered hills scattered with oak trees into a wooded hillside of mixed exotic trees, within which carefully sited shingled houses commanded panoramic views of San Francisco Bay. This landscape was in effect a continuous public garden punctuated by a series of private gardens. The irregular blocks of houses were stepped back into the hillside slopes, and a rambling network of paths threaded through the center of each block. Existing trees and rock outcrops were carefully retained, and the local stone was used to pave many garden paths and build low retaining walls, as in Maybeck's design for the Isaac Flagg garden. These winding paths created a sense of intimacy and mystery and made each individual garden seem larger.

Isaac Flagg garden, Berkeley, 1901. Garden and house designed by Bernard Maybeck. Maybeck's gardens invariably used local-stone paths and a naturalistic arrangement of plants.

Photo: Saxon Holt, 1993

One principle expounded by the Hillside Club was "A house should not stand out in a landscape, but should fit in with it."[7] Its members carefully selected colors that would make each house appear to be an organic element, with the prevailing brown hues of the hills determining the color of the houses. This chromatic principle was not, however, extended to the selection of plants. Fearing that indigenous plants might appear "dull in color and lacking in character," Keeler recommended (at Maybeck's suggestion) that California gardens have "a massy bloom at all periods of the year."[8] Maybeck remained committed to this idea for the remainder of his professional career, but the gardeners of Berkeley appear to have adopted it with less enthusiasm, seeming to prefer a rather subdued palette of colors.[9] They appear to have been content with gardens in which a small number of plants were in bloom throughout the year, providing accents of color that contrasted with the pervasive green foliage.

A completely different form of hillside garden was created in San Diego by Kate O. Sessions, working in association with the architect Irving Gill. The mesalike landscape of this city with its steep canyons lacked native trees and never developed the luxuriantly wooded character of the Berkeley hills. These southern hillside gardens featured a variety of drought-tolerant plants and low walls built of local cobbles or red Camp Kearney stone. Gill's plain concrete houses were poetic interpretations of Spanish houses and were, as he said, "plain and substantial as a boulder." Their ornamentation was left to nature, which added tone with lichens and softened contours with vines and shadows.[10] The house he designed in 1911 for a Miss Teats (later occupied by B. F. Chase) was typical. The simple, cubic concrete walls rose from the edge of the canyon, with Italian cypress, banana, and eucalyptus trees providing vertical contrast to the horizontal shrubs on the terraces.

Sessions was especially sensitive to the need for an approach to gardening that acknowledged San Diego's dry climate. Her nursery in the Pacific Mission Hills section of San Diego flourished from 1913 until her death in 1940. It offered many native plants, such as matilija poppy, golden flannel-bush (*Fremontia californica*), and blue-flowered ceanothus (*Ceanothus caeruleus*), as well as plants from South Africa, Australia, and Brazil with bold colors and forms, such as the silver tree (*Leucadendron argenteum*), bougainvillea, and *Eucalyptus ficifolia*. She also used pride of Madeira (*Echium fastuosum*) and numerous types of mesembryanthemums (*Mesembryanthemum chilense, crystalinum, edule,* and *nodiflorium*), whose kaleidoscopic carpet would, she believed, be "the envy of every frosty section of the United States and Europe."[11] One customer's request for hollyhocks received the tart response: "I let them alone. They do not like us and I don't like them. We have plenty of plants that do like our climate so I don't have anything to do with hollyhocks."[12]

~~~

B. F. Chase garden, San Diego, 1911. Garden designed by Kate O. Sessions; house (at center) designed by Irving Gill (as were the other houses in this photo). Drought-tolerant trees and shrubs such as eucalyptus and cotoneaster species were planted on the slopes below the house; bougainvillea decorates the walls. Photo: c. 1933

A. H. SWEET
GARDEN

The A. H. Sweet garden (1914), by Mead and Requa, former assistants of Gill, in association with Paul Thiene, was a more formal essay in hillside gardening. The house was placed at the top of a steep hillside and commanded views from both floors. The living rooms opened onto an outside room defined by walls, with wall fountains and a colonnade permitting views out. This architectonic space was wreathed with vines and glossy-leaved plants so

Below. A. H. Sweet garden, San Diego, 1914.
Plan of the house, by Frank Mead and Richard
Requa; garden by Mead and Requa with Paul
Thiene. Photo: *Western Architect,* October 1915

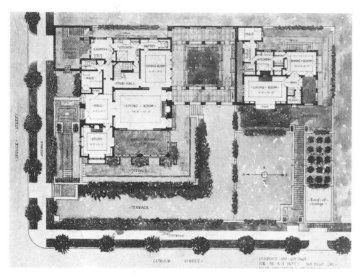

Right. A. H. Sweet garden. This view from the
upper terrace looks toward the arched
openings of the inner patio and emphasizes
the architectonic simplicity of the design, in
which the formal planting reinforces the
shapes of the architecture.

Photo: Carol Greentree, 1986

❧

**A. H. Sweet garden. This view of the stairway entrance to the guest cottage shows the
striking contrast, in color and form, of an aloe against bare white walls.**

Photo: Carol Greentree, 1986

that the severely plain walls served as a backdrop to the picturesque form of the plants. Below
the house is a series of terraces planted with drought-tolerant species. *Eucalyptus ficifolia* at the
edge of the highest terrace provides a bold and colorful contrast to the white mass of the
house. Plain concrete stairs decorated with tiled panels lead up through the terraces to the
front door in a circuitous route reminiscent of the Generalife gardens in Granada, Spain.

Patio gardens were especially popular in the Southland because of their associations
with Hispanic California and Italy. Helen Hunt Jackson's *Ramona* (1884) and her articles on
California, together with essays by George Wharton James, had renewed interest in the Mexican ranch-house patios. The advantage of the patio was that it could be used for a variety of
purposes: some housed swimming pools, others were covered with permanent or retractable
glazed panels or removable canvas panels to create an additional enclosed room.[13]

Many of Gill's houses were designed around a paved patio that was defined on three sides by colonnades and on the fourth side by a wall with glazed openings to a walled garden beyond. Furnished with vines, a banana or small palm tree, wicker tables and chairs, and rugs, these patios were used as rooms. Until its demolition the Homer Laughlin house in Los Angeles (1907) was a typical example that, like its Spanish precedents, provided a transition from the interiors of the house to the full sunlight of the walled garden. Gill, no doubt with advice from Sessions or Thiene, planted these architectural rooms with vines, dark green shrubs with glossy leaves, and brightly colored flowering shrubs and trees. Permanent color was provided by fountains, ceramic pots, vases, and glazed tiles on paths and on benches, which enhanced the garden at those times of the year when nothing was in bloom. Gill achieved what he called a "second blooming" on the walls of these garden rooms by placing red geraniums close to walls that were tinted by mixing primary colors with white paint.[14]

Homer Laughlin garden, Los Angeles, 1907. Garden and house designed by Irving Gill. The wisteria-draped pergola bisected the main garden and connected it to the enclosed patio at the heart of the house.

Photo: c. 1912

Walter Dodge garden, Hollywood, 1916. Garden designed by Irving Gill and Wilbur
David Cook, Jr.; house designed by Gill. The walled main garden, seen here, was adjacent to the terrace of the house. The *Beaucarnea recurvata* (a treelike member of the lily
family), in the foreground, provided a contrast to the simple formality of the garden.

Photo: Julius Shulman, 1954

For his larger houses Gill designed walled patios that became garden rooms, with creepers and vines draping the walls enclosing rectangular green lawns. The dark-leaved vines on the walls, the carefully placed trees, and the paths (made either of concrete stepping stones or of brick) were carefully balanced in an integration of geometric forms and nature that complemented the extreme simplicity of Gill's concrete houses. The finest and largest example was the Walter Dodge house in Hollywood (1916), designed in association with the landscape architect Wilbur David Cook, Jr. The green of the grass and of the plants on the walls was set off by an elaborate mosaic wall fountain. The house and garden were destroyed in 1975.

The open-landscape garden is particularly associated with the architects Charles and Henry Greene and their work in Pasadena. Many of their gardens are subtle evocations of Japanese gardens that contrasted strikingly with the lavish flower gardens generally favored in this conservative, upper-middle-class community. Neither brother had ever visited Japan, but their work became infused with a subtle poetry after an admiring client gave Charles Greene a book of photographs of traditional Japanese houses, temples, and gardens.

One of the finest surviving examples of such work is the winter home of Mr. and Mrs. David B. Gamble, constructed in 1908 on the edge of Pasadena's Arroyo Seco. (Mr. Gamble was a second-generation member of the Proctor and Gamble Company of Cincinnati and had retired in 1894.) The gently sloping lot faced west and was dominated by two groups of eucalyptus trees, which determined the position of the house. In three alternative design studies,

❧⸰⸱⸰☙

David B. Gamble garden, Pasadena, 1908. Garden and house designed by Charles and Henry Greene. The garden and house were conceived as a harmonious unit in which every element, even the paving of the driveway, was treated as a work of art.

Photo: Marvin Rand, c. 1977

Left. David B. Gamble garden. These stepping stones, which led to the clothes-drying yard at the side of the house, were positioned with as much artistry as those in the path across the main lawn.

Photo: Leroy Hulbert, c. 1910

Above. David B. Gamble garden, terrace. Two preexisting eucalyptus trees, brick-and-quarry-tile paving, and a wall of clinker brick and boulders were united in an asymmetrical composition around a small pool, capturing the spirit of a Japanese garden.

Photo: Leroy Hulbert, c. 1910

the house was placed around the tree masses, which shaded the building and opened its internal spaces to the breezes blowing across the site. Ultimately the house was sited so that one group of trees rose from the private terrace, with their upper limbs passing through the roof eaves; the other group was in the fenced service yard. Both groups have since died, but originally they served as visual anchors, diminishing the apparent size of the house as well as contributing shade. The house was visually tied to the ground by a terrace wall of clinker brick and boulders taken from the arroyo. The dark forms of the irregular bricks were carefully fitted into abstract patterns around the boulders. This wall has always been planted with the vine *Ficus pumila* (sometimes called *F. repens*), which originally provided a delicate mantle of lacy vegetation but over time has thickened into a mat that obscures the intended integration of structure and nature.

The exquisite grading of the lawn into softly undulating forms carried this integration of house and site further. From the street the sloping lawn appears to rise gently to the front-door steps. In fact, a semioval brick drive is hidden behind this graded berm. Subtle solutions were provided for the most mundane design problems. The point where the drive branches off to the garage is marked by an octagonal tile, which unifies the radiating brick lines into a flowing abstract composition. The drive also serves as an open drainage channel; where the drive crosses the sidewalk, water is channeled into open narrow grooves through the walk.

The main living rooms lie to one side of the long hall that bisects the house. A series of terraces and sleeping porches surrounds these spaces, protecting them from the bright light and keeping them cool. On the arroyo side the terrace expands to encompass the site of the original eucalyptus trees and a small pool. At one end the balustrade rises to support a slender glazed lantern, then dips down to rise up again behind the pool. This curving profile is balanced by the battered retaining wall and by the smooth brick steps that ascend to the quarry-tile floor of the terrace. The artistry of this design melds angular forms with the seeming randomness of the natural world.

Although the Arts and Crafts style had generally lost its popularity by the time of World War I, two of the gardens that most completely realized its ideal of harmonious naturalness were not created until the 1920s.

DAVID L. JAMES GARDEN

The first, designed by Charles Greene, is the David L. James house (1921) in Carmel Highlands, which is one of the most extraordinary fusions of house and site ever made in North America. Rugged bluffs along the dramatic triangular promontory rise abruptly from the ocean, broken only by the opening to a huge cavern directly beneath the house. The story of Greene's transformation of this extraordinarily beautiful site is appropriately romantic. James, an antiques dealer from Kansas City, and his wife were camping with friends on a rocky plateau near Big Sur. They became so enchanted by this beautiful area that they decided to acquire the property and build a modest summer home on it. A few days following their purchase they recounted their good fortune at a party in Carmel. The story intrigued a short man with long hair, who obtained their permission to visit the site, which he had long admired and wished to paint. A few days later the man, Charles Greene (who had retired to Carmel from

his practice in Pasadena), visited their camp and gave them watercolor sketches of a house that he thought would be appropriate for their site. The Jameses were delighted with his ideas and awarded him the commission.

Randall Makinson, Greene's biographer, has suggested that Greene's fascination with the ruins of Tintagel Castle in Cornwall, England, had a powerful influence on his design. The Jameses' V-shaped house was carefully placed close to the lip of the cliffs, enclosing a courtyard on the landward side and opening onto a paved terrace on the ocean side. The steep cliffs with deep fissures required the construction of very high foundation walls, which rise so effortlessly from the rocks that in places it is almost impossible to tell where the site ends and a wall begins.

There is no separate garden distinguished from the landscape, but succulents and yuccas were planted in small protected crevices in the walls and rock faces below the terrace that opens from the living room. The cliffs between the house and the road are crowned with

the dark mass of a grove of Monterey cypress trees. The seamless continuity of rock and retaining walls, the succulents planted on the ocean side, and the grove of bent, wind-swept Monterey cypresses create an effect of inevitability that results from Greene's wholehearted response to the genius loci. Frank Lloyd Wright has been justly praised for achieving this in some of his finest houses, such as Fallingwater in Pennsylvania. But the Jameses' house exceeds even this as an almost mystic expression of the spirit of place.

Unlike the craftsmen of the Middle Ages, who were allowed considerable freedom to exercise their own artistic skills, Greene's masons remained under his adamant control, receiving specific instructions about where to place each stone. Sections of new wall built during his numerous absences would be torn down on his return and rebuilt so frequently that the house was still unfinished when he was finally dismissed in 1923 by his exasperated clients. Greene was recalled in the 1940s to complete the basement.

Green Gables, Woodside. Garden and house designed by Charles Greene, 1911, for
Mortimer and Bella Fleishhacker; water garden designed by Greene, 1926–28. The long
reflecting pool and the arcade lead the eye toward the Santa Cruz Mountains.

Photo: David C. Streatfield, 1975

Green Gables (1911 and 1926–28), also by Charles Greene, is the largest garden in the country by an Arts and Crafts designer.[15] The understated monumentality of Greene's attempt to come to terms visually with the sublime Santa Cruz Mountains landscape is at variance with the simple, almost rustic, vernacular generally sought by Arts and Crafts designers. There is no record of why Mortimer and Bella Fleishhacker hired Greene for the job—an unlikely choice, since they wanted an English house with a thatched roof, like the Devonshire cottages they had seen while traveling. They disliked the Japanese-inspired bungalows in Pasadena for which Greene was known, but they may have disliked even more the work by the historicist Bay Area architects. Whatever their reasons for hiring him, over a period of some seventeen years Greene created for them one of his most beautiful designs. The 75-acre (30.4-hectare) property contained rolling meadows, clumps of live oaks (*Quercus agrifolia*), and panoramic views of the Santa Cruz Mountains to the south and west. The large lot, the shortage of water, and the difficulty of adjusting a modestly conceived summerhouse to the dramatic site made it Greene's most challenging commission.

The garden was designed in two stages. Below the house and its broad brick-paved terrace surrounding a huge oak tree is a rectangular lawn, at the end of which is a T-shaped pool. This extremely severe design was enlivened only by golden brown glazed pots at the corners of the pool and by a planting of poplars and Atlas cedars (*Cedrus atlantica*) at the top of the steep bank beyond the pool. These trees framed views of the mountains from the terrace and diagonal views across the lawn. Despite its formality, this austere design may be a reinterpretation of the simple English landscape garden of Studley Royal, in Yorkshire, which Greene visited in 1909.

Over the years Greene was invited back to design more projects for the Fleishhackers, the most important being the commission "to do something" with the area below the main lawn. His design—featuring a monumental 300-foot-long (91.5-meter) pool, curved at both ends—resolved the lack of a harmonious link between the garden foreground and the distant mountain panorama. The highly successful solution provides no glimpse from the house of the water garden, which can be seen only from the top of the stairs. Two broad flights descend to a wide terrace overlooking the pool. Huge flower pots made of small, carefully graduated courses of brick provide color and detail. From the terrace two flights of stairs embrace the inner end of the pool.

A stone arcade at the far end of the pool partially veils the view and suggests a ruined Roman aqueduct. Several studies were made for this feature, but the arcade was unquestionably the most appropriate solution. It is adorned with green glazed flower pots, as are the paths leading to it. Rather surprisingly, no source of water was provided to sustain these plants, so

the gardeners have had to clamber up and down a narrow ladder with a watering can. The open arches of the arcade are echoed by arched recesses in the wall below the staircase terrace. This latter feature and the bold swirling forms of the double-branched staircase evoke Italian Baroque gardens. Greene had visited Frascati on his honeymoon and must have been familiar with its gardens. The planting of two Monterey pines at the head of the staircase was another subtle allusion to Italy. The careful selection of three different stones for the paving of the staircase and the dark red-brown brick for the balustrade suggested considerable age.

Greene's understated references to English and Italian sources were a poetic response to the character of the landscape. The style of the house had been dictated by the client, but the garden was an artistic achievement directed entirely by the designer. It enhanced and emphasized the surrounding landscape by providing views of it and by incorporating the same materials as that landscape. Greene's exquisite craftsmanship and appropriation of historicist references yielded a new landscape that celebrated the genius of the place.

The Arts and Crafts movement was devoted to ideals of craftsmanship and regional identity. The broader meaning of Green Gables and the James garden (especially the latter) lies in their demonstration of how the spirit of place could be achieved in landscapes of sublime splendor.

Opposite. **Green Gables. The monumental staircase descends the hill in two broad flights to a terrace supported by a retaining wall with arched recesses.**
Photo: David C. Streatfield, 1975

Right. **Green Gables. The arcade at the outer end of the water garden suggests a Roman aqueduct. The glazed flowerpots along the top of the arcade introduce decorative flourishes of color when filled with plants.**
Photo: David C. Streatfield, 1975

4

IMPORTED STYLES: NORTHERN CALIFORNIA

HIGURASHI-EN

I n the San Francisco Bay Area early in this century, second-generation descendants of the raucous, extravagant entrepreneurs who had fashioned estates from Mexican ranchos sought to transform themselves into genteel patricians and their estates into country houses and country clubs. Their considerable fortunes made in banking, mining, lumber, and transportation were now directed toward creating a West Coast version of European aristocratic society.

In the gardens of these country houses the designers attempted to bring order to the floral prodigality of the nineteenth-century garden. As the Bay Area artist Bruce Porter remarked in his introduction to Porter Garnett's *Stately Homes of California* (published in Boston in 1915):

> If our houses garner increasingly the arts of all ages and all countries, so our Californian gardens hospitably take in and nourish, in sunshine and brisk air, aliens of every habit and every zone. These transmigrations and domestications offer an absorbing range of wonder to any saunterer along the bright paths. There is something prodigal in the manner of their thriving that perhaps makes us love them less than if they sickened a little and had to be fussed over and comforted till acclimatized. Instead of calling for any endearing ministrations of our hands these horticultural aliens are much more likely positively to riot among us, climb all over us in their first season.[1]

Many of San Francisco's leading citizens at the turn of the century owned estates for summer use on the Peninsula. Several of these had been created by subdividing earlier Victorian estates and hence were smaller than the grand estates then being developed on Long Island, New York. The designers in California borrowed from a variety of sources, including Japanese and Mediterranean design traditions, the French Baroque, and English gardens, both formal and naturalistic. Those eclectic sources, presented either singly or in combination, well suited owners whose previous experience with gardens had been derived from travel abroad or from fantasy. These reconstructions were achieved in defiance of the local landscape.

A local passion for Japanese gardens had been stimulated by the garden created by George Turner Marsh at the California Mid-Winter Exposition, held in San Francisco in 1894. After that, practically every large estate in California had some kind of Japanese garden—usually a tea garden, traditionally the smallest and least contrived of Japanese gardens. Entering a tea garden signified a passage from civilization to wilder nature. One of the few California tea gardens that still survives was designed in 1907 by Makoto Hagiwara for Eugene de Sabla, a pioneer in hydroelectric power. It was located at El Cerrito, the earliest Peninsula estate, which had been established by the Howard family in the early 1850s. After John McLaren became the Howards' head gardener in 1876, El Cerrito's gardens were much embellished by the conifer trees he planted in the manner of an English estate. By the time El Cerrito was acquired by de Sabla, the 1,500-acre (607.5-hectare) estate had been reduced to 20 acres (8.1 hectares).[2]

Hagiwara's Higurashi-en (garden worthy of a day of contemplation), which occupied less than half an acre, was sited apart from the main gardens and treated as a rural retreat. To frame the garden Hagiwara retained the native oaks, laurels, and madroñas (*Arbutus menziesii*), as well as a number of the magnificent evergreen specimens planted by McLaren, including a Spanish fir (*Abies pinsapo*), several Canary Island pines (*Pinus canariensis*), an Atlas cedar, and a deodar cedar (*Cedrus deodara*). Several tons of soil and Japanese volcanic rock were trucked in

Higurashi-en, Hillsborough, 1907. Tea garden designed by Makoto Hagiwara for
Eugene de Sabla, as part of his estate, El Cerrito. The lake at the center of the garden
is planted with trees and shrubs that provide a green structure for most of the year,
enlivened by delicate blossoms in the spring and strongly colored foliage in the fall.

Photo: David C. Streatfield, 1974

to build a miniature mountain, which became the principal background element and the source of an artificial stream that cascaded down a waterfall and expanded into a lake.

Combining elements of an artificial hill garden and a stroll garden, Higurashi-en was designed to evoke a sense of rustic solitude and to serve as a setting for the tea ceremony. (Both the hill garden and the stroll garden were styles codified by rules that governed the arrangement of plants and the placement of stones. The hill garden was essentially a miniaturized mountain landscape; the stroll garden usually involved a path following an irregular line around a feature such as a lake.) The garden is entered through a wooden gate constructed, without nails, from several different kinds of wood. Inside, a path directs the visitor through a sequence of different views, leading across stepping stones, around a lake, up the miniature mountain, back down over volcanic rocks, and across a stone bridge to the teahouse.

The effect of the garden changed with the seasons. Pale sheets of blossom shimmered in the spring; in the autumn, striking yellow and crimson foliage was reflected in the lake. The teahouse faced east, and its veranda overlooked the lake and the mountain. This positioning allowed visitors to enjoy the moon-viewing ceremony in September, the month of the most beautiful moon. Hagiwara planted trees and shrubs that had symbolic meanings: ginkgos for longevity; pines, bamboo, and plum for the continuity of life; and plum to announce the coming of spring. The stone bridge is inscribed with Chinese and Japanese characters that read "The Bridge of the Divine Immortals," a Taoist reference.

Completed in 1907, the garden immediately became popular with the de Sablas' friends and was frequently illustrated in magazines. At night tiny electric lights illuminated the paths and the waterfall. One visitor wrote, "The trees and shrubs look as if they were the haunt of fireflies and the ground seems sprinkled with glow worms."[3] The de Sabla property was subdivided in 1947, when the teahouse was incorporated into a new house; Higurashi-en survives in excellent condition as a private garden.

Japanese gardens place great value on restraint and order—qualities that have often been lacking in California gardens because with enough applied water almost any plant could be grown in them. The abundance of growth in California's gardens caused Bruce Porter to lament the absence of "appeal, of tenderness, of the hint of a delicate care bestowed, that gardens speak of in more difficult climates where lavish growth and bloom is a definite attainment on the part of everybody and everything concerned."[4] As designers sought to balance the extravagance of the local plant life with more formal design modes, they turned to precedents derived from Renaissance Italy, Baroque France, and Islamic Spain. This diversity of styles was encouraged by a dawning respect for the inherent nature of California's landscape and climate, which resembled those of the Mediterranean region. Herbert Croly, editor of the magazine

Architectural Record, suggested that adopting the Italian style of architecture and hillside terrace gardening made more sense in California than anywhere else in the country because the landscape itself was "classic" and resembled that of Italy.[5] Stephen Child, a Boston architect who also practiced in California, shared his enthusiasm: "The real garden should adjoin the house, windows, and doors opening upon its terraces, paths, and parterres, its fountains splashing in invitation. . . . The spirit of cheerfulness and the close connection between art and everyday living which are expressed in the Italian villa-garden make the Italian treatment appropriate in California."[6] Certainly the style made more sense in California than Charles Adam Platt's Italianate gardens did along the eastern seaboard.[7]

Several designers adopted Croly's advice but continued to use some plants that had been popular in previous decades. The resulting lush effect was criticized by the architect Melville McPherson. "The Italian cypresses in rows of military regularity lose something of their formality when screened by the portière boughs of a pepper tree, the clipped edge is less austere with a rose clambering over it and lemon trees won't stay dwarfed for earthen vases. Altogether the Italian villa as found in California has no exact counterpart in Italy."[8] The Italianate elements in California gardens—particularly balustraded terraces and parterres enlivened with pools and fountains—were often concentrated in the area immediately surrounding the house; beyond them, gardens invariably became open lawns and groves of trees. This hybrid quality was perfectly captured by the English writer Marion Cran in describing the estate Arcady in Montecito: "It looks like Italy and England mixed."[9]

The rather stiff, scholarly Italianate designs produced by such architects as Robert Farquhar, Willis Polk, and Myron Hunt may very well reflect the fact—as noted by Chesley Bonestell, chief designer for Willis Polk—that they were often based on specific historical models. For example, the garden of The Uplands, C. Templeton Crocker's estate in Hillsborough, was based on an Italian villa garden.[10] The most successful Italianate gardens were designed by Bruce Porter, the Bay Area artist who was highly respected by architects as an arbiter of taste.

NEW PLACE Porter approached garden design in a thoroughly romantic and painterly fashion.[11] His design for New Place (1905), William Crocker's 700-acre (283.5-hectare) estate in Hillsborough, was one of the earliest Italianate gardens in California. With its extensive parklands casually but artfully planted with a variety of pine and oak specimen trees, and with its formal gardens surrounding the house, New Place was intended to evoke the villas on the outskirts of Rome. Porter's simple yet romantic design suggests a garden of considerable age. The balustraded gravel terrace overlooks a simple lawn with a scattered planting of large trees and rectangular pools with single jets of water. The vines carefully placed on the house, the

New Place, Hillsborough, 1905. Garden designed by Bruce Porter for William Crocker.
The balustraded gravel terrace opens from the drawing room, at left. Planted with
Italian cypress trees (*Cupressus sempervirens*), it overlooks a formal water garden. New
Place survives in good condition as a country club. Photo: c. 1928–32

massive Italian cypresses (*Cupressus sempervirens*), the large terra-cotta pots, and the umbrella-like forms of the Italian stone pines (*Pinus pinea*) combine to create an orderly Italianate effect.

By the early years of the twentieth century marked differences had developed between the preferences of patrons on the East and West coasts. Rich Californians tended to venerate the openhanded patterns of informal living that Helen Hunt Jackson had celebrated in *Ramona* and in her essays on California, whereas wealthy easterners generally adopted architectural and garden styles associated with aristocratic European cultures. The French Baroque style, for example, was very popular for East Coast gardens, but far less favored in California. The framing of sweeping, axial vistas and the brilliant manipulation of terraces and geometric shapes first practiced by André Le Nôtre, the great seventeenth-century French landscape architect, were far more appropriate to the relatively flat, watery expanses of northern France than to California's boldly dramatic landscapes.

CAROLANS

A few moneyed Californians did succumb to the French Baroque style nonetheless. Had it been completed, the most ambitious French garden not only in California but in the entire United States would have been Carolans, the estate of Harriet Pullman Carolan (the Pullman car heiress) and Francis Carolan, her fox-hunting husband.[12] In 1913 Harriet Carolan decided to transform a steep hillside into an elaborate formal landscape. The 500-acre (202.5-hectare) site commanded spectacular views eastward over the Crystal Springs Lakes, San Francisco Bay, and the Oakland hills and northward to San Francisco. The estate was to be

Carolans, Hillsborough, 1915. Garden designed, but only partially executed, by Achille Duchêne for Harriet Pullman Carolan and Francis Carolan; house designed by Ernest Sanson. This plan for the main vista was reproduced in *Gazette illustrée des amateurs des jardins*, 1923.

designed by the architect Ernest Sanson and Achille Duchêne, a landscape architect from Paris, with Willis Polk as the local coordinating designer. Duchêne was a brilliant scholar of seventeenth-century gardens, several of which he had restored. His water parterre at Blenheim Palace in England was one of the most imaginative historically inspired gardens of this century.[13] His garden scheme for Carolans was one of the most ambitious ever proposed for a California site, and had it been completely executed, it would have been his largest design. Its importance lies in Duchêne's attempt to apply a carefully coordinated and very subtle system of design to a vast property with sweeping vistas.

Duchêne's design positioned the house on a low east-west ridge, with a formal paved entry court on the south side, which had the least interesting view. The principal rooms were approached by a top-lit staircase hall one floor above the entrance court. The disposition of the rooms was determined by the time of day they would be used and when the views would be particularly beautiful. The dining room faced east to the sunrise, the living rooms were on the west side to command the sunset, and the bedroom on the north looked toward the city lights. The axes of the east, north, and west facades were extended outward as formal gardens. The parterre on the east was broken into two sections; the longer, most easterly section terminated in a low staircase guarded by Lombardy poplars (*Populus nigra* var. *italica*) framing the view to the Crystal Springs Lakes. The short north garden, also open at the end, was flanked by two small loggias covered with wisteria.

The most impressive of the formal gardens was the one to the west. A terrace opened from the living rooms to a broad path that bisected low boxwood-hedged parterres filled with clipped lavender. A long formal lawn, or *tapis vert* (literally, "green carpet"), flanked by fountains and trimmed shrubs led to a grand parterre of brightly colored annual flowers. To the north and south this parterre culminated in slightly raised semicircular gardens enclosed by latticed pergolas covered with climbing plants. Groups of oak trees and eucalyptus framed the *tapis vert* and the pergolas. Behind the central parterre was a wall of fountains with monumental staircases at each side. This served as an important midpoint in the vista. Above the wall a terrace overlooked the house and the panoramic vista. Beyond a slightly narrower *tapis vert* the paths at the side terminated in a formal terrace backed by a monumental columned portico set "like a white blind against the giant eucalyptus grove."[14] The view from this point was the most impressive, sweeping from a distant glimpse of San Francisco to the broad line of the East Bay hills, with the Crystal Springs Lakes and the house below. On one side of the upper *tapis vert* was a grove of Monterey cypresses and climbing roses, which faced a bank of camellias on the opposite side.

Duchêne's design owes much to Le Nôtre's work, especially at Vaux-le-Vicomte, but the design is also notable for the way it departed from that and similar precedents. In a classic French Baroque garden the eye is directed along a central allée, with a series of radial minor allées cut through a surrounding forest. Carolans opened up to views in three directions with axes in the foreground; the middle distance was treated as a parkland that merged visually with the distant landscape. The various formal gardens established viewing platforms from which to look out at the panorama.

Duchêne's magnificent perspective drawings published in the *Gazette des jardins amateurs* are all that survive to record this ambitious conception. By 1917 only the terraces immediately surrounding the house had been finished; Harriet Pullman Carolan Schermerhorn subdivided the estate in the late 1920s, leaving the house on only 6 acres (2.4 hectares).

La Dolphine (1916), the house of Senator and Mrs. George Newhall, was the most ambitious French-inspired design to be actually realized in California. The design, executed on a flat site in Hillsborough by the architect Lewis Hobart, orchestrated the principal elements of the garden in a Latin cross. The entrance drive occupied the cross-axis, and the house was placed just below the intersection of the two axes. The living rooms opened onto a broad balustraded terrace, from which a flight of stairs, as wide as the central block of the house, descended to a formal garden centered on a rectangular reflecting pool with apsidal ends. Enclosed on three sides by raised walks beneath rows of plane trees (pollarded, or pruned, to form solid masses of foliage) that are behind low-clipped cypress hedges, the garden incorporated elements of Italian Renaissance and French Baroque designs. This lower garden, like the upper *tapis vert* and the main terrace, was furnished with numerous wooden *caissons de Versailles* (wooden boxes, often on wheels, in which small trees are grown) containing pruned orange trees. These did not have to be consigned to orangeries in the winter, as in France, but remained outside all year.

Beyond the reflecting pool was a long *tapis vert* flanked by facing rows of white and pink hawthorn trees. This burst of color and the background planting of large clumps of euca-lyptus trees were untraditional departures from the French Baroque garden tradition of using allées cut through planted forests, and they stamp this design as distinctively Californian. The eucalyptus has such a shaggy silhouette that it is singularly ill-suited to provide the effect of a dense forest that was such a central feature of the French Baroque garden. The citrus orchards located just outside these gardens were not visually integrated into their formal framework.

La Dolphine was subdivided in the 1950s. The long *tapis vert* no longer exists and the central pool has been converted into a swimming pool, but otherwise the formal areas around the house are still intact.

FILOLI   In the first two decades of the twentieth century, most California gardens were mixed in character, without clear fidelity to a particular style. The tendency for gardens to open up to informal areas at the perimeter derived from the precedent of the English picturesque landscape park, in which such areas often provided a transition to the outer landscape. More formal English precedents were sometimes invoked in California as well. The most notable example of these is William Bourn II's garden at Filoli (an acronym for "fight, love, live"), in Woodside.

The scion of a distinguished family of New England sea captains, Bourn was an extremely ambitious and successful businessman who dominated the development of public utilities in the San Francisco Bay area. Educated at Cambridge University, he developed a keen appreciation for the English country estate, seeing it less as a symbol of social and political power than as the embodiment of a way of life rooted in place. In 1909 Bourn acquired Filoli, his principal estate, because its beauty reminded him of an old English country house. The brick mansion (designed by Willis Polk) on its low, oak-covered knoll commanded northerly views over the Crystal Springs Lakes. After Bourn rejected a proposal submitted by Chesley Bonestell of the Willis Polk office for elaborate formal terraced gardens facing the house, he hired Bruce Porter in 1916 to take over the design.

Porter's romantic, even painterly approach is more apparent here than at New Place. The main axis follows the low point of the shallow valley located immediately to the west of

Filoli, Woodside, 1917. Garden designed by Bruce Porter for William Bourn II; house designed by Willis Polk. This principal axial vista, looking north toward the Crystal Springs Lakes, is flanked by columnar Irish yews (*Taxus baccata* var. *stricta*) and pyramidal golden yews (*T.b.* var *aurea*). Photo: David C. Streatfield, 1969

Filoli. Irish yews and a small pool mark a cross-axis in the walled garden. This formality is countered by the loose forms of a flowering cherry.

Photo: Robert M. Fletcher & Associates, 1984

the house. Below the house the axis passes through one arm of an L-shaped terrace, open to views of the landscape on its outer side, and continues through a walled garden. Beyond that garden, flanked by rows of Irish yews (*Taxus baccata* var. *stricta*), the axis passes through a large kitchen and cutting garden and then terminates in a semicircular space formed by yews, poplars, and wisteria-clad columns. A remarkable feature of this design is the lack of an emphatic terminal at either end. Porter's intention seems to have been to maintain open views of the landscape as a visitor progressed in either direction along this axial path. The single element of contrast is a diagonal axis within the walled garden linking a terraced platform to a teahouse on the north wall. The principal cross-axis, which is aligned on a sunken garden beneath the cupola of the garage block, passes through the other arm of the L-shaped terrace.

Visual relationships to the outer landscape were established through the careful selection of plant colors. The clipped Irish yews emphasize the main path and pick up the dark greens of the native oaks and laurels. Poplars and plane trees provide washes of lighter green, and the deodar cedars on the drive and the olive trees outside the walled garden provide a gray-green cast, recalling the grayish light at the top of the mountains. Inside the walled garden a group of Italian stone pines echoed the darker colors and balanced the mass of the western tree-covered hills.

Porter's original concept has been somewhat blurred by the alterations made by Mr. and Mrs. William Roth, who acquired Filoli after Bourn's death in 1936. They added another line of yew trees to the east-west arm of the L-shaped terrace, focusing the view toward the mountains and obscuring its original openness. Numerous changes were made in the walled garden, despite the Roths' retention of Isabella Worn, a talented horticulturist who had originally selected the plants for Porter. In 1976 Mrs. Roth gave Filoli to the National Trust for Historic Preservation, and it has been open to the general public ever since.

Today the walled garden remains the center of the design. Its introverted, almost medieval character was made possible by a number of devices: the path was made narrower inside the walls, and the garden was divided into several subsidiary gardens to establish a sense of intimacy and mystery. Originally designed to satisfy the Bourns' desire for symbolic references to places that they admired, the garden encompasses a Dutch garden formed with low

Filoli, sunken garden, looking west toward the Santa Cruz Mountains. The walled garden lies to the left; the pavilion and the line of yew trees on the right were added in the late 1930s by Mr. and Mrs. William Roth. Photo: David C. Streatfield, 1969

boxwood-edged parterres planted with yellow and purple pansies and the Chartres Window Garden (on the east side), which is supposed to replicate the central window of Chartres Cathedral, with boxwood hedges forming the tracery, holly hedges as the lead glazing bars, and vivid pansies and petunias supplying the color of the glass panels. Brilliant washes of color are concentrated throughout the walled garden at different seasons, as Porter intended. In the spring the color comes from pink and red flowering cherries, rhododendrons, camellias (planted in the 1940s), azaleas, and beds of petunias and tulips. The deeper reds of begonias originally lit up the dense shade beneath the Italian stone pines. In the fall, maples and elms create washes of flaming reds and golds.[15]

Porter's criticism (mentioned in his introduction to Garnett's *Stately Homes of California*) that California gardens lacked the appeal, "the hint of a delicate care bestowed, that gardens speak of in more difficult climates," could perhaps be applied to his own surviving masterpiece, although that garden does display a sophisticated order.[16] In fact, it is doubtful that any of the patrons of the gardens described in Garnett's book were at all concerned with such appeal; rather, their extensive travels led them to create edited versions of what they had seen in Europe.

The eclectic gardens described in this chapter reflect the national penchant for borrowing Asian and European stylistic motifs, but they differ from their elaborate counterparts in the East and Midwest. Their smaller size suggests a more modest approach to formal living, and their greater simplicity suggests a higher level of inventiveness in manipulating the conventions of popular historical styles.

Filoli, gate to walled garden. The wrought-iron gate and the detailed decoration of the archway above it recall English gardens of the seventeenth century. Photo: Jerry Pavia, 1992

❦

Filoli, walled garden. The elaborate formal patterns of the Chartres Window Garden,
created with boxwood hedges and annuals, provide a brightly colored foreground to a
magnificent pair of Italian stone pines (*Pinus pinea*), which have died since this
photo was taken. Photo: David C. Streatfield, 1969

5

IMPORTED STYLES: SOUTHERN CALIFORNIA

Pages 102–3. **Willis Ward garden, Montecito, 1916. Designed by Francis T. Underhill.**

Photo: Saxon Holt, 1993

B efore the 1920s most of California's great gardens were created in the northern part of the state, a fact that reflects the dominance of the state's economy by San Francisco banks. But by the early 1920s the expansion of the movie industry, the discovery of oil at Signal Hill (near Long Beach) in 1923, and aggressive real estate development made Los Angeles the fastest growing urban region in the country. The 1920s was the greatest decade in California's garden history, a period when more fine large and small gardens were created in the Southland than at any time before or since. This happened because of a number of factors: abundant water was diverted to Los Angeles from the Owens Valley; fine nurseries cultivated an extraordinary range of plants; new technology that enabled the moving of large trees was developed; and a cadre of sophisticated garden designers, as well as hordes of sophisticated clients, arrived to make the best of these resources.

The clients came from various social groups in the Southland. There were "old money" clients, from New York and Chicago and other parts of the Midwest, who wintered in Santa Barbara and Montecito. They tended to be highly educated and well traveled, with sophisticated but usually conservative tastes. Often second- or third-generation members of rich families, they were accustomed to getting exactly what they wanted, and many of them had owned or created fine gardens elsewhere. Another group of clients comprised the movie moguls, businessmen, and industrial entrepreneurs who lived in Los Angeles, Beverly Hills, Pasadena, Riverside, and Redlands. Many of these were newly rich and had grown up if not in poverty then without an inherited tradition of fine taste. Such clients also found inspiration in their own travel experiences, but often they depended heavily on the predilections of their designers. Some of the gardens created for them were indistinguishable from those of the "old money" group, but in others the differences are clearly evident. Middle-class clients had more limited budgets, but this did not deter them, or their designers, from creating some exquisite gardens. Indeed, some of the smaller gardens of this period are more successful than the larger estates because they were spatial extensions of the houses, and because their owners, often ardent gardeners themselves, were more involved in their care.

EL FUREIDIS

Well before the 1920s, there was a notable example of stylistic eclecticism in the Southland: El Fureidis, designed by Bertram Grosvenor Goodhue for J. Waldron Gillespie in Montecito. A rich bachelor who owned several other houses elsewhere in the United States and in Cuba, Gillespie developed an extensive arboretum on this 40-acre (16.2-hectare) estate during the last decade of the nineteenth century. This included an avenue of *Cocos plumosa* palms along the entrance drive, 125 other varieties of palms, and 25 varieties of acacias. In 1901 he engaged Goodhue to design a villa with Persian gardens. In search of inspiration, Gillespie and Goodhue took a trip around the world the next year, visiting Spain, Italy, and

Persia—where they rode 400 miles (640 kilometers) on horseback, from the Caspian Sea to the Persian Gulf, visiting Isfahan and Shiraz. They saw gardens in these cities by day and by moonlight, when they were especially mysterious and romantic. Not surprisingly, the trip made a considerable impression on Goodhue.

Goodhue's design for El Fureidis (Arabic for "pleasant place") was clearly inspired by some of the gardens that they had visited, but the results were unmistakably American. The living rooms of the house opened directly onto a long, narrow, paved upper terrace centered on a rectangular pool. Below this was a simple parterre of four pools of water framed by brick-paved paths; a small circular central basin contained a simple fountain reminiscent of those in

El Fureidis, Montecito, 1903.
Garden and house designed by
Bertram Grosvenor Goodhue for
J. Waldron Gillespie. The upper
terrace, with its long narrow pool
(center), is located along the
western facade of the house.
El Fureidis has been extensively
remodeled.

Photo: Robert M. Fletcher
& Associates, 1983

California mission gardens. It was originally surrounded by beds of red geraniums; tall Cocos palms immediately below the house provided a delicate transparent screen contrasting with the low horizontal form of the house itself. A long staircase led down the hill between tall clipped cypress hedges to three narrow, shallow terraced pools in front of a casino or teahouse overlooking a creek. Surrounding this simple, formal setting was an extensive series of groves of tropical trees and a handsome formal reservoir, a Japanese temple, a tilework shrine to the Madonna, a naturalistic water garden, and meadowlike spaces.

El Fureidis epitomized two conflicting design ideas. The central formal gardens were an exquisite expression of the precious nature of water, emphasizing its scarcity, while the outer gardens expressed the Victorian delight in exotic, well-watered abundance.

Also in Montecito just before the 1920s began were two amateur designers, Francis T. Underhill and Helen (Mrs. Oakleigh) Thorne, who created notable formal gardens. Underhill is one of the least known yet most important garden designers of this period. A member of an old New York family and a close friend of Theodore Roosevelt, he was educated by tutors and spent the last four years of his education traveling around the world. His interest in livestock led him to buy several ranches in Santa Barbara, where he settled in the mid-1880s. A yachtsman, horse fancier, breeder of cattle and hogs, world traveler, and raconteur, he took on architectural and landscaping projects for friends as a gentlemanly sideline rather than as a profession.[1]

Underhill experimented with designing at a variety of scales, ranging from the intimate areas close to his house to a larger scale that made a transition to the encompassing landscape. He used little color but effectively exploited the textures of plants. The simplicity of his gardens is astonishing and anticipates the work of Lockwood de Forest and Thomas Church (see chapters 6 and 7).

WILLIS WARD
GARDEN

Much of Underhill's work shows a propensity for formal spatial arrangements, both at a relatively modest and at a grand scale. The 40-acre (16.2-hectare) Willis Ward estate (1916), at the east end of Montecito, exemplifies the latter. The site includes a low ridge commanding a magnificent view north up San Ysidro Canyon and a sweeping panorama south to the ocean. Underhill's scheme was bold and simple, playing up the northern view. The house originally envisioned for the site (it was never executed) was to look down on a water garden comprising three terraced oval pools above a large grass meadow. The symmetrical space enclosing those elements is defined by a planted forest of redwoods punctuated by giant arborvitae (*Thuja plicata*) and *Lagunaria patersoni*. The forest is encircled by a drive that provides a one-way circulation pattern. The proportions of the pools to the meadow and to the trees were orchestrated to draw the eye toward the bottom of the distant canyon so that the entire mountain panorama appears to be part of the landscape. Springs provide sufficient water for year-round irrigation of the entire garden, but the meadow below the lowest pond has never been irrigated.

Extensive beds of ivy used as ground cover combine with numerous large rocks (already on site), the lawn, and several oak trees to create a simple landscape around the present owners' modest single-story house, designed by Chester Carjola in 1959, which occupies the site of Underhill's proposed mansion. A pair of superb Norfolk Island pines provides the only exotic flourish in this grandly scaled simplicity. The garden itself remains virtually unchanged from Underhill's original design.

LAS TEJAS

Most California garden designers during the 1910s and 1920s avoided grappling with issues of water conservation. Helen Thorne, of Millbrook, New York, was a notable exception in the work she did at Las Tejas (the tiles, 1918), her winter home in Montecito. She stated that "a dependence upon irrigation is, I believe, an economic factor forcing California gardening into those formal lines which lend themselves to its practice. A hedge is much more readily watered than broad irregularly planted borders." Thorne used quantities of what she called "the evanescent, decorative planting consisting of practically the same material which

Willis Ward garden, Montecito, 1916. Designed by Francis T. Underhill. Outcrops of
native boulders and a grove of oak trees were carefully retained to provide contrast
with large sweeps of lawn and clumps of hydrangeas.

Photo: Saxon Holt, 1993

supplies color in our Eastern gardens," but she also used drought-resistant shrubs as the backbone of her garden and "reduced the grass to a negligible and ornamental quality."[2] (Modern gardeners would nonetheless be appalled by her regular watering of her native oak trees—a practice that inevitably resulted in root rot.)

Thorne's extensive gardens at Las Tejas included a wildflower field, a small masonry gazebo with brick arches and fifteenth-century Romanesque-style columns from southern France, a knot garden, a heliotrope garden, a Spanish garden, a Japanese garden, a rock garden, orange and apricot orchards, and a small cactus garden, created later by Anne Stow-Fithian. This mélange of garden types and productive places was not unlike the mix seen at the more sumptuous Imperial Roman villas. Like many rich amateurs of the age, Thorne had highly eclectic tastes derived from extensive travel, but she showed a subtle and unusual restraint in her garden, and she was very much in control of its design and development. According to those who knew her, she taught herself how to use a surveyor's theodolite and staked out the two principal gardens herself.[3]

The main vista is Thorne's principal achievement. The southern facade of the house was remodeled into a version of Vignola's Casino at Caprarola, Italy (1547–59).[4] It faces a series of axially organized garden rooms descending to a three-arched teahouse pavilion. Each room was created with hedges, the central space being left open. The design is impressive when viewed from either direction. Apart from the repetition of three arches facing each other, the role of architecture is relatively slight, and the Italian Renaissance has been poetically evoked by the formal architecture of plants.

In front of the house is a formal rose garden flanked by groves of Italian cypresses and tall palm trees. The slope below this terrace is planted with a juniper ground cover, punctuated by a series of axially sited oval basins with small, delicately carved shells at their outer edges.

There is no exact precedent for this cascade, which was a most convincing and artistic essay in the Mannerist and Baroque manner.

Below this, the next terrace holds a large rectangular pool enclosed on the east and west by high hedges of eugenia, which make a short return on the south side to frame the view of the next terrace. This is a large rectangular lawn flanked by wisteria-covered pergolas with barley-sugar columns. At each terrace level the retaining walls, built of local Calabasas stone, are covered with ivy and vines. The southernmost terrace is occupied by a formal pool overlooked by the low teahouse pavilion. The visual interest of this sequence of terraces lies in the contrast of shapes and texture of the red eugenia hedges with the dark green of the columnar yew trees, above which float the foliage of palm trees and the filmy gray foliage of the olive trees.

In the mid-1920s Frank A. Waugh, professor of landscape architecture at the Massachusetts College of Agriculture, Amherst, wrote: "Now the first thing I feel in California gardens is their independence. Perhaps this is one of the best things. It is more notable in domestic architecture than in garden design." He continued, "California is now engaged in one vast and spectacular experiment in domestic architecture."[5] Waugh's comments capture the somewhat ambivalent character of the 1920s gardens. By 1920 the Spanish Colonial Revival and various Italian modes, all of which were often grouped under the rubric "Mediterranean," had been adopted as the dominant architectural styles in the Southland. But no comparable

༄──༄

Left. **Las Tejas. The southern facade of the house, designed by Francis W. Wilson after the Casino at Caprarola, Italy, overlooks the main vista of an extensive series of formal gardens.**
Photo: c. 1928–32

༄──༄

Opposite. **Las Tejas. Here the main vista is seen from the bottom of the garden, with clipped hedges in front of masses of trees, including olive groves.**
Photo: c. 1928–32

uniformity prevailed in garden design. The areas immediately surrounding Mediterranean houses were often designed as formal patios, parterres, and terraces—and often adorned with appropriate tilework, fountains, and statuary—but they invariably gave way to expansive naturalistic areas. The problem with the latter, as the landscape architect Charles Gibbs Adams pointed out, was the overabundance of plants that could be grown there. "The embarrassment of riches is upon us; and we need to develop restraint and temperance to resist that danger."[6]

Individual visitors to California during the 1920s reacted differently to what they found there. For Mrs. Francis King, the popular writer, it was color that defined California and its gardens. "Not climate first, nor its fruits or flowers, forests or valleys, seas or mountains—but color, color, color ineffable, color like a miracle, color unearthly in its variety and soft loveliness."[7] For Mabel Choate, creator of one of the finest gardens in the East (Naumkeag), it was not their color or their floral richness but how they were used that characterized the state's gardens. She drew attention to the use of the garden as an "outdoor living room" in California, which she attempted to emulate back home. Californians inhabited the formal terraces and patios surrounding their houses with sensuous enjoyment, though the outdoor rooms favored in the 1920s were still rather genteel places in which the sunlight was experienced at a distance, under the partial shade of loggias, verandas, and porches. Indeed, most houses were carefully sited so that the living rooms, indoors and out, did not directly face the hot afternoon sun.

In the typical Southern California garden of the 1920s a series of paved spaces adjoined the house, and paths connected formal gardens to informal lawns and wooded areas at the perimeter. The John Severance garden (1922), designed by Paul Thiene in Pasadena, was typical. Its main feature was a large grove of live oaks on sloping ground. The almost tropical character of this area was intensified because they were approached through a series of lavishly planted formal gardens. The paved terrace of the house abutted a long rectangular lawn, which was flanked by deep borders backed by low clipped hedges; next to the lawn was a paved platform surrounding two picturesque oak trees. This overlooked a long rectangular pool on a lower terrace, at the far end of which stood a large pavilion, modeled on the main facade of the Pazzi Chapel in Florence. From the house this facade appeared to be a distant object veiled by the oak trees.

The austere pavilion served as the principal entry to the oak grove. Beneath the half-shade of the oaks, Thiene planted a lavish collection of New Zealand tree ferns (*Cyathea dealbata*), bamboos, and cycads. The English garden writer Marion Cran described its lush qualities, with "azaleas, ferns and running streams—drifts of forget-me-nots, red-berried cotoneasters, masses of clivias, the queer bird of paradise strelitzias, and sparaxis-like billbergias

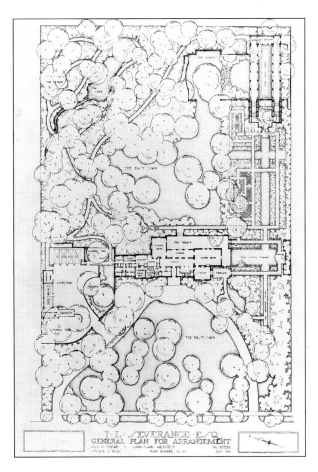

~~~

Left. **Plan of John Severance garden, Pasadena, 1922. Designed by Paul Thiene.**

~~~

Opposite. **John Severance garden. A lush tropical quality was achieved by planting tree ferns, azaleas, clivias, strelitzias, and billbergias beneath the oak trees.**

Photo: 1920s

with their long drooping stems hung with green bells. Under the camellias grew carpets of cyclamen and violets."[8] The exotic textures and colors of this garden could be conjured up only by the lavish application of irrigated water. The fungus that affects and eventually kills over-watered oak trees had not yet made itself known. It was a mark of the prevailing horticultural ignorance that Thiene continued to mix oaks with such tropical or subtropical gardens for the remainder of his career.

CASA DEL HERRERO

A garden that maintained considerable fidelity to Spanish models was Casa del Herrero (house of the blacksmith, 1925) in Montecito, one of the most exquisite houses and gardens of the Spanish Colonial Revival period. Its owner, George Steedman, retired from his engineering firm in Saint Louis at a relatively early age, and with his wife, Carrie, focused his highly inventive artistic abilities on the creation of his estate. The Steedmans were friends of

Arthur and Mildred Stapley Byne, the foremost authorities on Spanish houses and gardens. The Bynes traveled with them to Spain on several occasions and guided their purchases of doors, ironwork, ceilings, and other items for their house. Together they acquired large quantities of Spanish tiles for garden paving and benches, as well as Algerian tiles, with abstract patterns curiously reminiscent of Art Deco designs, that were used on the walls of the house and throughout the garden.

The initial design of the Casa del Herrero garden—by Ralph Stevens, a landscape architect who practiced in Santa Barbara from the late 1910s until the mid-1950s—was not specifically Spanish; rather, its stylistic origins lay in the Italian Renaissance villa and the English landscape tradition. Most of Stevens's design was implemented, but in the late 1920s the curving drive that approached the house from the road was replaced by an entry court paved with pebbles, and the lawn below the south facade was redesigned by Lockwood de Forest. Stevens's planting of the entry court with bananas and *Phoenix roebelini* palms at its four corners is tropically lush. On the north and south sides of the house great care was exercised in placing trees, shrubs, and vines to frame or enhance different features of the house. On the south facade the framing fan palms (genus *Washingtonia*) are pulled sufficiently far away from the wall so that they cast delicate shadows onto it, and their foliage stretching above the roof of the house reduces the scale of the house when seen from a distance.

Axes extend eastward and southward from the house. The eastern cross-axis passes through a paved patio at the side of the house to a rectangular lawn and semicircular exedra, below which is a fan-shaped rose garden—a sort of secret garden approached by a pair of

≪—≫

Casa del Herrero, Montecito, 1925. Garden designed by Ralph Stevens and remodeled by Lockwood de Forest; house designed by George Washington Smith for George and Carrie Steedman. The entry court is paved with multicolored pebbles in a simple geometric pattern around an octagonal fountain. At the corners of the courtyard are planting beds filled with subtropical species.

Photo: Russell Beatty, 1985

Casa del Herrero. The main lawn, in front of the southern facade of the house, is enlivened by a star-shaped pool and a tile-lined rill, both of which are part of a closed water system that recycles its own water.

Photo: Robert M. Fletcher & Associates, 1984

Left. Casa del Herrero. The patio opening
from the living room, on the east side of the
house, was used as an outdoor room,
furnished with aluminum chairs made by
George Steedman and benches lined with
Spanish ceramic tiles.

Photo: Russell Beatty, 1973

Below. Casa del Herrero. The eastern axis terminates in another outdoor room—a paved
exedra with a tile-lined fountain and benches.

Photo: Russell Beatty, 1985

Casa del Herrero. The southern axial vista terminates in this paved garden room, shaded by tree ferns and graced by an elegant little cast-iron fountain in a tiled basin.

Photo: Russell Beatty, 1973

narrow staircases. The patio, screened by an open arcade, has a typical four-part Spanish plan, with a low central fountain and small tiled water channels in the paths. Three of the quadrants are occupied by rectangular panels filled with plants; paving takes the place of the fourth panel. The outside of the arcade is covered with carefully trimmed ficus vines, so that from a distance it looks like a clipped hedge. The exedra is centered on a more elaborate tiled fountain, framed by benches inset with Spanish tiles. This patio was used from the 1920s on as an outdoor room and, like the rest of the garden, was furnished with cast-aluminum chairs made by Steedman in his workshop, which opened off the service court. Their perforated seats and backs emulate in appearance, if not weight, the heavy wood-and-leather Spanish chairs used inside the house.

The main southward axis also links a series of spaces to each other. Below the south facade of the house is a square lawn with deep beds at each side containing oak trees and small vine-covered pergolas. This area was considerably modified at the design stage, and surviving drawings by Lockwood de Forest are covered with Steedman's annotations, which show that he took keen interest in even the smallest details of the brick paths.

Steps between the pergolas lead down to a long *tapis vert,* with deep beds on both sides backed by high clipped eugenia hedges. At the end, shaded by tall tree ferns and oak trees, is an intimately scaled terraced garden, enclosed by stuccoed walls decorated with Algerian tiles and low benches. Its floor is paved with stone panels separated by grass strips, and the shade is enlivened by the sparkling light reflected from a very small fountain. From here one can look either back to the house or into a desert garden below. Beyond these formal spaces structured by walls and hedges there was originally an extensive citrus orchard threaded by narrow paths.

One of the most playful and enchanting parts of the garden is the exit from the service court at the west end of the house into the herb garden. It demonstrates how imagination could enliven even the most mundane features. On the west side of the house is a drain pipe that debouches into an open channel formed of pantiles, which directed the rainwater into a large jar. A bougainvillea vine draped over this exit provides a romantic touch to a practical feature.

At Casa del Herrero the tiled details on the walls and paving are for the most part authentically Spanish and reflect the strong influence of the Bynes. However, the layout of the garden, with its strong visual axes and its combination of flower gardens with productive orchards, is Italianate. A similar conflation of sources occurred in many of Florence Yoch's designs. Her design for Parley and Gipsy Johnson's garden (1925) in Downey also looked to Spanish sources, but Gipsy Johnson specifically commissioned "a Spanish garden with an English accent"[9]—this latter quality being achieved in the colorful flower beds, which are definitely not Spanish in style. The flat site, just under one acre (.4 hectare), was originally surrounded by a 70-acre (28.3-hectare) orange orchard. The house was placed toward the rear of the site so that the garden occupied the front portion; enclosed by high stuccoed walls, it was designed as a secluded oasis. A perspectival sketch by Yoch (collection of Gipsy Johnson) evokes the simplicity of Moorish gardens, matching their discipline with an asymmetrical yet balanced planting scheme. The basic geometry of the beds provides a framework for the complex rhythmic patterns established by hedges and by rows of orchard trees, which are further enlivened by the random placement of flowering trees and cypresses. The juxtaposition of cypress trees, a crape myrtle tree (*Lagerstroemia indica*), a lemon-scented gum *(Eucalyptus citriodora), Phoenix reclinata,* scarlet eucalyptus (*E. ficifolia*), and a large preexisting peppertree suggests a romantic garden occupied by several generations and slightly neglected.

The design is a subtle orchestration around a central lawn of a *ramada,* a rose garden, an orchard, a cutting garden, a kitchen garden, and a secret garden. The living rooms open onto a loggia and patio that are paved as a continuous plane. At the center of the patio is a low octagonal fountain, which is linked by a tiled channel to a basin in the far wall of the house. Potted plants provide spots of bright color on the patio and near the wall basin. The planting around the patio typifies Yoch's constant striving to plant formal spaces informally, with trees, vines, and shrubs. It is not unlike some of Gertrude Jekyll's designs, but Yoch's use of trees introduces a vertical element that Jekyll never employed.

⟋⟍⟋⟍

Parley and Gipsy Johnson garden, Downey, 1925. Designed by Florence Yoch. The house and the design of the gardens around the central lawn are Spanish in character, but the plants and the lawn itself recall English gardens. This garden survives in good condition. Photo: David C. Streatfield, 1978

The cluster of exuberant, colorful gardens provides a contrast to the simple rectangular lawn. The loggia leads directly to a rustic *ramada* made of massive stuccoed columns supporting unpeeled wooden poles clad with jasmine, Silver Moon roses, and clematis. Beyond the *ramada* the path expands around a wellhead and leads to an elevated platform surrounding the peppertree. The path continues from the terrace at right angles through the rose garden at the south end of the lawn and then makes another right-angle turn and returns through the kitchen garden to the house. Great diversity was achieved in the Johnson garden by using a variety of formal features traditional in Spanish gardens, such as the *ramada* and the loggia. But the circulation through the various parts of the garden is more idiosyncratic than traditional.

During the 1920s references to the past in Southern California gardens were sometimes made with a careless freedom that bordered on vulgarity. The influence of filmmakers in evoking lavish historical periods, such as the decadent days of the Roman Empire, was certainly strong. But flamboyant behavior was not an invention of the movies, having been an important aspect of California life ever since motley crews of immigrants had started pouring into San Francisco during the gold rush. William Randolph Hearst's ranch, San Simeon (more familiarly known as Hearst's Castle), was the most theatrical embodiment in garden form of this aspect of Californian identity.

San Simeon was dedicated to entertaining guests. But unlike the smaller gardens of the 1920s—which were developed as a backdrop to unpretentious, comfortable, and old-fashioned hospitality for friends and relatives from a homogeneous social world—the gardens at San Simeon had to accommodate entertainment on an extravagant scale for guests from many different milieus. Actors and actresses, politicians, artists, comedians, sports figures, and business associates were entertained there with princely liberality.

William Randolph Hearst had grown up in San Francisco and with his family had camped regularly on what is now known as the Enchanted Hill, at San Simeon, 220 miles (352 kilometers) north of Los Angeles. His father, Senator George Hearst, who had made a fortune from mining, had purchased the Pietra Blanca ranch at San Simeon in 1865. Some 1,600 feet (488 meters) above sea level and five miles (eight kilometers) from the Pacific Ocean, the site typifies the softly rounded forms of the coastal range. William Randolph Hearst transformed it from a virtually treeless site into a series of lush, almost tropical gardens, containing sculptures ranging from ancient Egyptian to streamlined Moderne in a setting of transplanted oaks, cypresses, palm trees, and flowering shrubs.[10] The sumptuous vulgarity of these gardens recalls imperial Roman gardens such as those at Hadrian's Villa near Tivoli.

The transformation started in 1919, when Hearst inherited his mother's estate. His original modest intention of creating an informal "Swisso-Jappo Bungalow" surrounded by three guesthouses ultimately evolved into a grandiose estate with a main house that was a cross between a cathedral and a palace. This remarkable scheme appears to have expanded from a sketch by his architect, Julia Morgan, of a tree-covered hill with three guesthouses at its base and a tower rising from within the trees. Neither the buildings nor the gardens were originally conceived as part of a predetermined design; instead, they were created by Morgan, assisted by the landscape architect Charles Gibbs Adams, in response to the exigencies of the site and to Hearst's ever-expanding visions, as well as his obsessive and far-flung enthusiasm for collecting.[11]

The grassy hilltop, with its few scattered oak trees, was transformed into a series of terraces without a clearly defined sequence. Hearst, like many others in California, apparently disliked treeless slopes. Beyond the gardens Adams planted some twenty-four varieties of conifers, including cypresses, cedars, spruce, pines, firs, and sequoias (including giant sequoias). The trees were selected in part because they would be unpalatable to Hearst's menagerie, which included giraffes, gazelles, and gnus.[12] Many of the trees had to be planted in holes dynamited in the thick rock. Thousands of tons of soil were transported by truck to fill these holes and to form raised beds. Many fully grown Italian cypresses, palms, and oaks were brought to San Simeon as boxed specimens. Adams recounted that Hearst spent ten thousand dollars moving two six-hundred-year-old oak trees, and that one hundred fan palms were transplanted from an old garden 200 miles (320 kilometers) away.[13]

In front of the principal facade of the twin-towered main house is a large paved terrace, which expands around a quatrefoil-shaped pool containing a sculpture of Galatea on a dolphin. Beneath the large cypresses and palm trees are planting beds containing magnolias, Chinese magnolias, orange trees, camellias, azaleas, and rhododendrons. Linked to the main terrace by a modest staircase is a broad, roughly semicircular promenade, below which are the three guesthouses and more terraced gardens that descend the hillside. The staircase flanks a Moderne basin in which sit diorite figures of the lioness-faced goddess Sekhmet dating from the eighteenth and nineteenth Egyptian dynasties (1570–1200 B.C.). Behind the fountain stand two Italian Gothic columns. This wild eclecticism occurs again in the juxtaposition at various places along the promenade of Roman sarcophagi, Italian Renaissance fountains, Greek terra-

San Simeon, San Luis Obispo County, 1922–40. Garden designed by Julia Morgan and Charles Gibbs Adams; house designed by Morgan for William Randolph Hearst. The broad promenade below the main house provides access to the three guest houses and offers views over the ranch lands to the Pacific.

Photo: David C. Streatfield, 1969

San Simeon. The large quatrefoil-
shaped pool on the main terrace
contains a sensuous statue of
Galatea on a dolphin surrounded
by a *Scirpus*.

Photo: David C. Streatfield, 1969

cotta storage jars from southern Italy, and copies of classical statues, of famous sculptures such as Antonio Canova's *Three Graces,* and of Art Deco pieces. The exoticism of this mélange of old and new is intensified by clumps of azaleas, rhododendrons, oranges, avocados, loquats, grapefruits, limes, and quinces beneath the towering oak trees. These various fruit trees were cultivated as much for their colorful appearance and scent as for their fruit.

The garden was made for promenading and for viewing Hearst's remarkable art collection as well as the expansive vistas of the ranch landscape backed by the sapphire blue waters of the Pacific Ocean. The social heart of the garden, below the promenade on the west side, is the immense Neptune pool, which is 140 feet (42.7 meters) long, with semicircular ends and a rectangular alcove on one side. On the south side is what appears to be an Etruscan temple facade, its pediment tympanum containing a Renaissance sculpture of Neptune. The pool was enlarged in three successive stages, the final enlargement being necessary to accommodate an elaborate white Carrara marble group in which Venus rises from a large shell supported by merfolk. The entire sculptural ensemble was commissioned from Charles Cassou and made in his Parisian workshops. The sensuous, pure white objects; the white marble arcades defining the pool and its surrounding geometric pavement; and the deep turquoise blue of the swimming pool all contrast strangely with the rather crude classical balustrade and the series of

Greco-Roman–style herms holding lamps, all cast in concrete. This combination of sumptuous and mundane materials again shows an odd fascination for mixing old and new in a visually compelling way. The monumentality of this part of the gardens recalls the scale of D. W. Griffith's and Cecil B. De Mille's epic movies.

Maintained as a weekend house rather than a permanent residence, San Simeon was only one of Hearst's residences; others included apartments and hotel suites in Los Angeles and New York and a castle in Wales. San Simeon was a highly specialized form of resort, a beautiful pastoral landscape where wild fantasies could be indulged for brief periods as an escape from daily routine. After Hearst's death, his heirs gave the house and gardens to the state of California, which accepted with great reluctance, thinking it would become a white elephant. It is now the most popular park in the state's system.

MERRITT
ADAMSON
GARDEN

San Simeon is impressive for its exuberant conflation of styles, plants, and art objects and for its lack of fidelity to aesthetic convention. A similar exuberance infused many of the movie palaces created during the 1920s and 1930s. This tendency to emphasize flamboyant forms, patterns, and colors at the expense of historical accuracy is illustrated particularly well in Stiles Clements's romantic design for the Merritt Adamson house in Malibu (1929). Composed with vague references to Andalusian farmhouses, the house was enlivened by brightly colored panels of tiles around the windows and at other prominent places. A wildly improbable tribute to the exoticism of the Hispanic world can be seen in the fountain on the living-room terrace, with its showy tiled peacocks parading on either side of a turquoise vase. Similar panache is evident in the large tiled panels on the exterior walls of the house, with their bold

∂~∾

**Merritt Adamson garden, Malibu, 1929.
Designed by Stiles Clements. The principal
ornamental feature of the living-room terrace
is this tile fountain decorated with
flamboyant peacocks.**
Photo: David C. Streatfield, 1992

scrolling curves. Such settings surrounded the Adamsons and their guests with a highly romanticized fantasy world far removed from the reality of the Hispanic past.

Although the popularity of the Italian Renaissance style for houses and gardens was
greatly diminished compared to previous decades, a number of beautiful villas and ambitious
gardens were created in this mode during the 1920s. Its reduced popularity may have been due
to its association in the Southland with highly formal patterns of living. Marion Cran, for
example, found Harold Lloyd's Italianate villa far too pretentious for the likable and casual
comedian. She wrote: "As one ecstatic female says: The Harold Lloyd estate is comparable
only with the gardens of the Caliphs. Oh, poor Harold."[14]

LA TOSCANA   La Toscana (1929), the Kirk Johnson estate in Montecito, was one of California's most
splendid estates inspired by Italian Renaissance villas, and it is still very well maintained.[15] The
previous owners, the Oothouts, had planted the gently rising site with some fine trees, such as
pines and cedars, that had grown to a considerable size by the time the Johnsons built their
estate. The house was designed by George Washington Smith, and A. E. Hanson laid out the
gardens after the plans for the house had been completed. The landscape's composition took
full advantage of the magnificent preexisting trees and of the splendid northward views of the
mountains. Paved terraces—which open out on the north from the dining room and on the
east from the entrance hall—overlook a series of axially organized formal gardens. On the south
side of the house a large parklike lawn falls away to a thick grove of oak trees. The garden
therefore offers a series of formal and naturalistic spaces. The formal spaces are close to the

❧

**La Toscana, Montecito, 1929. Garden designed
by A. E. Hanson; house designed by George
Washington Smith for Kirk Johnson. The
southern facade of the house is framed by
masses of pines, cedars, and other trees
planted by the original owners, the Oothouts.**
Photo: David C. Streatfield, 1976

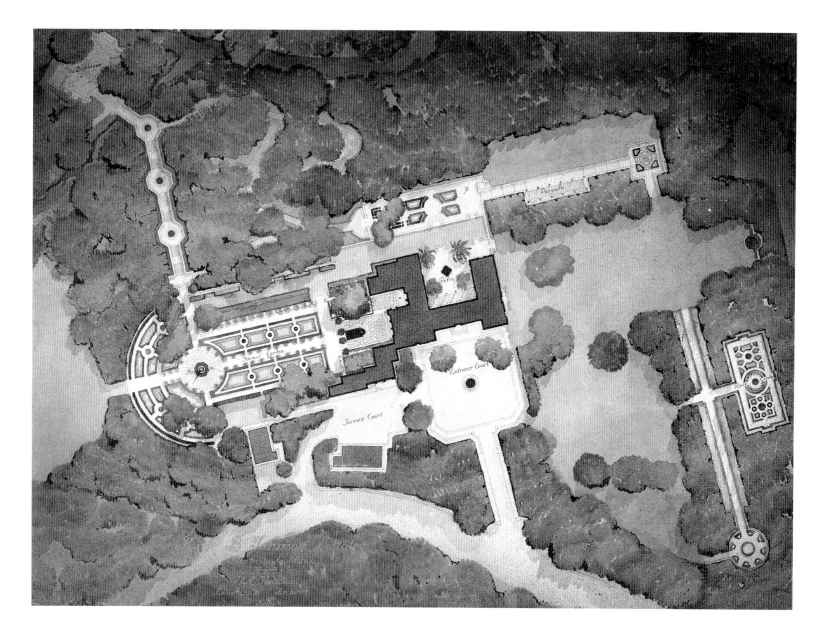

∽∾

Above. Plan of La Toscana.

∽∾

Opposite. La Toscana. The drive leading to the entry court is lined with clipped hedges
and was designed to direct the eye toward the fountain at the center of the court.

Photo: David C. Streatfield, 1969

house, then there is a meandering circuit walk that passes through the grove of trees at the edge of the lawn and provides oblique views back to the house.

A short, straight drive rises between high clipped hedges of *Pittosporum undulatum* to a formal entry court on the west side of the house. From the road the low fountain at the center of the court appears to sit at the top of the inclined plane. Three sides of this court are formed by clipped hedges contained by a low wall. The contrast of the dark greens, the simple plane of raked gravel, the low fountain (derived from a fountain at the Villa Medici in Rome), the asymmetrical positioning of two large Monterey cypress trees—a powerful example of *sharawadgi* (the practice in Oriental gardens of placing asymmetrical elements in formal settings)—and the careful painting of the facade to suggest weathering combined to establish a sense of tranquil maturity.

The terrace opening from the dining room faces an inclined path, flanked by terracotta pots holding small orange trees, which rises to a paved circle with a central fountain. As in the entry court, foreshortening was employed so that from the dining-room terrace the column of the fountain appears to rise right from the top of the path, directing the eye to La

Cumbre, a peak in the background. Live oaks frame this view and break the geometry of the circle. The circle is paved with a series of scallops, evoking a wavelike sensation. Incidental features such as the gardener's shed and other service structures at the edge of the garden were orchestrated into picturesque compositions by their relationship to the arching branch of a pre-existing oak tree. These compositions form a subtle counterpoint to the symmetry of the house.

An upper terrace opens from the main living room on the east side of the house and is flanked by the single-story wings of the living room and the master bedroom; it is closed on the west side by a linking arcade. At the center of this terrace is a fifteenth-century Italian wellhead, and a large dragon tree close to the living room provides a carefully considered point of asymmetry. This space offers a variety of places to sit, both in sunlight and in shade. Below it is a simple parterre of clipped boxwood, whose formality was originally broken by an asymmetrically placed lemon-scented gum tree (*Eucalyptus citriodora*). On the south side of the house the great mass of the trees along the southern boundary and the extensive lawn provide the dogleg views typical of English landscape parks. The views from the perimeter path at the southern edge of this lawn of Smith's carefully composed Italianate villa recall the views glimpsed from the expansive parks of the villas in and around Rome, such as the Villa Doria Pamphili.

IRA BRYNER
GARDEN

The Ira Bryner garden in Pasadena (1929) is a much smaller garden, with gentler references to Italianate themes. Mr. and Mrs. Bryner moved to Pasadena from Pennsylvania, and the house that Roland Coate designed for them makes overt references to the character of a Pennsylvania farmhouse. The garden, designed by Florence Yoch and maintained in excellent condition by its present owner, is just under two-fifths of an acre (.2 hectare) in size and slopes diagonally down toward the street, rather like a shallow amphitheater. The house was positioned on a high terrace at the top of the site, commanding views of the San Gabriel Mountains beyond the arroyo. The curving drive immediately below the house divides the site into two parts. The unusual shape of the site, its steep topography, and the placement of the house created a series of oddly shaped spaces, which Yoch transformed into a set of diverse and intimate gardens by using subtle references to numerous historical sources, terraces and staircases, varied plantings to break down rigid geometric patterns, and perspectival devices to open up a sense of space.

On the south side of the house a deep loggia fronts the drawing room. The loggia is narrowed at both ends: on the west side by a stairway down to the entry court, and on the east by shallow steps that lead up to a low arched arbor—which because of the visual relationships looks almost like a piece of trompe l'oeil—with an asymmetrical boxed kumquat tree in the

La Toscana. A simple boxwood parterre, located below the patio, leads the eye toward
La Cumbre Peak in the Santa Ynez Mountains.

Photo: David C. Streatfield, 1969

Ira Bryner garden, Pasadena, 1929. Garden
designed by Florence Yoch; house designed by
Roland Coate. The loggia faces a triangular
rose garden to the right and terminates in an
arbor made of steel pipe, at the end of which
is an Indian plaque.
Photo: David C. Streatfield, 1974

foreground and an Indian sculptured plaque at the rear of the arbor. Formal steps lead up from the loggia to a triangular, terraced rose garden, in which the seemingly random path layout and a scattering of fruit trees visually expand what would otherwise seem like an odd leftover space.

The area below the drive is terraced in three levels. Adjacent to the drive is an orchard, below which stairs lead down to a path following the curve of the drive. At this middle level is a small formal rose garden (whose plan recalls the hippodrome in the reconstructed plan of Pliny's villa at Tuscum), which leads to a wooded area. The lowest level is occupied by a rectangular lawn, from which a path flanked by white azaleas leads up gentle steps through the wood to a latticed garden pavilion. On the axis of the stairs is a small pool, which from the path looks almost like a panel of black glass floating in space. This part of the garden is reminiscent of some of the Jacobean gardens that Yoch photographed on her trips to England. Its simplicity is a carefully calculated contrast to the richly planted terraced spaces above it.

Ira Bryner garden. The angular formality of
the small, dark pool at the end of the lawn is
offset by the graceful arcs of the oaks' trunks.
Photo: Robert M. Fletcher & Associates, 1983

Harvey Mudd garden, Beverly Hills, 1920s–40s. Garden and service buildings designed by Edward Huntsman-Trout; house designed by Elmer Grey, 1920. The service road, made in 1929, wound past a parrot cage, on the left, to the dog kennel, lathhouse, greenhouse, and gardeners' office. Photo: 1950

HARVEY MUDD
GARDEN

The Norman-French style was one of the most popular styles nationally in the 1920s, but it was used for only a few houses and small commercial buildings in the Southland and only rarely in gardens there. Edward Huntsman-Trout's design for the service buildings on the Harvey Mudd estate in Beverly Hills was an isolated example of this style, derived from the small stone, brick, and half-timber mansions and village streets of Normandy. Huntsman-Trout worked on this estate almost continuously from the mid-1920s until the early 1940s. The large, ungainly neo-Tudor house was surrounded by a series of terraced formal gardens, which made subtle reference to Jacobean, Italian, and French Baroque gardens. The diverse historical allusions were handled with such mastery that they blended effortlessly into each other.

At the rear of the house a single-lane road led up a narrow canyon to a series of service buildings, including dog kennels, greenhouses, lathhouses, woodsheds, and an elaborate parrot cage. The road, treated like a winding country lane between masonry walls, was designed to achieve a sense of rightness in which the hand of the designer disappeared. In the 1950s Huntsman-Trout used the term "commonplace" to describe this approach.[16] The picturesque arrangement of structures had a timeless quality that was dependent on superb materials used with exquisite craftsmanship. That such subtle attention should be given to the quarters of gardeners, dogs, and parrots rather than to their master's quarters was not unusual, for designers in this period invariably treated the service areas of an estate as handsome features along the circuit of the grounds. This area of the garden was destroyed when the estate was subdivided in the 1960s.

MRS. FRANK
EMORY GARDEN

The garden of Mrs. Frank Emory in Pasadena (1929), which survives in excellent condition, is perhaps the most consistently English garden created in California during the 1920s. The house, by Myron Hunt, suggests a large half-timber manor and is surrounded by extensive lawns, shrubbery, terraces, pools, and gardens (created by Hunt in consultation with Yoch) that recall formal Elizabethan rose gardens, Tudor fish ponds, Jacobean terraces, and small eighteenth-century landscape parks. The fine oak trees were underplanted with shrubs to screen out views of the street and to provide a sequence of hidden and open views of the house along the drive.

The entry court, apart from the detailing of its balustrade, is a typical product of the 1920s, with the masonry paving laid in grass, a detail used for all the principal paths in the garden. A long path connects the terrace opening off the living room to a large formal rose garden completely enclosed by high shrubs and to a long rectangular reflecting pool, carefully sited beneath a highly picturesque oak. Such details create a romantic mood and imply that the garden has evolved over several centuries. Like its eighteenth-century models, the garden has a sense of open, natural spaciousness, and it was designed to look endless, with the limits of the space carefully concealed. The garden's lush greenness is in striking contrast to the aridity of the outlying landscape.

Elaborate gardens such as La Toscana and San Simeon were part of a privileged and private world, meticulously maintained by well-trained gardeners for the delight of their rich owners and their guests. Yet, surprisingly, some of them were shared, albeit indirectly, with the rest of the world. During the 1920s, and to a lesser extent in the 1930s, these gardens were used as locations for numerous movies; it was obviously cheaper and more effective to film a garden in Beverly Hills or Pasadena than to create an elaborate set.[17] The Severance garden and at least fifty others were made available for filming through the Assistance League of Los Angeles.

Mrs. Frank Emory garden, Pasadena, 1929.
Garden designed by Myron Hunt, with
Florence Yoch; house designed by Hunt. The
entry court is defined by a cast-stone
balustrade in the Jacobean style, now
embowered with a heavy planting of roses; it
is paved with cast-stone slabs separated by
narrow strips of grass.
Photo: Robert M. Fletcher & Associates, 1983

Mrs. Frank Emory garden. The highly romantic reflecting pool recalls images of formal ponds in English Jacobean gardens.

Photo: Robert M. Fletcher & Associates, 1986

Movies conveyed subtle messages about taste, and so the designers who did work for them helped shape the aesthetics of an entire generation. Not until the 1930s did professionally trained designers such as Lloyd Wright (Frank Lloyd Wright's son) and the architect Lutah Maria Riggs begin to design movie sets. In the early 1930s Ralph Cornell, a distinguished landscape architect, designed a set for Fox Movietone that could be adjusted very slightly to provide three formal gardens in completely different styles.[18] Florence Yoch made one of the earliest contributions to the fantasy world of the movies by designing the Capulet garden and the graveyard for the first sound film made of *Romeo and Juliet,* directed by George Cukor in 1936. The garden's general ambience evokes the Italian Renaissance, but many details, such as the paving, typify California gardens of the 1920s.

Movie making was the only sector of California's economy not adversely affected by the Depression. Everyone associated with movie production seemed able to find work. Movie stars, directors, and producers made enough money to live handsomely, and their house and garden commissions enabled several designers to avoid the worst of the economic slump.

During the 1930s elaborate houses were commissioned by rich businessmen in addition to movie stars, directors, and producers, albeit on a scale somewhat less lavish than that of the previous, pre-crash decade. Many of these houses were built in such fashionable suburbs of west Los Angeles as Santa Monica, Beverly Hills, Bel Air, and Holmby Hills. These estates were still planned with features such as large terraces for entertaining, rose gardens, vegetable gardens, tennis courts, and swimming pools, but they differed in a number of ways from similar estates of the 1920s. The sites were often smaller, and different architectural styles were preferred. In the 1920s various versions of Mediterranean, Norman-French, and Tudor styles had been popular. In the 1930s the rise of modern architecture challenged landscape architects to adopt styles that seemed more up-to-date. The Moderne became a popular compromise between overtly historical design and radical modernism. Its stylized, usually rounded forms were used by a number of landscape architects, including Thomas Church and Benjamin Morton Purdy.

JAY PALEY
GARDEN

An elaborate example of Moderne forms combined with Baroque elements, exotic references to natural phenomena, and some Art Deco sculpture occurs at the estate of Jay Paley (president of the Columbia Broadcasting System in the 1930s), which was designed by Edward Huntsman-Trout and Paul Williams. The site in Holmby Hills is roughly triangular, surrounded on two sides by roads, with a ridge descending to a point. The house is positioned at the upper end of the ridge; a 700-foot-long (213.5-meter) axis links the entry court, the house, a putting green, a large formal lawn, a swimming pool, a cabaña, a tennis court, and a path to the road. Outside this central area the hillside was terraced and used for a citrus

Above. Aerial plan of Jay Paley garden,
Holmby Hills, 1936. Garden designed by
Edward Huntsman-Trout; house designed by
Paul Williams. The garden was slightly
modified in execution.

Right. Jay Paley garden. The mass of the two-
story master-bedroom wing on the left was
balanced by the immense rubber tree (*Hevea
brasiliensis*) at right, which was transplanted
from a Pasadena garden.

Photo: 1930

orchard. This combination of productive elements and spaces devoted to pleasure gardens was somewhat unusual by this period.

A curving drive ascends from the road, passing between an orange orchard on the right and a cutting garden, greenhouses, and lathhouse on the left. It terminates in an oval entry court, defined by a single-story garage block on the left; at right angles to it is the rather plain two-story facade of the house, enlivened only by a fanciful balustrade and a handsome doorcase. The facade's severity sets off the sumptuous paving design. At the center of the oval court is a bronze plaque, from which lines radiate to the periphery of the paving, with semicircular loops at the end of each wedge-shaped panel. This stylized Baroque design typified the process of simplifying the basic elements of historicist forms, a process used by many traditional designers. The entire design was executed in different forms of tinted concrete aggregate. The superb craftsmanship is a splendid tribute to the skills of concrete masons and contrasts strikingly with work by modernist designers who insisted on using new materials.

A visual counterpart to the magnificent entry court is the playful swimming pool. This oval pool, placed at right angles to the main axis, is flanked at each end by small white-sand

❧

Jay Paley garden. The shallow end of the swimming pool is decorated with twelve signs of the zodiac in a flamboyant sunburst design.
Photo: David C. Streatfield, 1984

beaches. The shallow end of the pool is paved with colored tesserae in a bold sunburst containing the twelve signs of the zodiac, adding a burst of bright color to the landscape.

On the garden side of the house Huntsman-Trout and Williams devised an effective and dramatic piece of *sharawadgi:* the two-story semicircular porch of the master-bedroom suite on the left was balanced by the huge mass of a rubber tree at right. Huntsman-Trout found this large specimen in a garden in Pasadena, and it was moved to Holmby Hills on rollers through city streets. The rubber tree has since died, but otherwise the Paley estate survives in excellent condition.

By the 1940s most landscape architects had embraced modernist ideas, many of which grew out of a conscious attempt to create designs appropriate to the regional landscape. But the adoption of nationally fashionable styles and the creation of personal fantasies did not disappear. Some designs by the Pasadena landscape architect Jacques Hahn reveal the same fascination with riotous color that had characterized Victorian and early twentieth-century gardens.[19]

The most remarkable continuation of Californians' fascination with floristic exuberance was Madame Ganna Walska's garden, Lotusland (1941–84), in Santa Barbara. This estate encompasses several gardens, each of which celebrates one aspect of California's tropical potential. Madame Walska was a flamboyant opera singer who came from a modest Polish family and married six very rich men—one of whom was Harold McCormick, chairman of the International Harvester Company. In 1941 Walska purchased from Humphrey O. Clarke the 40-acre (16.2-hectare) estate Cuesta Linda, which the E. Palmer Gavitses had developed in the 1920s; she renamed it Lotusland, after the lotuses on one of its ponds. The property was a small part of an estate originally formed in the 1880s by Kinton Stevens and known as Tanglewood, from the state of its undergrowth. Stevens, one of the most prominent nurserymen in the Southland, had cleared a number of oaks to make space for his collections of exotic plants. His son, the landscape architect Ralph Stevens, designed the gardens for the Gavitses, who had built their house in the late 1910s and developed a series of gardens containing different plant collections, including cacti and succulents, in the 1920s and 1930s.

After World War II Madame Walska began to make considerable changes among the extensive groves of oak trees and the immense cedars, pines, and *Araucaria bidwillii* that remained from Kinton Stevens's time. Her changes supplemented and complemented what already existed in spectacular and highly unusual ways. Walska added an outdoor theater with a collection of grotesque dwarf figures brought from her chateau in France; created a floral clock; and developed collections of bromeliads, palms, cacti, euphorbias, and cycads. What distinguishes these collections is the prodigality with which they were planted and the bold manner in which they were arranged. The three most extraordinary gardens so created at

Lotusland are the Blue Garden, the Aloe Garden, and the Cycad Garden.[20] The ethereal Blue Garden, which was developed in the 1960s, consists of a grove of blue Atlas cedars (*Cedrus atlantica* var. *glauca*), Mexican blue palms (*Erythea armata*), furcraeas, and blue spruce (*Picea pungens*), which provide a moderately dense level of shade. The ground is planted with blue fescue grass (*Festuca ovina* var. *glauca*), and the winding path is lined with broken pieces of slag glass left over from the production of Coca-Cola bottles. This completely blue environment has no precedent in garden history and expresses Walska's highly poetic imagination.

Equally unusual is the Aloe Garden, which was originally created in the late 1950s and completely rearranged in 1975 by Charles Glass, a cactus and succulent specialist, in collaboration with Walska. At that time nearly all of the plants in this garden were removed; new soil was reworked with quantities of sand, gravel, topsoil, and planter mix; and several hundred black volcanic rocks were brought from eastern California. All of the work was done by hand so that adjoining areas would not be disturbed. There are hundreds of different aloes in this garden, with each type planted in large numbers, including the tree aloes *Aloe bainesii, A. dichotoma, A. speciosa,* and smaller kinds such as *A. striata, A. brevifolia,* and *A. vera* (Barbados

Opposite. Lotusland. Beneath Mexican blue palms (*Erythea armata*), blue spruce (*Picea pungens*), and blue Atlas cedars (*Cedrus atlantica* var. *glauca*), the Blue Garden is carpeted with blue fescue grass (*Festuca ovina* var. *glauca*), and the paths are edged with lumps of blue glass.
Photo: Saxon Holt, 1988

Right. Lotusland. Aloe Garden, designed by Charles Glass with Madame Walska, 1975. The pool is lined with abalone shells, and the fountain consists of giant tridacna clamshells mounted on a coral column.
Photo: Jerry Pavia, 1990

aloe). Botanical specialists, gardeners, and artists can all appreciate the remarkably subtle salmon pink flowers and grayish foliage of these plants. Their lushness is enhanced by a shadowed pool at the center of the garden, which has a curb lined with abalone shells. A number of giant tridacna clamshells set on a coral column form a fountain in which the water slowly drips from one shell to another.

Facing the paved entry court in front of the house is a grove of immense dragon trees, forming a large-scale living sculpture. This magnificent tree, imported from the Canary Islands, was frequently planted as a specimen in California gardens of the 1920s.

The last major garden created by Walska, the Cycad Garden, was also designed by her in association with Charles Glass, in 1978–79. The cycad, though resembling a palm tree, is more closely related to pines; it is a gymnosperm that bears cones rather than flowers. The Cycad Garden is divided into beds of Australian, African, Mexican, and Asian cycads. Gentle hills and hollows were graded to enhance the experience of visitors moving through the landscape of these remarkable plants. Paths are placed in hollows from which it is possible to study the bold and often sculptural trunks of these trees that arch up into space.

~⚶~

Above, left. Lotusland. Dragon trees (*Dracaena draco*) were frequently planted in the 1920s
as specimen trees, but never in the prodigious quantities seen here.

Photo: Robert M. Fletcher & Associates, 1990

~⚶~

Above, right. Lotusland. Cycad Garden, designed by Charles Glass with Madame Walska,
1978–79. This garden, which contains an important and representative collection of
these ancient plants, was designed to emphasize their sculptural forms.

Photo: David C. Streatfield, 1988

Lotusland. The highly eccentric forms of *Euphorbia ingens* were exploited with characteristic flair by Ganna Walska at the southern entrance to the motor court.

Photo: Robert M. Fletcher & Associates, 1989

Pasadena garden, c. 1965. Designed by Ruth Shellhorn. The main lawn recalls
the spacious qualities of an English landscape park.

Photo: David C. Streatfield, 1990

The drive to the house is lined with an extraordinary collection of cacti, whose unusual forms have been orchestrated into a fantastical collection of grotesqueries. Like all of the other Lotusland gardens this area contains botanical rarities, and the plants have been skillfully arranged in compositions of unusual forms, colors, and textures. Walska died in 1984 and left her estate to a nonprofit foundation; it can be visited by appointment.

Ganna Walska's inspired eccentricities have never been matched. But the impulse to impose different cultures on the California landscape continued through the period dominated by the rise of modernist ideals. Created by such skillful designers as Joseph Copp, Jr., many of these later gardens are handsome and effective. One of the most impressive is Ruth Shellhorn's remodeling, in the mid-1960s, of an old garden above the arroyo in Pasadena, in a masterly revival of the ideas and techniques of the English picturesque style. Shellhorn had worked briefly for Florence Yoch, and in the 1940s and 1950s she designed some of the finest shopping centers in the Southland, at Santa Ana, La Habra, and Sherman Oaks.

The large half-timber house in Pasadena resembles an old English mansion. This, coupled with the presence of some magnificent oak trees, determined the English character of Shellhorn's design. By using carefully massed groups of shrubs beneath the trees and by adjusting their textural values from coarse to fine, she created extremely subtle spatial effects.

Pasadena garden. The plants along the garden path were carefully selected to provide gradations of texture from delicate to coarse.
Photo: Robert M. Fletcher & Associates, 1986

The prosceniumlike opening at one side of the main lawn gave the illusion that the smaller lawn in front of the tennis court was farther away than it really was. The masterly choice of foliage, colors, and textures provided a delicate range of receding forms and planes in space.

Shellhorn has described her work as the creation of pictures.[21] This garden demonstrates powerfully that the ideas of earlier theorists, such as Uvedale Price, can still be invoked in the production of memorable gardens. This is a predominantly green garden in which shifting tones and the contrast of light and dark modulate the spaces. Superb in its understatement, it emphasizes the ongoing passion for green in a dry land.

In a manuscript on garden design Florence Yoch, while admitting the appropriateness of Mediterranean gardens for California, surprisingly suggested that, despite the considerable effort involved in its creation and maintenance, a green lawn was still the finest and most desirable feature of a garden.[22] Her statement suggests that even a very sensitive designer, who practiced in this semiarid landscape for many decades, subscribed to a landscape ideal that was an imposition on, rather than an accommodation to, the local landscape. Eclectic practice, supported by the available technology, enabled choices that were cultural, not regional, in nature.[23]

Lutah Maria Riggs's design for Villa San Giuseppe in the Los Feliz district of Los Angeles is more obviously historicist, complementing the large and romantic house designed in 1924–30 by Bernard Maybeck for the flamboyant Packard dealer Earle C. Anthony. The house sits on a narrow ridge at the center of an 8-acre (3.2-hectare) property designed in the manner of a late eighteenth-century picturesque landscape garden by the talented urban planner, landscape architect, and architect Mark Daniels. The principal feature of Daniels's design was a formal space axially related to the arched loggia of the drawing room. The end of the axis embraced, in Daniels's words, "a view of distant city and mountains that cannot be surpassed from any terrace on the slopes of Fiesole."[24]

The property was purchased in 1964 by Daniel and Bernardine Donohue, who wished to provide a more formal entrance to the house that would recognize the expanded needs of automobile access and accentuate the illusion of a late medieval Italian country villa within a High Renaissance garden. They finally engaged the distinguished Santa Barbara architect Lutah Maria Riggs to redesign the garden, in 1966–67. She terraced the steep hillside with new concrete retaining walls and installed a new drive, which winds gradually up the hillside. This roadway terminates in a circular court, on the edge of which is an open domed temple brought from Europe, framed by pine trees, through which is seen a distant view of the San Gabriel Mountains. From this court a drive leads to the front door; a flight of stairs on its axis descends below the drive to a series of formal terraced gardens. The finest of these is paved with red gravel and surrounds a raised fountain pool with deep scalloped edges. This spirited design playfully recaptures the exuberance of the Italian Baroque. Maybeck's oval swimming pool was accommodated in a new paved and walled court, in which freestanding old columns brought from Italy transform the irregular space into a composition that is modern in character, although it incorporates styles spanning the fourteenth century to the 1920s.

Riggs's gardens so perfectly complement Maybeck's eclectic design that they appear to have been created by the same hand. Her most memorable design was the transformation of Daniels's formal garden into a long paved space terminating in a large tiered fountain brought from Italy. The paving is a simple series of fan shapes in buff and umber that recalls Italian

Villa San Giuseppe, Los Angeles. Garden designed by Lutah Maria Riggs for Daniel and Bernardine Donohue, 1966–67; house designed by Bernard Maybeck for Earle C. Anthony, 1924–30. The fountain on the lower terrace evokes the exuberant spirit of Italian Baroque gardens.
Photo: Richard Barnes, 1992

Renaissance designs. It is contained by low clipped hedges and rows of pollarded trees within the stone balustrades designed by Maybeck. The latter enfold the design and terminate with statues flanking the fountain. The view out, with the paving, fountain, and statues, is now even more comparable to views from Fiesole than it was in Daniels's design.

Both Shellhorn's design in Pasadena and Riggs's Villa San Giuseppe demonstrate an effortless ability by those designers to work imaginatively within the conventions of older design genres. To a considerable degree this can be attributed to the Beaux-Arts system of education, with its rigorous attention to functional planning and its command of a broad range of historical styles. These designs are equally significant in emphasizing the continuity of clients' needs for symbolic connections that go beyond the vagaries of changes in fashion.

Villa San Giuseppe. The main garden, with its wavelike paving and elegant fountain, captures the essence of an Italian hillside villa. Photo: Richard Barnes, 1992

6
REGIONAL GARDENS

Any region is both a physical place in the landscape and a concept. Regions have been defined as clearly by political, economic, and cultural boundaries as by the geographic and biological elements that define them as physical places. Designers have defined regional character by identifying the physical patterns of vernacular landscapes such as villages, fields, farms, and other building and garden types that represent an adaptation to place over long periods of time. The building and garden types that these traditions produced were created with local materials and were advocated by the Arts and Crafts movement as models to be emulated. This concept led to the creation of some notable California gardens—the first made during the state's industrial period to successfully establish a regional character. The eclectic gardens created at the same time were often concerned with issues of regional character as well but were more reflections of their owners' personal preferences in style.

Regional character in California gardens of the 1920s was achieved by only a few designers—often without their intending to create a specifically regional garden. They achieved regional character by rigorously adhering to a design tradition from a similar landscape region (usually the Mediterranean Basin), by designing for patterns of use that took full advantage of the California climate, and by using native plants or other drought-tolerant plants.

California designers recognized early in the century the physical similarity of the state to Spain and Italy. By the 1920s Spain had become the more popular tradition to emulate, due to some extent to California's own Hispanic past. The farmhouses of Andalusia were much admired by many architects and garden designers for their appropriateness for California, and the Santa Barbara architect George Washington Smith was greatly attracted to Spanish gardens. "In the Spanish garden, the long open vista of the Italian garden is transformed into a vista through many gateways so that a feeling of intimacy and mystery is achieved, rather than an effect of formality and grandeur. One is never overcome by seeing it all at once, but one has new surprises as he progresses through the gardens."[1]

CASA DEL GRECO

Smith demonstrated this effect at Casa del Greco (house of the Greek, 1920), his own house in Montecito. The L-shaped building, placed around an entry court at the west end of the site, looks eastward into the garden. A long brick path establishes a central axis linking a series of elements. Adjacent to the living rooms is a brick-paved terrace, with a vine-covered pergola supported on substantial piers. This provides a shaded place to sit and look at the various compartments of the garden. Beyond the terrace the main axis passes through a large circular area, defined by low boxwood hedges and tiled benches, with an octagonal fountain basin. A narrow tile-lined channel leads beneath a row of trees to the end of the garden. The cedar trees outside the circular space have become very large, throwing a dense shade, but originally this short vista was a carefully organized sequence of openness, filtered shadow, and dark

shade. (In the house, by contrast, Smith adopted the traditional Hispanic treatment of the interior as a series of dark spaces.) To the side of the central path are a complex boxwood maze, a rose garden, and numerous oak trees. It is essentially a garden of strong, geometric green forms (requiring relatively little water or maintenance), enlivened by the colors of the tilework and of flowers in numerous terra-cotta and glazed pots. Smith treated his house and garden as separate worlds, and the lack of integration of interior and exterior space is conspicuous.

MRS. RICHARD
B. FUDGER
GARDEN

Florence Yoch and the architect Roland Coate produced another Andalusian-style garden that provided simple and appropriate outdoor living spaces, for Mrs. Richard B. Fudger's Los Angeles town house. The U-shaped house, on a relatively confined and oddly shaped site overlooking a country club, was integrated around two patios. The garden was originally separated from the street by a double row of olive trees, behind which a high wall

Casa del Greco. The boxwood
maze, to the south of the main
axial walk, is centered on a small
ornamented sculpture.

Photo: David C. Streatfield, 1986

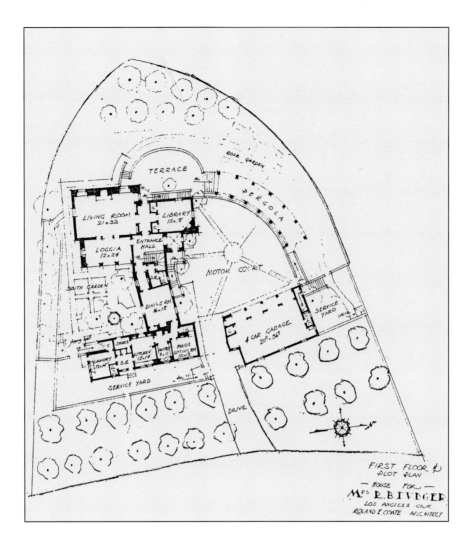

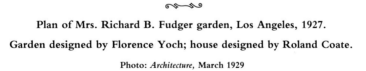

Plan of Mrs. Richard B. Fudger garden, Los Angeles, 1927.

Garden designed by Florence Yoch; house designed by Roland Coate.

Photo: *Architecture,* March 1929

screened the service yard and the garage. The drive passed through the wall into a paved semi-circular entry court, which still serves both as a turnaround and parking area and as a patio for the house. From it, stairs rise to the front door of the house and to a pergola that follows the curve of the patio and gives access to a rose garden at the upper level. On the south side of the house all the living rooms open onto a patio with a small formal garden of boxwood hedges

Mrs. Richard B. Fudger garden. The careful
placing of the vines on the walls and the trees
in the entry court typifies both the architectural nature of many regionalist gardens of the
1920s and the attention devoted to entry spaces
during that period. This garden has been
considerably altered.

Photo: *Architecture*, March 1929

and two olive trees. On the west side of the house a semicircular terrace once overlooked and gave access to a small orchard. The rambling relationship of terraces, loggias, and pergolas recalled the architectonic yet essentially informal character of Moorish Spanish gardens, an effect reinforced by Yoch's retention of an old olive orchard. The olive trees both defined the edge and reinforced the introverted character of the garden.

ISADORE EISNER
GARDEN

Except when working on hillside sites that commanded dramatic views, California landscape designers invariably provided a screen of trees around the perimeter of a site so that the overall impression was of a carefully ordered series of formal gardens within what appeared to be a forested setting. Paul Thiene's design for the relatively small garden of the Isadore Eisner house in Los Angeles is an extremely successful example of this approach. The drive

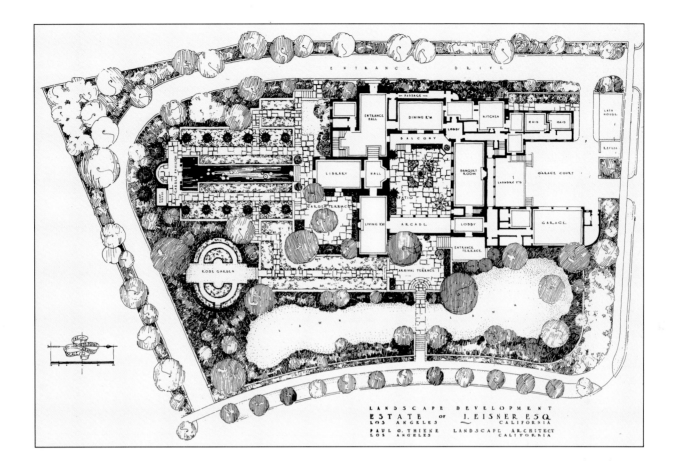

Plan of Isadore Eisner garden, Los Angeles, 1926. Designed by Paul Thiene.

was pushed against the interior boundaries of the site, so that the house occupied the northern section of the property while the remainder was developed as garden. A thick planting of evergreen trees along the property lines screened out views of the adjacent houses, maintaining the successful illusion of a house and garden in a wooded setting. At the south end of the garden were a pedestrian entrance garden and a formal water garden. All the gardens were planted informally, with olive trees and flowers linking them together with a circuitous system of platforms and stairs. The garden was laid out by Thiene's chief designer, A. E. Kuehl, while Thiene was responsible for the planting. The design created the illusion of much greater space, an illusion intensified by the irregular movement through space and by the blurring of the edges of the paving and walls with shrubs and low plants.

❧

Isadore Eisner garden. The long ornamental pool, on an axis with the library, is
flanked by flowerpots and beds of purple verbena (*Verbena teucrioides*). The specimen
olive trees add an air of maturity to the garden. Photo: 1920s

Just as there is a mixing of styles in eclectic gardens, so can regional gardens be achieved in multiple ways. Certain interests—such as maintaining long-established local traditions of hospitality or studying indigenous plant communities—are related to the region rather than to imported styles. The garden at Rancho Los Alamitos in Long Beach, created by Florence Green Bixby, has a characteristically Californian modesty that recalls gardens like that at Rancho Camulos (see chapter 1). Diametrically opposed to flamboyant eclecticism, Rancho Los Alamitos exemplifies a number of ideas that became popular in California. In an understated, casual way appropriate to the ranching tradition, it made reference to California's Hispanic past and to the garden as a site for personal retreat and private domestic tranquility as well as for generous but not extravagant entertainment.

Rancho Los Alamitos (cottonwood ranch) originally comprised some 300,000 acres (121,500 hectares) in what is now the city of Long Beach. Manuel Nieto received it as a Spanish land grant in 1794; disputes with his heirs later broke the ranch into five separate parcels, one of which retained the name Rancho Los Alamitos and the original adobe house built by Nieto. The house was expanded in 1840 by Don Abel Stearns, a Yankee trader and landowner, who sold the ranch to John Bixby, a sheep farmer from Maine, in 1873. His wife, Susan Bixby, surrounded the house and the ranch roads with avenues of peppertrees to provide much-needed shade.[2] Their eldest son, Fred, inherited the ranch in 1909, and from that time until 1936 Fred's wife, Florence, concentrated on creating a series of garden enclosures around the house, carefully preserving the existing trees and other features.

Florence Green Bixby had grown up in a typical Victorian middle-class household in Berkeley and graduated from the University of California in 1898. Shy and introspective, she loved poetry and gardening and never developed any real appreciation for the rough life on a cattle ranch. She was frightened of snakes and never learned to ride a horse. Nevertheless, by creating her gardens with clear respect for her husband's ranch lands, she strongly affirmed the continuity of the ranch mythology as central to the California experience.

The old, low house (now the oldest surviving adobe in the Southland) was surrounded by a series of garden spaces that were used as outdoor rooms. On the north side of the ranch house Bixby created what has always been known as the Old Garden, centered on an octagonal fountain underneath a huge peppertree that is said to have been planted by Stearns. Beneath the peppertree is a patio with low walls, against which were placed benches. This patio was furnished with Indian rugs and rustic furniture. The pleasantly mild climate of the Long Beach area enabled the Bixby family to spend much of their time here in the dappled shade, enjoying an orderly world of white flowers, bold textures, numerous scents, and productive plants such as peaches, sapotas (*Sapota achras*), and bananas. Low-clipped boxwood and

Rancho Los Alamitos, Long Beach, c. 1922. Garden designed by Paul Howard for, and in close association with, Florence Green Bixby. The large paved patio in the Old Garden, furnished with rustic furniture and Indian pots and rugs, was used as an outdoor room by the Bixby family and their friends.

Photo: Albert E. Cawood, 1928

myrtle hedges established order and defined the flower beds. A paved area adjoining the drawing room was also used for sitting. Stretching a canvas tarpaulin over this area and sprinkling it with cornmeal converted it into a dance floor for the Bixby children and their friends. It was lit by lanterns carefully concealed in the trees, and the music wafted from a small orchestra playing inside the house.[3]

At the end of the bedroom wing and opening off the entrance garden was the Secret Garden, created in the late 1920s. Its walls were enlivened with vines, decorative plaques, and a small ceramic fountain. In this tiny sunny space Florence Bixby often looked after her numerous grandchildren, nephews, and nieces, or indulged her own need for privacy. In a poem written in 1922 she refers indirectly to the need for a "secret place."[4] She may well have needed respite from her considerable domestic and social duties as wife, mother, and prominent social figure. The name she gave this garden implies that it was to be used as a haven, but all of her garden spaces served this purpose.

Every year Fred and Florence Bixby held a large barbecue party on the expansive lawn in front of the old house beneath the shade of two enormous Moreton Bay fig trees (*Ficus macrophylla*), which had been planted as saplings by Susan Bixby in the 1880s. Guests would eat barbecued beef and chicken and watermelons on tables covered with red-checkered tablecloths

Rancho Los Alamitos. The Secret Garden was
used by Florence Green Bixby as a private
outdoor retreat.

Photo: Albert E. Cawood, 1928

scattered in the shade of the trees. Pens enclosing small domestic animals were set up to entertain the children.

The inner circuit of gardens appears to have been designed by the landscape architect Paul Howard. It was contained by the existing drive and rows of peppertrees on the south and west sides and on the east by a curving avenue of Canary Island palm trees that Florence planted in 1909. These avenues of trees marked the zones of social and private spaces directly related to the house.

Across the drive on the south and east sides is a series of gardens, created between 1922 and 1936, that provides a somewhat labyrinthine circuit of paths as well as places to sit and look out over the ranch lands and toward the ocean. The formal terraces on the south side were designed by the Olmsted Brothers and represent an attempt to mask the ugly oil wells that began to pierce the landscape after the discovery of oil on the ranch in 1923.

The gardens to the east of the drive are centered on the tennis court, which was installed in the late 1910s as part of Howard's plan. Tennis playing was advocated by Florence Bixby as a way to promote suitable social contacts—and hence marriages—for the three Bixby daughters, but it was disdained by Fred Bixby as an unsuitable activity for a ranch. The court was surrounded on one side by a pergola supporting Concord grapes, beneath which grew

Rancho Los Alamitos. The eastern facade of the house overlooks a large lawn dominated by two Moreton Bay fig trees (*Ficus macrophylla*), planted by Susan Hathaway
Bixby in the 1880s. Photo: Jerry Pavia, 1990

artichokes (a favorite of Fred's); on the second side by a wisteria-covered pergola; and on the third side by the Friendship Garden. As a keen gardener Florence Bixby was the grateful recipient of many plants from her gardening friends, one of whom suggested that she create a special place to plant all of her gifts. The Friendship Garden is a small hourglass-shaped lawn surrounded by beds jammed with an odd assortment of plants, reflecting the very warm regard of Florence Bixby's friends.

At the north end of the tennis court is the Desert Garden, which contains a collection of cacti assembled with the help of William Hertrich, designer of the Huntingtons' gardens in San Marino. Florence Bixby had developed a fascination with desert plants after being sent by her husband to the desert to collect cacti so he could win a bet that spineless cacti could provide an alternative source of water for the cattle on one of his ranches in Arizona.

Adjoining the Desert Garden is the Native Garden, which developed from a series of failed attempts to create a rock garden. The idea of making a garden with native plants was most unusual in the late 1920s. Helped by Allen Chickering, a college classmate, and Ed Howard, of the prominent nursery Howard and Smith, Florence Bixby created a wild garden with small flowing streams, waterfalls, and pools in a hummocky landscape of herbaceous plants, shrubs, cottonwoods, and toyons (*Heteromeles arbutifolia*). It is remarkably like a descrip-

Rancho Los Alamitos. The small Friendship Garden was filled with plants given to Florence Bixby by her gardening friends.

Photo: Albert E. Cawood, 1928

Above. Rancho Los Alamitos. The Desert Garden was originally planted with *Cereus* species, agaves, and prickly-pear cactus (*Opuntia* sp.), rather than the aloes, barrel cactus (*Echinocactus acanthodes*), and creeping-devil cactus (*Lemaireocereus eruca*) that occupy the foreground in this contemporary view of the garden.

Photo: Jerry Pavia, 1990

Right. Rancho Los Alamitos. Florence Bixby developed the Native Garden during the late 1920s as a place to display native plants and replicate their habitats.

Photo: Albert E. Cawood, 1928

tion in her eldest daughter's classic book *Trip with Father:* "Branches of trees arched over a soft, small trail. Vines with little blossoms, berries and wild roses, lichens on rocks, and rivulets of water, it was the kind of country Mother loved."[5]

Both the Desert and the Native gardens were attempts to re-create fragments of the natural world, intended not so much as botanical collections as evocations of particular natural landscapes. The Native Garden also celebrated one of California's cultural traditions: figures of Saint Francis set in small niches on trees attracted the Bixby's Mexican ranch hands, who were welcomed into this part of the garden on Sundays.

Despite the number of professional designers and experts consulted by Florence Bixby, these gardens were entirely her creation. She also played the role of head gardener, supervising intermittent help by ranch hands and doing most of the hand-watering herself. Her simple, understated gardens, created with robust plants rather than a wide range of exotics, were in visual harmony with the original adobe house, which had been extended into a rambling, U-shaped structure. Together they were the quintessence of what the English garden writer Marion Cran called "Old California."[6]

OLIVE HILL

At the same time that Florence Bixby was continuing and expanding aspects of California's Anglo-Hispanic traditions of garden design and hospitality, a group of progressive architects was exploring the fundamental visual principles in Mayan and Mexican design traditions as well as a progressive use of garden space as outdoor rooms for theatrical performances and uninhibited outdoor living. Hollyhock House (1920), on the large site in Hollywood known as Olive Hill, was commissioned by the oil heiress Aline Barnsdall. There Frank Lloyd Wright and his associates Lloyd Wright, Rudolph Schindler, and Richard Neutra developed an alternative to what Wright called the "toothpaste flamboyance" of the worst Spanish Colonial Revivalism. At Hollyhock House, and in a subsequent series of concrete-block houses, Wright turned to the Mayan and other pre-Columbian traditions of Central America, which he believed were the true American vernacular. Wright proposed this as a potent antidote to what he called "the eclectic progression of to and fro in the rag-time and cast-off of all the ages."[7]

Hollyhock House, built on a Los Angeles hilltop, was a series of single-room wings enclosing two large courtyards; additional walled courtyards on the perimeter of the house opened up to views over the city. The inner court, onto which all the major living rooms opened, was used both as an outdoor living room and as a theater for dramatic performances. Barnsdall dreamed of turning Olive Hill into an arts center, and this central area was conceived as the principal place for outdoor performances—an idea consistent with modernist European ideals about the garden as usable space. The audience sat in the courtyard and on the roofs of

Hollyhock House, Olive Hill, Los Angeles, 1920. Garden and house designed by Frank Lloyd Wright for Aline Barnsdall. A small stream originally linked the pool in the fore-ground to a pool in the living room at the far end of the garden court. Photo: c. 1923

the house, which were linked to the court by open staircases. At the far end of the court was a second-story corridor joining the two sides of the court and providing a proscenium for the stage area. The courtyard itself comprised a lily-filled semicircular pond, beyond which a series of shallow semicircular steps rose to a thick backdrop of eucalyptus trees. In designing this integrated indoor-outdoor space, Wright adopted the Mayan tradition of treating a building as a series of solid wall planes, broken only by relatively small window and door openings. Within the intimate privacy of this inner court, however, long banks of windows and doors open up the interior, physically and visually, to this green outdoor room.

Lloyd Wright garden, Hollywood, 1927. Garden and house designed by Wright for
himself. This view from the street shows how Wright eliminated the customarily
wasted space of the front garden and replaced it with a deep, low bed of ground cover
and vines that climb up the walls of the house. Photo: Saxon Holt, 1993

One of the oddest features of Hollyhock House is Wright's use of the hollyhock as the decorative theme for the house. There is, of course, nothing specifically Mayan about the hollyhock, and it is not a plant native to California. It was left to Wright's oldest son to incorporate regional plants into the structures he later designed himself. Lloyd Wright, who served as landscape architect for all of his father's concrete-block California houses of the 1920s, carried the integration of buildings and plant motifs to a level rarely achieved before or since. His own studio house in Hollywood (1927) occupies its tiny lot almost completely, leaving room only for planting boxes and for a very small walled courtyard on the perimeter. An Italian stone pine planted in the court has grown to a prodigious size and now acts as a huge parasol, keeping the structure cool. The house was treated as a heavy cubic mass, enlivened at the window and door openings by projecting cast-concrete blocks, in shapes abstracted from the Joshua tree (*Yucca brevifolia*), which is native to Southern California deserts. The form of these blocks contrasts with the blank walls, and the similarity of the effect to pre-Columbian forms was intended as a subtle reference to the Indian culture of the American continent. The rich surface of the cast concrete is complemented by the delicate range of textures in the vines, ground covers, succulents, and yuccas in the planting beds. Sliding doors open the living room to the tiny court, which was used as an extension of the room.

Lloyd Wright garden. The living room and the patio, which is shaded by a giant Italian stone pine (*Pinus pinea*), were designed as a single space.
Photo: Derry Moore, 1979

The concept of the garden as a series of outdoor rooms integrated spatially and visually with the interior of the house was explored in a thoroughly modern way by the architect Rudolph Schindler in his own house. An émigré from Austria, Schindler went to Los Angeles in 1921 to assist Frank Lloyd Wright in designing Olive Hill. Trained in the tradition of morally committed modernism associated with the Viennese architect Adolf Loos, Schindler was lured to California by its reputation as a place where the progressive and the unusual were wholeheartedly embraced. Both Wright and Schindler discovered that local sympathy for non-traditional values was more superficial than it was reputed to be—characterized by a penchant for nude sunbathing, physical exercise, healthy diets, and a simple life-style. Yet even though it seemed that the modern was ultimately just another fashion there, California produced more modern architecture than any other region in the country.

Schindler wrote about his plans for his own house:

> Our rooms will descend close to the garden and the garden will become an integral part of the house. The distinction between indoors and outdoors will disappear. Our house will lose its front- and back-door aspect. It will cease being a group of dens, some larger ones for social effect, and a few smaller ones (bedrooms) in which to herd the family. Each individual will want a private room to gain a background for his life. He will sleep in the open. A work-and-play room, together with a garden, will satisfy the group needs.[8]

Later Schindler wrote about his concept of a cooperative dwelling. "This theme fulfills the basic requirements for the camper's shelter: A protected back and an open front, a fireplace and a roof."[9]

Schindler's Kings Road lot in Hollywood was 100 by 200 feet (30.5 by 61 meters). Designed to be occupied by Schindler and his wife, and by his friend Clyde Chase and his wife, it was divided by high clipped hedges and concrete walls into a series of enclosures. At the center of this complex of enclosed spaces was a Z-shaped house with large windows that opened up the interior spaces to the gardens; both house and garden have recently been restored. The interior spaces were based on the idea that each occupant should have his or her own private retreat. Each family had an L-shaped unit in which a studio/living room was separated from an outdoor patio only by floor-to-ceiling sliding canvas panels, which could be removed in the summer. Each patio had an outdoor fireplace. There was one kitchen shared by the two families; the wives took turns cooking for everyone. Bedroom spaces were not provided; instead, "sleeping baskets," or porches, were placed over the two entrances. There are seven outdoor zones: a long, narrow entry path; a patio garden related to the northern part of

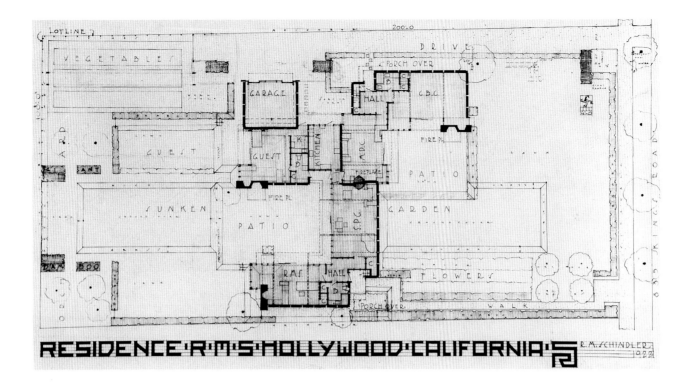

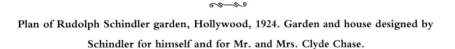

Plan of Rudolph Schindler garden, Hollywood, 1924. Garden and house designed by
Schindler for himself and for Mr. and Mrs. Clyde Chase.

the house; a garden related to the southern part of the house; a rear patio garden related to a
large central room; an orchard; a vegetable garden; and a service drive leading to a garage. The
plan of house and garden was organized rather like a De Stijl composition. Hedges divided the
area into subzones that were diversified by formal plantings of orchard trees, a clump of
bamboo by the service drive, and rectangular panels of ground cover defined by narrow borders of tall grasses.

The house embodies an odd mixture of ideas. Camping out had become popular in
the West, and this passion for contact with nature was urbanized in the form of the sleeping
porch, which had become extremely popular by the turn of the century. Schindler, with his
European roots, sought a more orderly urban contact with nature, in which nature was tamed
by geometry. In a sense, his house is an updated version of the Mediterranean courtyard house,
without the mediating pergola. Its architecture suggests both impermanence and stability. The
tilt-slab walls combined with wooden ceilings and sliding canvas doors create what Schindler
called a marriage between the solid, permanent cave and the open, lightweight tent.[10]

Rudolph Schindler garden. Only large sliding glass panels separated the living room in the Chases' part of the house (seen here) from their patio. Photo: Julius Shulman, 1950

Fascination with native plants played a significant role in developing a regional style of gardens. Theodore Payne, one of the most fervent advocates of their use, had acquired a keen interest in wildflowers and native California plants while he was a ranch foreman in Santa Ana Canyon in Orange County.[11] In 1903 he opened a store in Los Angeles selling seeds of native plants, and in 1915 he created a 5-acre (2-hectare) native-plant garden at the natural history museum in Los Angeles. By the 1910s some of the larger estates in Montecito had extensive areas of wildflowers and native shrubs, representing part of the collecting mania that was so characteristic of late nineteenth-century gardens. Never treated as the principal feature of a garden, they invariably lay beyond the immaculately maintained formal flower gardens around the house and enhanced that formality through contrast.

CIMA DEL
MUNDO

Payne's most extensive wildflower garden was developed during the 1920s at Cima del Mundo for Lora Knight. The Montecito site was unusually beautiful, with undulating grass meadows and large groves of oak trees. Payne enhanced this landscape by replacing the grass with extensive plantings of wildflowers that rolled over the soft forms of the landscape and came right up to the walls of the house. The kaleidoscope of spring colors was a celebration of one of the most pleasurable times of the year in central and Southern California. Regrettably, it proved impractical to grow wildflowers in small gardens, since they flourish best without the disturbance associated with normal gardening activities. The garden no longer exists.

Subtle, almost painterly references to historical styles, the use of drought-tolerant plants, and a concern for water conservation were the hallmarks of Lockwood de Forest's

Cima del Mundo, Montecito, 1925. Garden designed by Theodore Payne for Lora Knight. The courtyard, which looked out to the extensive wildflower meadows, was planted with native plants, a banana tree, and some strelitzia.

Photo: c. 1928–32

memorable garden designs. From the early 1920s until his grievously early death in 1949, de Forest was a gentleman landscape architect, designing gardens in Santa Barbara and Montecito with his wife, Elizabeth Kellam. He came from a prosperous old New York family; his father and namesake was a landscape painter and a leading authority on Indian art, which he collected for the Metropolitan Museum of Art. A member of the tightly interwoven network of moneyed and cultured families who dominated Santa Barbara society, the young de Forest was a flamboyant and engaging figure, said to have been rather like a character from an F. Scott Fitzgerald novel.[12]

Building a cabin in the woods on the campus of the Thacher School in Ojai and exploring the nearby mountains awakened de Forest's keen appreciation of the California landscape while he was still in his teens.[13] He undoubtedly also absorbed a great deal from his travels in Italy and Spain with his friend and client Wright Ludington, the art collector. De Forest began his landscaping practice in 1920 and almost immediately established a reputation for fresh and original designs.

LOCKWOOD DE
FOREST GARDEN

De Forest's own garden of 1926, located in Santa Barbara, anticipated many characteristics of the modernist California gardens of the 1940s.[14] It provided graceful access for the automobile, it incorporated many drought-tolerant plants, it was easy to maintain, and it dramatically employed the technique of borrowed scenery. The small house was planned around a

❧

Lockwood de Forest garden, Santa Barbara, 1926. Garden designed by de Forest for himself. The northern facade of the house faces the lawn and a deep bed of native plants.

Photo: Saxon Holt, 1988

tiny brick-paved atrium with large glazed doors that open up the house visually and cool it physically. A small tiled fountain and an olive tree provide the only contrast to this simple geometry. De Forest arranged the garden as a series of formal areas on the east, north, and west sides of the house. On the east side the kitchen, dining room, and library open onto a series of small gardens defined by clipped hedges and globes of myrtle along a path. The sophisticated nature of these plant collections contrasts with the decomposed granite path, the retention of boulders, and the simple curbs of local stone—all of which supply regional color. The concept that the colors of the surrounding landscape could be a principal ordering device for a garden was one of de Forest's most significant contributions to the theory and practice of landscape design.

The square lawn is defined by eighteen-inch-tall (forty-six-centimeter) stone walls, which go several feet below ground to prevent the lateral spread of the kikuyu grass (*Pennisetum clandestinum*). This tough and resilient South African grass has never been watered since the garden was installed. During the hot, dry months of summer, it turns a golden brown, like native grasses. The large bed beyond the lawn is planted with native bulbs, grasses, and drought-tolerant shrubs, which also cover the high berm against the boundary wall. The planting is so skillfully devised to frame the view that there is no apparent end to the garden. The lawn and bed are the foreground of an immense regional panorama that extends to the

~~⚬~~

Lockwood de Forest garden. The distant panorama of the Santa Ynez Mountains on the north side of the house is framed by trees on adjacent properties and by a deep bed of native plants. The oak tree on the right has died since this photograph was taken.
Photo: Robert M. Fletcher & Associates, 1982

Lockwood de Forest garden. The contrasting
colors of rosemary and lavender, in what had
originally been a rose garden, comprise part of
the palette of regional hues, complemented by
the colors of the rock and stone curbs.

Photo: Robert M. Fletcher & Associates, 1984

top of the mountains. A carefully placed live oak tree (which has since died) originally framed the view on the right-hand side. A paved area beneath it offered a place from which to look at the deep bed and a series of rock-lined pools providing the contrast of water that appears almost black. The garden survives in good condition.

WILLIAM
DICKENSON
GARDEN

De Forest's garden for the William Dickenson house (1928) in Hope Ranch (a large subdivision immediately west of Santa Barbara) was also designed as a poetic response to the landscape, again created with a mixture of native and nonnative plants. The house, by Reginald Johnson, was sited to save as many trees as possible in the existing oak grove. The house and its remarkable garden, which in recent years has been completely remodeled, originally exhibited restraint on a generous scale. The design made masterly and subtle use of a small palette of striking plants that complemented the forms and colors of the magnificent oaks. The house was planned around three courts: the entry court, garage court, and service court. The latter two were designed around oak trees. Only the entry court was empty, and that emptiness established a strong counterpoint to the rest of the garden. A simple cross-axial system linked the house, its courts, and the main lawn. Yet the diagonal line of movement through the landscape, either from the house or along the drive, established a continually changing set of focal points, foreshadowing Thomas Church's work in the 1940s (see chapter 7).

As in de Forest's own garden, the main lawn was defined by low walls that were a comfortable height for sitting. The lawn was treated as a visual field upon which the picturesque forms of the oaks became sculptural pieces, especially in the late hours of the afternoon, when the garden was most frequently used. The low sun threw long shadows on the ground, and silver light haloed the trunks and branches of the trees. This light established the garden's main color scheme, recurring in the beds outside the walls with yellow-green proteas, junipers, banksias, and silver trees, beyond which the silver ocean could be glimpsed.

The most dramatic feature of the garden, the silver allée, was reached by a path at the edge of the wall and could not be seen from the house. A long, narrow lawn was flanked by deep beds edged with low-clipped hedges in front of rows of silver trees, underplanted with bird of paradise (*Strelitzia reginae*). From a small rose garden at the far end were the best views of the ocean and the distant mountains. Unlike the main lawn, which acted as a transitional space of silvery half-lights, the allée was entirely silver, with foreground, middle ground, and the distant ocean and mountains bound together in a seamless unity of silver. This unusual effect was transitory, experienced only in the late hours of the day. The entire garden was an extraordinary achievement, uniting wilderness and the domesticated order of the garden.

Left, top. William Dickenson garden, Hope Ranch, 1928. Garden designed by Lockwood de Forest; house designed by Reginald Johnson. The sculptural form of a California live oak originally framed a view of the lawn and a deep bed of proteas.

Photo: David C. Streatfield, 1969

Left, bottom. William Dickenson garden, service court. De Forest achieved a powerful simplicity by surrounding preexisting oak trees with a simple lawn defined by clipped hedges featuring a range of carefully selected textures.

Photo: David C. Streatfield, 1969

Opposite. William Dickenson garden. A striking effect of silvery light was created in the silver allée by underplanting silver trees (*Leuca-dendron argenteum*) with bird of paradise plants (*Strelitzia reginae*).

Photo: David C. Streatfield, 1969

Val Verde, Montecito. Garden
designed by Lockwood de Forest
for C. H. Ludington and Wright
Ludington, 1926–39; house
designed by Bertram Grosvenor
Goodhue for Henry Dater, 1918. At
the north end of the garden, a
curving brick path placed beneath
preexisting oak trees follows the
edge of a steep slope. Wright Ludington's Renaissance plaques are
embedded in the wall.

Photo: David C. Streatfield, 1988

De Forest worked for two generations of the Ludington family revitalizing their Spanish Colonial Revival house designed by Bertram Goodhue. Built for Henry Dater in 1918, it was known as Días Felices (happy days). This large, lumpen house sat in the middle of a 25-acre (10.1-hectare) estate in Montecito, overlooking a terraced formal garden and a rectangular decorative pool. Outside this central area a network of formal paths threaded through palms, bananas, and other tropical trees. The estate was purchased in 1925 by C. H. Ludington, a prominent Philadelphia lawyer and the father of de Forest's close friend Wright Ludington. De Forest was commissioned to make the numerous alterations needed to convert the property from a winter retreat to a permanent residence, which was renamed Val Verde (green valley).

De Forest designed a collection of discrete single-story buildings to accommodate servants and garages, and he extended the gardens above the house up to an old water reservoir, which was no longer needed. The service buildings were designed around a series of small courtyards on the axis of the main drive. The drive's terminus was a stone fountain basin, reminiscent of one at the Villa Medici in Rome, in a simple brick-paved terrace contained by two walls. The plain walls were painted with numerous layers of paint and deliberately scraped to suggest decades of weathering. The carefully pruned branches of oak trees provided a light canopy. The branch of one of these trees passed through the upper portion of one of the walls, an unusual integration suggesting that wall and tree had always been there.

A door in the wall beneath the arching branch opens to a path following the edge of the hill, which drops away on the left side; a curving plaster wall follows the path on the right. The wall was treated as an abstract background for some of Wright Ludington's classical, medieval, and Renaissance bas-reliefs in stone and marble. Their presence suggests antiquity in

❧

Val Verde. On the slope below the east side of the house, de Forest added both a series of clipped boxwood hedges around the paths leading from Goodhue's staircase and the columns on the upper-terrace walk, which look almost like abstract sculpture from below.

Photo: Robert M. Fletcher & Associates, 1991

a space that is also distinctly modern because of its flowing shape and the changing abstract shadows thrown on the walls and the path. A melancholic mood is established by this mixture of references to different periods, and the mood changes throughout the day, depending on the quality of light. Such transitory effects were anticipated and celebrated by de Forest in a seemingly casual fashion on a relatively minor path.

Above the house was a freestanding water tower. Made obsolete by the establishment of the Montecito Water Authority in the 1920s, it was converted into bedrooms. The main irrigation reservoir became a swimming pool, and the tower was linked to the pool with changing rooms and a large gallery designed to house four Chinese paintings. After Ludington inherited the estate in the late 1920s, he added a separate atrium to hold several pieces of Greek and Roman sculpture. It was built with terra-cotta-colored Roman bricks, marble columns that recalled Venetian Gothic columns, and Spanish roof tiles around four mature olive trees. Walks through the atrium were lined with pots of tuberous begonias and primroses, which were changed seasonally. Like the other features in this garden, the atrium was an abstraction of historical precedents.

Below the art gallery were two irrigation basins, which de Forest converted into reflecting ponds. The concrete was painted a pale terra-cotta, almost pink, and the stepped portions of the pools were lined with white tiles. A stone terrace was added above the upper pool, with two large terra-cotta urns and a fountain between them. With careful selective pruning of the oaks, de Forest transformed this area into a landscape in which the reflecting pools were poised as panels floating in a carefully edited "nature" comprising undulating ivy ground cover and arching oaks. The effect foreshadows, by at least two decades, some of the more potent designs in New Jersey by the modernist designer James Rose.

In the late 1930s the vaguely Spanish tropical garden and the Beaux-Arts formal garden that abutted the house at Val Verde were transformed into a simple evocation of an Italian villa's garden. Wright Ludington had never liked the house or its dull formal gardens, which were not well related to the outer landscape. De Forest resolved these problems in an appropriate and powerful way that displays great poetic insight.

The lawns flanking the house were replaced by two pools on the long cross-axis of the house. On the north side of the house the dining room overlooks a narrow pool flanked by olive trees. The cross-axis was terminated with a simple exedra wall, in front of which is mounted a Roman herm. On the south side of the house a wider pool is flanked by long, narrow parterre beds with low boxwood hedges and dwarf orange trees. Beyond the pool a large, Roman female figure in white marble once stood out against the curving backdrop of dark oak trees. Thus, from the center of the house the view in either direction ended with a statue.

Val Verde. The hard-edged relecting pool at the south end of the living room accentu-

ates the sculptural character of the grove of oak trees beyond.

Photo: David C. Streatfield, 1988

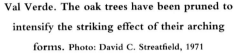

Val Verde. The oak trees have been pruned to intensify the striking effect of their arching forms. Photo: David C. Streatfield, 1971

Immediately adjoining the house and at the top of the slope is a 300-foot-long (91.5-meter) cross-axial path, which de Forest transformed into a remarkable terraced overlook. Beyond the house, the path is lined on both sides by square columns about 12 feet high (3.7 meters). They terminate in plain capitals but do not support, as one would anticipate, heavy wooden beams; instead, the beams appear to have collapsed long ago. The pergola hints at a mood of decay, but this is delicately balanced with the new life of the bougainvillea vines wrapping around the columns. The power of this "ruin" is best grasped by looking diagonally upward from the pool at the bottom of the garden.

Goodhue's garden design had been axial and directed the eye down the central staircase. De Forest created a strong tension by placing a Greek torso on the main axis as a focal point and by placing a long narrow pool at the south end of the original pool, with a head on a column within an apselike section of hedge. The eye is attracted to this minor focal point and is thereby directed over the woods to a distant view of the ocean. This sense of outward orientation is reinforced by the introduction outside this formal garden of new trees that have a predominantly grayish cast to their foliage. The grayish tone extends from the olive trees close to the house out to these trees and on to the grayish light of the mountains, visually relating the garden to the surrounding landscape.

The diversity of the gardens described in this chapter makes clear the lack of consensus about how to create regional character. Each of these gardens constitutes a personal response by the client and the designer to particular opportunities for creating harmonious spaces appropriate to each place.

Val Verde. The columns along the overlook terrace, immediately below the house, frame

views of acacias and olive trees at the edge of the garden. Photo: David C. Streatfield, 1988

7

THE NEW GARDEN

G arden design in California from the late 1930s to the mid-1960s was dominated by modernist ideals and forms. Modernist designers advocated the rejection of historical forms and the adoption of new technologies and materials, including plastics, asbestos cement, aluminum, and lightweight steel. The forms they favored were abstract, influenced particularly by Cubist painting and sculpture. As a state with a strong tradition of outdoor living and as the first state to adopt modernism enthusiastically, California became a major center of landscape design during this period. Indeed, the influence of the private California garden on public landscape designers both within the state and across the country was paramount. In shopping centers, university campuses, and suburban office complexes one can find designs whose character was derived from these modernist garden precedents.

Since landscape architecture had not been taught at the Bauhaus in Germany—the wellspring of modern design in pre–World War II Europe—the modernist approach to landscape architecture had not been clearly articulated. Modernist architects in Europe tended to envision their buildings as hermetic boxes, imposed on an undefined backdrop. The exciting spatial implications of Mies van der Rohe's Barcelona Pavilion (1929) were never fully explored, although they intrigued many American landscape architects in the late 1930s. Instead, landscape designers such as André and Paul Vera, André Lurçat, Pierre Le Grand, and Gabriel Guevrekian created abstract gardens in Paris and Provence that were self-consciously modernistic.[1] Only in Scandinavia—in the work of Erik Gunnar Asplund, C. Th. Sørensen, and Alvar Aalto—was there a sensitive integration of architecture and landscape.[2]

Californian designers were not directly influenced by these landscape precedents or by modern art until the late 1930s. Their eager embracing of modernism at that point can be explained in part by the Depression, which had greatly altered the state's economic and social circumstances. Even for the very rich, including the leading figures of the movie industry, lavish garden-making on the scale practiced in the 1920s had become prohibitively expensive. The new economic and social imperatives required a more pragmatic approach to designing gardens that emphasized function and reduced maintenance, both of which were implicitly part of the modernist agenda. This transition can be traced in the work of Florence Yoch and Thomas Church during the 1930s. Yoch turned away from her earlier eclecticism toward a less derivative and more abstract approach, evident in her design for the distinguished film director George Cukor. This graceful garden (1936) in the Hollywood Hills played a critical role in her subsequent development as a designer. Ruth Shellhorn, who worked for Yoch on this garden, believes that its challenges forced Yoch to reconsider the value of historicist design, and there was certainly an increasing freedom in her work thereafter.[3]

GEORGE CUKOR

GARDEN

⤾〰⤿

Pages 188–89.

El Novillero,

Sonoma, 1948.

Designed by Thomas

Church for Dewey

and Jean Donnell.

Photo: Felice Frankel, 1989

Steep, narrow streets somewhat reminiscent of those in an Italian hill town wind through the Hollywood Hills to Cukor's oddly shaped site. Seventy-five feet (22.9 meters) of the hill had to be leveled to provide a platform at one end of the V-shaped site for the long, one-room-wide, two-story dwelling, designed by J. E. Dolena. The junction of the two sides of the V was the lowest part of the garden; the swimming pool was placed there, serving as a visual focus from both directions and as the recreational heart of the garden. From the pool a curving path, punctuated with pots of plants, moved up to a pillared arbor overlooking Los Angeles; below the pool was an extensive rose garden.

Next to the swimming pool a large paved terrace with an outdoor fireplace provided a range of places to sit in full or partial shade beneath the jacaranda trees. Cukor's garden epitomizes the decisive changes in garden design that occurred during the 1930s. In the 1920s only avant-garde artists and ardent health-seekers had spent much time in their outdoor living rooms. By the 1930s deep tans had become stylish, and clients wanted to spend as much time as possible in the garden in the sun, and even though the gardens created during and after the Depression were smaller, facilities for recreation occupied more space in them.

Trained in the theater and a discriminating art collector, Cukor was perhaps the most cultured member of his generation in the movie industry. He had given Yoch carte blanche,

George Cukor garden, Hollywood, 1936. Garden designed by Florence Yoch; house designed by J. E. Dolena. The swimming pool was the focal point of this relaxed setting. The garden survives, but in a greatly altered state.
Photo: Fred Dapprich, 1930s

George Cukor garden. A curving path led beneath the jacaranda trees and up to a columned overlook. In the 1940s Cukor replaced the low flowerpots with French statues, much to Yoch's annoyance.

Photo: Fred Dapprich, 1930s

specifying only that she provide a garden that was "Italian in feeling."[4] Not wanting to make overt references to specific Italian gardens, Yoch achieved this by using a few well-placed statues and some beautifully crafted masonry retaining walls, built by her crew of Mexican workmen. But this Italianate garden was also remarkably abstract and highly appropriate for informal outdoor living.

Thomas Church, like Yoch, was trained in the Beaux-Arts tradition, which required mastery of historical styles. After graduating from Harvard in 1926 he traveled in Italy and Spain, and the integration of house and garden and the restrained plant palettes that he observed there inspired his own work for the remainder of his career. Church's early gardens were highly simplified versions of Italian and French formal gardens. In a 1933 article about the Villa d'Este he wrote, "We, today, who stand on the brink of a modern and sensible approach to our garden problems may well revive and restudy the underlying principles which make the Italian Renaissance gardens the greatest achievement of garden building in history."[5] But he also believed that the garden had to be redefined to suit the new economic circumstances, and a few months earlier he had written: "The small garden is like a small room. It must be neat. Houses have changed. They are down off their stilts. Everything points to the increasing intimacy of the house and its garden."[6]

In 1938 a model of Church's design for a swimming-pool garden (never built) was included in the *Exhibition of Mural Conceptualism* held at the San Francisco Museum of Art.[7] Church's garden was conceived as a setting for an abstract panel of iron and concrete by Flo-

192   THE NEW GARDEN

rence Allston Swift, an avant-garde sculptor. Surrounding the free-form pool and cabaña structure were low walls and plants arranged in an abstract composition of planes and objects around an irregular path. Each element, whether a structure or a plant, was placed to create a cumulatively rich sequence of visual experiences. The flat ground plane incorporated a series of different surfaces, including grass and several paving materials, in a way that recalled the overlapping planes and textures of Cubist collages. Church's designs have been interpreted as being derived from modern art, especially the work of painters such as Joan Miró and Jean Arp,[8] but there is no evidence to support this assertion. His elegant use of abstract forms just as likely came from other sources, such as the compound curves of nineteenth-century French park design and objects by the Finnish designer Alvar Aalto.[9]

There is a striking similarity between Church's Mural Conceptualism garden design and the radical modernist work then being developed by Garrett Eckbo (who had been an undergraduate at the University of California, Berkeley) and James Rose as students at Harvard, especially the series of gardens designed by Eckbo and published the previous year.[10] Eckbo and Church were not aware of each other's work, and the similarities between them should not obscure the fundamental differences between Church's inclusive eclecticism and Eckbo's purposeful radicalism. Nonetheless, the appearance of these designs by Yoch, Church, and Eckbo marked the beginning of treating the California garden as an abstract space. For older designers such as Yoch, Church, and Edward Huntsman-Trout, the garden remained primarily a place that was devoted to private social purposes but that could also become a work of art. Younger, more socially committed designers such as Eckbo, Lawrence Halprin, and

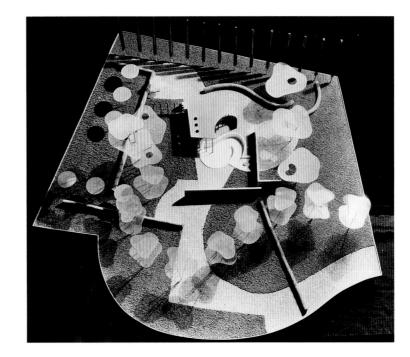

∽≈⁓

Model for Mural Conceptualism garden, 1938. Designed by Thomas Church, with an iron-and-concrete panel by Florence Allston Swift, for an exhibition at the San Francisco Museum of Art. The design focused on a swimming pool and a single-story pavilion at the top of the model.

Robert Royston—all of whom had been influenced by Christopher Tunnard's book *Gardens in the Modern Landscape* (1938)—sought to take Tunnard's radical reconsideration of art, nature, and society as the basis for restructuring land-use practices for the entire environment.[11] It is one of the tragedies of the American landscape that they were successful only in a limited sense. However, by using the garden as a site for experimenting with the treatment of outdoor spaces, they invigorated the design of public and commercial spaces in the 1950s and 1960s. Lawrence Halprin's design for Old Orchard shopping center (1955) in Skokie, Illinois, for example, is a good example of the use of the forms of the new garden in another context.

The new garden designs united indoor and outdoor space to create a setting for a relaxed, often hedonistic way of living. For the first time in the century gardens were fully used as outdoor rooms, and the success of that merger depended on the collaboration of architect and landscape architect. William Wurster expressed this particularly well. "Architecture and Landscape Architecture are one thing when they are separated only as to materials and technique, not as to basic approach."[12] He continued:

> This same emphasis on unity can be applied to the product of these professions. Structure gives protection from the elements, but it rises to be architecture only if it does this with beauty. Landscape architecture follows the same path when it sets a fine plan and lifts the choice and placing of planting into a like beauty. The treatment of space can provide similar spiritual satisfaction be it indoors or outdoors.
>
> In California this kinship has been widely accepted because it reflects, and in turn facilitates, indoor-outdoor flow of living which is probably unique. . . . At least the architect and landscape architect together provide a simple frame for a special way of life.[13]

Such collaboration also involved the client and other artists, especially sculptors. The sculptor Claire Falkenstein celebrated the fact that in the 1940s landscape architects collaborated as never before with artists, who were inspired to use new materials such as sheet steel, extruded metal, and transparent plastic, as well as more traditional materials. "Poised in delicate balance, sculpture is a concentrated expression of its environment. It tends to clarify, suggesting the order and degrees of man-made freedom such as may be apprehended in the most minute plant structure of nature or in the design of the whole garden."[14] Landscape architects also experimented with some of these materials, as well as with asbestos cement and poured concrete.

The new garden was greatly reduced in size as a result of economic necessity. Older estates were frequently subdivided into smaller lots, ranging from a few acres to an area as small as 60 by 25 feet (18.3 by 7.6 meters). This could easily have produced a sense of claustrophobia, and numerous devices—such as diagonal walks, "borrowed scenery" (through which the garden became a foreground to views of the regional landscape), and the revival of the ha-ha (the sunken fence used in English eighteenth-century gardens)—were employed to visually expand the apparent space of the garden. The massive expansion of Los Angeles and the Bay Area after World War II led to building on steep hillsides, which had hitherto been undeveloped because of the engineering problems they presented. Integrating inside and outside was comparatively easy on flat sites, but it could be accomplished on hillsides only through the extensive use of decks, which were especially characteristic of gardens in the San Francisco Bay region but also were used in the Southland.

The differences between the north and the south, familiar in earlier periods, were still evident. The softer forms of the Northern California landscape—with hillsides forested with redwood, live oak, and laurel, or with planted groves of eucalyptus—often encouraged more enclosed designs. The treeless and arid character of the Southland still led to the planting of rapidly growing trees and subtropical plants. Unlike those in the Bay Area, Southland nurseries (most notably Evans and Reeves in Santa Monica) continued to introduce new varieties of plants such as hibiscus, bougainvilleas, acacias, erythrinas, grevilleas, callistemons, bromeliads such as billbergias, hardy orchids, and fuchsias. The more flamboyantly hedonistic culture of the Southland encouraged an atmosphere of experimentation strikingly different from the Bay Area's traditional ideal of harmony with nature.

Gardens by professional designers exerted a considerable influence on popular taste. The San Francisco Museum of Art held exhibitions on landscape architecture in 1948 and 1958, and an exhibition on garden furniture in 1948; numerous garden shows in the Bay Area presented examples of modernist designs. Work by landscape architects such as Douglas Baylis, Thomas Church, Garrett Eckbo, Lawrence Halprin, Theodore Osmundson, Robert Royston, and Geraldine Knight Scott and by the architects Richard Neutra and William Wurster appeared in magazines such as *California Arts and Architecture, House Beautiful, House and Home,* and *Sunset.*[15]

What distinguished Church's work from that of most modernist landscape architects in California was his concentration on the client. Some clients were passionately devoted to gardening, some loved to entertain elegantly in their gardens, some used their gardens as intensely private places for their own pleasure. Each required a different design. This explains why some of Church's later designs refer overtly to historical sources, since that was what his clients wanted. Several friends and architects who knew Church believed that he had absorbed this sensitivity to the client through his exposure to gardens by Lockwood de Forest, who also was determined to provide a perfect setting for his clients.

Church's designs were based on four principles: unity, function, simplicity, and scale. Interior and exterior spaces were united visually and functionally through the use of large sheets of plate glass and the adoption of new foundation techniques that permitted the treatment of the living-room floor and the outside patio as a continuous plane. Church was responsible only for the design of the garden, not the house, but his masterly designs were so successfully integrated with the architecture that the results appear to be the product of a single hand. Invariably, he would create four separate but interrelated spatial zones. The entrance zone, including parking and entrance courts, related to the street and neighborhood. The service zone, normally quite small, related to the kitchen and included the service entrance, storage areas, the garage, vegetable and cut-flower plots, and lathhouses and greenhouses. The social zone accommodated spaces for outdoor entertaining, and the recreation zone provided areas for children's play as well as tennis and swimming.

Church achieved simplicity by using a greatly reduced plant palette. Low maintenance was often accomplished with ground-cover plants such as ivy and juniper, native plants, and clipped hedges (especially boxwood, which looked pleasant throughout the year), as well as with paved surfaces of concrete, brick, stone, and red rock. Church was careful to ensure that each of the design elements—including paved areas, plant masses, swimming pools, and structures—was in scale with the others. Unlike younger landscape architects, Church did not use new materials such as asbestos cement, plastics, and lightweight metal, but he did use plants in new ways. The floral abundance that had generally prevailed in earlier California gardens was replaced by a selective use of plants chosen for their textural and sculptural qualities, including New Zealand flax, philodendrons, and pampas grass. Existing trees were carefully retained and pruned to enhance their sculptural character.

Church orchestrated these elements into simple compositions with a complex multiplicity of focal points, creating an effect that he called "visual endlessness." As he said, "The lines of the modern garden need to be moving and flowing so that it is pleasing when seen from anywhere inside or out."[16] But this dynamism had to be handled with restraint. As Church wrote: "All is calculated to give complete restfulness to the eye. If the eye sees too many things it is confused and the sense of peace is obliterated."[17]

EL NOVILLERO

The masterly and understated character of Church's work is most notably demonstrated at El Novillero (the young bullfighter, 1948), a large cattle ranch near Sonoma. Overlooking San Francisco Bay, the property featured extensive areas of sensuously contoured grass-covered hills, dotted with clumps of live oak. There Church created one of the finest

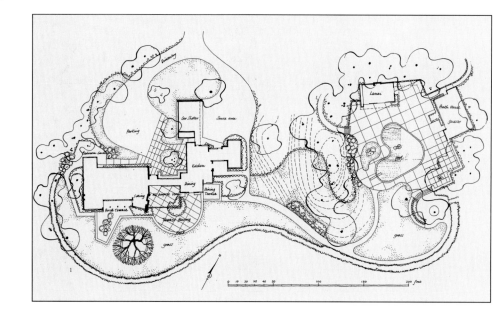

Plan of El Novillero, Sonoma,
1948. Designed by Thomas Church
for Dewey and Jean Donnell.

modern garden designs in the country—a significance recognized early on by George Rock-rise, the architect of its two structures. "We knew from the beginning that we were doing something important here."[18] Building restrictions after World War II prevented the construction of new houses, but a swimming pool could be constructed on a ranch, since the water could be used for fire fighting. Church chose a site on a tree-covered knoll for a pool, cabaña, and lanai. After preliminary design work started, he began to remove selected oaks from the site, retaining only those that framed the panoramic views over the winding salt marshes below the ranch and toward San Francisco.

The soft forms of this expansive coastal landscape of hills, marshes, and oxbow bends are skillfully related to the pool and the garden. As one approaches the garden along the gently winding drive, which is a former cattle trail, each curve reveals new aspects of the topography, including its rocks and clumps of round-headed oak trees. The entry court in front of the low L-shaped house is partly defined by a large group of oak trees, carefully thinned so that in the afternoon back lighting transforms their trunks into striking silhouettes.

The front door opens onto the "gathering room," which separates the bedroom wing from the dining room and service quarters and leads directly to a paved terrace. The view from the terrace extends across a narrow area of mown lawn around the house to a low-clipped juniper hedge. The flowing line of this broad hedge distinguishes the realm of the garden, as a place of art, from the landscape beyond, recalling Humphry Repton's similar distinction between art and nature.[19]

El Novillero. The swimming pool is surrounded
by a patterned plane of concrete paving;
the lanai by George Rockrise is at the back.

Photo: Felice Frankel, 1989

From the house, the pool garden looks like a low tree-crowned hill, whose mass is emphasized by the lines of the path that crosses it. The path splits at a high point on the slope, one branch leading to the main entry to the pool and the other providing a short cut to its deep end. Jean Donnell established the position of the latter by taking the most comfortable route across the slope; Church followed her, marking the center line of the path with his heel as he walked backward down the hill. Much of the garden was similarly designed on the ground, without preparatory drawings. Construction drawings for the pool were prepared in Church's office, but after careful inspection of the site, the pool's axis was shifted to capture a better view.

El Novillero. The design of the swimming pool employs two Cubist devices. The lines
at the edge of the pool simultaneously "explode," directing the eye to the salt marshes
in the valley below, and "implode," leading to the sculpture by Adaline Kent in the
center of the pool. Photo: Russell Beatty, 1987

From the steps at the main entry to the pool area the visitor looks across a level platform, cut from the hill. The inner end is retained by a masonry wall, above which is a grove of
trees. A glazed lanai, designed by Rockrise in 1950, occupies the angle in the wall; on the
right is a concrete cabaña that doubles as a guesthouse. The principal part of the platform is
paved with square panels of concrete. That grid continues across the lower part of the hill as a
wooden deck, through which rise the trunks of more oak trees. This device ensured the retention of the oaks, whose contrasting presence was essential to the design. Large boulders found
on the site were placed as contrapuntal forms in a small free-form grass panel within the concrete paving. At the center of the pool is a concrete sculpture, by Church's friend Adaline

Kent, that plays a unifying function in this richly layered composition. An early proposal had been to place a large rock in this position, but Church rejected it as uncomfortable to sit on and potentially dangerous for inexperienced swimmers.[20] Kent's concrete sculpture can be sat on and swum through.

As one moves around the pool, the lines in the paving, the open volume of the lanai, and the closed volume of the cabaña all seem to expand and contract in relation to each other and to the masses of the oak trees. When seen from the lanai, the composition comes to rest. The lines of the edge of the pool "implode" into the spiraling forms of the sculpture and "explode" out to the salt marshes and golden brown hills. This simultaneous convergence and divergence is another technique drawn, probably unconsciously, from Cubism. The abstract forms of the pool have a poetic power, whether in the rain, under gray skies, or in full sunshine, whether empty or peopled with a large company of swimmers. The garden survives in excellent condition, except that the oak trees that originally framed the view out over the salt marshes have succumbed to oak-root fungus.

Church's distinctive designs for several small gardens in downtown San Francisco were an important part of his accomplishment. Narrow little rear gardens had been a characteristic of the city ever since it was platted in the nineteenth century. These spaces were used either as naturalistic enclaves of plants or as service yards. Church's designs of the late 1930s had demonstrated their potential as usable space and as a visual focus for the living rooms,[21] and much of his subsequent practice was devoted to addressing this design problem.

THOMAS
CHURCH
GARDEN

Church's own garden on Hyde Street went through three major transformations from 1934 until it assumed final form in 1954. Unlike most other San Francisco gardens, it lies between the house and the street, serving as both entry and outdoor space. The simple Victorian house was remodeled in 1954, at which point the double-branching staircase to the front door was linked to the street by a curving concrete path. The stairs are framed by a pair of junipers pruned into poodle shapes. Behind the tall wooden fence a row of plane trees has grown up to form a high and light canopy. Beneath it palm trees and New Zealand tree ferns establish a feathery, tropical quality, which is picked up in the textures of clivias, agapanthus, lilies, and zoysia grass around a small sunken sitting area. Victorian garden furniture, an eighteenth-century Chinese figure, and an eighteenth-century street lamp acquired on a trip to Copenhagen provide personal grace notes.

∽—∾

Thomas Church garden, San Francisco, 1954. Designed by Church for himself. The Victorian house was remodeled with a double-branching staircase to the front door, flanked by a pair of poodle-trimmed junipers.

Photo: Saxon Holt, 1986

This garden, which survives in excellent condition, has a quiet mood that contrasts with the busyness of the outside street. The plants, from many different zones, may look natural but represent "created nature." A totally different treatment was used on the south side of the house, on the rear part of the adjoining lot, which Church acquired in 1940. In the 1950s he built an apartment building at the street, leaving a space behind it that was less than 25 feet (7.6 meters) square. Seen from the kitchen of the Church house and from the apartments, this garden is bright with color and quite unlike the quiet green space of the front garden. Raised planting beds provide areas to sit and places for pots of red pelargoniums. Their color plus the yellow of coreopsis, the delicate pink of a flowering cherry, and the white blossoms of wisteria on an arbor add bright washes of color.

Church's influence on garden design in Northern California was significant, and for several years his office was like an atelier. Baylis, Eckbo, Halprin, Royston, Osmundson, and Donald Carter all worked for him. His close friendships with the architects William Wurster and Gardner Dailey led to collaborations in which he was treated as an equal; this in turn elevated the profession of landscape architecture to a level of respect it had not previously enjoyed in the Bay Area. The extent of Church's influence on the younger designers who worked in

Thomas Church garden. The long, delicate racemes of wisteria soften the formal structure of the small south garden.

Photo: Saxon Holt, 1986

Thomas Church garden. In the south garden a small gate provides a touch of
trompe l'oeil (by implying that there is a space beyond it that can be entered) in a formal
setting of clipped Japanese boxwood hedges (*Buxus microphylla*), flowering cherries,
and potted pelargoniums. Photo: Saxon Holt, 1986

his office varied considerably. Baylis's approach probably came closest to Church's in his concern that clients not suffer because of his own desire to experiment.[22]

Baylis's design for his own garden in San Francisco, begun in 1951 and finished in 1956, also addressed the classic problem of the San Francisco rear garden. The very small wooden house on a narrow alley was remodeled by Gordon Drake, who added a two-story glazed space opening onto a long, tapered redwood deck that almost completely filled the rear of the lot. Designed in a grid of alternating redwood slats, punctured by a huge old fig tree, the deck was used as an outdoor room. Furnished with a variety of planting beds, an old cooking cauldron, a low raised table, and other furniture, it provided a sunny outdoor room in the middle of the city. This garden survives in good condition.

Halprin's early work clearly owed much to Church's superb craftsmanship and understatement, but he later moved in a different direction. For Halprin, garden design is based on the idea that gardens are "formalistic conceits within a framework of natural phenomena—they owe an act of courtesy to the landscape within which they appear."[23] His gardens were designed not to be natural, "but for the people in them to feel natural."[24] Central to his search for a fusion of natural order and human enjoyment has been Halprin's experimental design workshops with his wife, the dancer Anna Halprin. Her experimental work in dance attempts to set the dancer into motion in a way that frees the body from physical constraints.

Douglas Baylis garden, San Francisco, 1951–56. Designed by Baylis for himself; house remodeled by Gordon Drake. The severe architecture of the house is continued in the architectonic deck, which is enlivened by garden furniture, an old fig tree, and plants in pots and in an old cast-iron cauldron.

Photo: Morley Baer, 1956

Perspective drawing, 1953, of the Lawrence Halprin garden, Kentfield, 1955. Garden
designed by Halprin for himself; house designed by Wurster, Bernardi, and Emmons.

Their own garden (1955) at Kentfield, near San Rafael, was designed to encourage
movement through the landscape and to encourage self-discovery through exposure to a
variety of garden spaces. The steep 4-acre (1.6-hectare) site is covered with madroñas, redwoods, bay trees, live oaks, and tanbark oak trees (*Lithocarpus densiflora*), with an understory of
bracken fern, sword fern, and wild blackberry. The house, at the end of a narrow winding
lane, was designed by Wurster, Bernardi, and Emmons as a set of sophisticated shacklike structures perched at the edge of the hill and looking out at Mount Tamalpais. The space of a
brick-paved terrace, to quote Halprin, "explodes outward to the view on the downhill side—
it is, in effect, an outdoor room opening across a broad expanse of tree tops forming a green
almost level carpet to the view."[25] The steep hillside below this platform was choreographed as
a series of penetrations through the woods, down winding stairs, to a multilevel redwood deck
poised in a group of oak trees. The deck is used for eating, sleeping, conversation, and contemplation, but its main function has been as a setting for Anna Halprin's dance experiments.[26]

Lawrence Halprin garden.
Redwood trees grow up through
the wooden deck on the north
side of the house.

Photo: Lawrence Halprin, 1992

Lawrence Halprin garden. The
deck at the bottom of the garden is
used for avant-garde dance
performances.

Photo: Lawrence Halprin, 1989

Halprin's garden for Spencer Grant in
lent condition, is a less complex design for
selected the architect Joseph Esherick for his
devised a scheme in which the redwood-sided
a Swiss barn, was placed on a series of masonry
wisteria-clad pergola, to an octagonal gazebo.
scape and provide a diagonal view across the s
of oak trees. The swimming pool beneath thes
stone used in the retaining walls. The lavish p
masonry create an effect reminiscent of the o
Zones of irrigation increase inward from the p
the house are small, heavily watered areas. Th
garden in a way that reveals the character of the

Spencer Grant garden. Hillsborough, 1956. Garden designed by Lawrence Halprin; house designed by Joseph Esherick. The soft lines of the plants below and above the wisteria-draped pergola make a visual transition to the more drought-tolerant plants at the edge of the garden. Photo: Saxon Holt, 1993

Left. Spencer Grant garden. A wisteria-draped pergola links the house to a garden pavilion overlooking the swimming pool.

Photo: Lawrence Halprin, 1973

Below. Spencer Grant garden. The masonry terraces and the siting of the house were inspired by old Italian villas. The free-form swimming pool provides a strong contrast to them and a visual focus.

Photo: Lawrence Halprin, 1961

Hilltop, Pasadena, 1948.
Garden and house designed by Thornton Ladd
for his mother, Lillian Ladd. The house sat on a plateau facing
a dramatic view of the San Gabriel Mountains.

HILLTOP   A fundamental tenet of modernist thought was the complete rejection of references to the past. When traditions were still invoked by a few modernist designers, it was in highly abstract ways. Hilltop (1948), designed by Thornton Ladd for his mother, was an extremely subtle synthesis of ideas derived from Italian and Spanish courtyard houses, Japanese Zen gardens, and De Stijl painting and sculpture.

The hilltop site in Pasadena commanded unlimited views to the east of the Rose Bowl, the Arroyo Seco, much of Pasadena, and the Pacific Ocean. The foundations and basement of a half-finished Georgian Revival house were retained, and the entire hilltop was developed into a series of closed, partially open, and completely open garden spaces in which horizontal and vertical planes appeared to be poised in space, veiling or defining various views. The courts around which the house was designed were visually anchored by a long horizontal trellis, suspended two or three feet above the ground, which formed the southern boundary of the swimming pool. This trellis passed behind (and from below appeared to pass through) an

open concrete structure at the southwest corner of the garden. Under a long floating roof to
the left was a sand garden, in which a slightly raised wooden box was divided into four rectangular panels filled with raked white sand. The materials of a typical Zen garden were used here
as an abstract composition that could be changed into different patterns every day. A bonsai
juniper tree provided a counterpoint of form and color.

At the center of the house a large, square peristyle garden offered views of the outdoor
gardens, including the sand garden; a "Mondriaan garden" of sand, wood, carefully arranged
succulents, and grass; and a Japanese water garden, which lapped around the bedroom. The
peristyle was a simple grass-floored space. Transparent wooden screens, panels of frosted glass,
and slatted horizontal panels appeared to float above the walls of the peristyle's colonnades.
These elements, together with carefully placed panels of sculpture and hanging baskets, provided subtle enrichment of the plain walls.

Ladd's control of space was masterly. Each area had a distinct character and was carefully conceived in relation to the others. Circulation through the garden was directed along
routes at right angles to each other, with the changes in direction arranged to provide framed

﹏

Hilltop. Bonsai juniper trees, seen here at night,

punctuated the abstract sand garden in front of the dining room.

Photo: 1950s

Hilltop. In the peristyle garden the planes of the horizontal trellises and the solid walls created an abstract composition that was offset by the rocks and agaves in the foreground and by the vines on the walls.

Photo: Ezra Stoller, 1956

Hilltop. The raked-sand panels and the beds of succulents in the Mondriaan garden formed a visual foreground to the peristyle garden.

Photo: Ezra Stoller, 1956

views. Below the entrance drive was a small studio building, axially related to the open cube in the garden. Complementary to the visual complexity of the main house, it was designed as "a single rectangle, steel frames, wood joists, concrete shear walls, strictly speaking one single room with screens for visual partition, one roof detail, one screen detail, one sliding door and glass detail."[28] The studio's simple space was approached by concrete pads that stepped down the hillside. Ivy, yuccas, succulents, olive trees, a philodendron, and a vine anchored this steel-frame box to the landscape.

The work of Edward Huntsman-Trout was at times more overtly historicist than that of his modernist colleagues, for he developed a theory of "inevitability," according to which the elements of a design were derived both from the character of the site and from tradition. "It has always been my firm conviction that the planning which we do should seek the obvious, the straightforward answer, the least common denominator, the inevitable. . . . I like it best when what I have done seems not to have been contrived. It was just there." Huntsman-Trout conceded that "we are bound every day to indulge in borrowing from the past and the world about us in some degree." But he also believed that landscape architecture should be practiced "with good judgment and full aesthetic realization, and a generous accompaniment of skepticism."[29]

EDWARD HUNTSMAN-TROUT GARDEN

Huntsman-Trout's own house in West Los Angeles, begun in 1945 and never quite completed, embodied this theoretical approach in a setting for informal outdoor living. The straightforward house and garden recalled the modesty of California's Hispanic tradition and the craftsmanship of the Arts and Crafts period without making explicit references to either.

Before the design was begun, Huntsman-Trout's family picnicked on the site almost every weekend for more than ten years. His wife recalled that he would climb up into the branches of the beautiful sycamore trees at the bottom of the site and study their shadow patterns for hours.[30] Such familiarity with a site is reminiscent of the Japanese approach to garden design and was central to the design's success. The T-shaped house was placed at a forty-five-degree angle to the cardinal points of the compass. It is approached by a large graveled entry court, about 80 feet (24.4 meters) square, that is screened from the road by a thick planting of tall dark green shrubs.

The lower walls of the house are soft, honey-colored Bel Air sandstone. This beautiful masonry, sited beneath an arching canopy of sycamores, implies a rootedness, as does the large rock beside the entry path. The placing of the rock was quite accidental: it rolled off a flatbed truck and proved to be so hard to move that the house was built around it. Behind it sit a classical urn, and fragments of other antique sculpture can still be found throughout the house and garden, which survives but has been altered. During his long career Huntsman-Trout scoured

builders' yards and antique shops, searching for objects of character. This was motivated not by any need to own valuable things, although some of his purchases were expensive; rather, it was impelled by a desire to embellish the garden. This utterly unpretentious combination of high art and vernacular materials reflects Huntsman-Trout's philosophical and scholarly inclinations as probably the best-read landscape architect of the century.

The main part of the garden was a brick-paved patio in the angle formed by the two-story house and the adjoining one-story music room. Beyond this rectangular area, a low masonry terrace wall supported a sloping area of rough grass, beyond which shallow ramps led up to a high masonry wall at the base of the steep part of the hill. The patio was in constant use during the summer as a place for meals, work, and conversation. The brick paving of the patio extended into the music room, which in winter was separated from it only by shoji screens. When these screens were removed in the summer months, the music room became a large, deep, cool porch to which one retreated to escape the sun. The placing of the house in relation to the trees, the soft colors of the brick paving and the stone walls, the large number

❧

Above, left. Edward Huntsman-Trout garden. A fragment of Gothic tracery was artfully placed against the trunks of sycamore trees in the entry court. Photo: David C. Streatfield, 1979

❧

Above, right. Edward Huntsman-Trout garden. Sycamore trees frame this view of the shoji screens of the music room, seen in early spring. Photo: David C. Streatfield, 1979

of flower pots, and the subtle grace notes of the beautiful pottery and carefully selected antiques all contributed to the subtle yet dynamic integration of structure and landscape.

In his passionate pursuit of modernist forms, Garrett Eckbo has been the most ideological and the most experimental of the modernist landscape designers. As a graduate student in landscape architecture at Harvard, he argued for new materials and new ideas, suggesting unconventional but valuable approaches to the use of space, line, color, form, and texture. "Why must we be slaves to the ages?" he asked.[31] Improvisation has been at the core of his career, which he claims "has been based on rejecting traditional vocabularies and developing new ones."[32] Connections with abstract painting and sculpture underlie Eckbo's work. He has noted that sculpture is the art most similar to landscape architecture, but he also frequently composes the ground plane in ways that recall the work of painters such as Pablo Picasso, Georges Braque, and Jean Arp. In his gardens freestanding structures, paved surfaces, fences, and walls provide a hard framework that is often deliberately contrasted with the soft, loose forms of plants.

GOLDSTONE GARDEN

In the Goldstone garden (1948) in Beverly Hills, designed by Eckbo for a Georgian Revival house, the ground plane was treated as an abstract composition of several materials: brick, grass, and poured concrete articulated with redwood boards. Walls set off the lawn, swimming pool, and bathhouse complex at the end of the garden. The north wall was built of pumice blocks, brick, and broken bottle ends gathered from the rear alley and poured in concrete. These textures were accentuated by projecting and perforated concrete blocks set into the wall. Additional contrast was provided by a planting of *Callistemon viminalis* and American redbud (*Cercis canadensis*) against this wall and beneath the shade of a jacaranda tree.

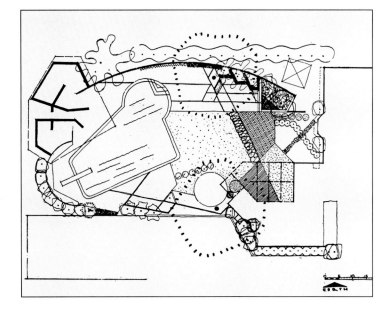

Plan of Goldstone garden, Beverly Hills, 1948. Designed by Garrett Eckbo. The irregular shape of the changing rooms at left and the curving wall across the top complement the abstract ground plane with its concrete paving, panel of grass, and free-form swimming pool.

Goldstone garden. A complex three-dimensional sculpture was formed by the combination of the trellis of the changing-room structure with the wall of concrete, brick, pumice blocks, and bottle ends. This garden no longer exists. Photo: Garrett Eckbo, early 1950s

Harryman garden, Whittier, 1950. Designed by Garrett Eckbo. Large white stones create the illusion of a dry stream running through the grass and rising up to a heavily planted mound at the edge of the garden. Implied lines of movement spiral through the fluid forms of the berms, with philodendrons, yuccas, Canary Island pines (*Pinus canariensus*), and loquats (*Eriobotrya japonica*) providing textural counterpoints.

Photo: Frank J. Thomas

Robert Royston, who was in partnership with Eckbo from 1946 until 1956, designed gardens that were also explorations of form. Royston's own house in Mill Valley (1948) was one of two very small houses designed by Joseph Stein, built using low-cost standard-panel construction, on a terrace cut into a wooded hillside site with sweeping views of San Francisco Bay. A remarkable sense of spaciousness pervades both of those houses and gardens, despite their small size. This was achieved by organizing the interior spaces on a single floor plane that extended along diagonal sight lines through the house and out into the space of the garden. The repetitive rhythm of floor-to-ceiling glazed panels creates a transparency that contrasts with the solid fences and plant masses outside the house. The fences and plants define small, intimate, free-form enclosed spaces on the hill side, while the view side opens up to the mountains beyond.

In the Royston garden a partially open screen of redwood posts, designed in collaboration with Florence Allston Swift, frames square spaces that are either left open or filled with decorative panels of asbestos cement and wire. This screen continues the transparent quality of the architecture and introduces art into the garden, framing views and blocking out unattractive adjacent areas. In more recent years Royston has designed a simple wooden deck, poised at the edge of his garden in such a way that only the dramatic views of the mountain are seen, not the houses lower down the hill. The deck is furnished with simple wood-and-canvas chairs designed by Royston in the 1940s.

Plan of Robert Royston garden, Mill Valley, 1948. Garden designed by Royston for himself; house designed by Joseph Stein. This elevation of a long wall sculpture on one of the property boundaries, designed in association with Florence Allston Swift, shows both open panels and panels filled with abstract compositions in wire.

The landscape itself became a potent force for another group of designers. Richard Neutra, a significant figure in the history of the modernist garden, sought the ancient animistic ideal of oneness with the world. In 1951 he wrote:

> Before destruction by civilization, Nature, its objects, its constellation of stars or landscape, its natural sites were regarded as animated. They had a physiognomy which conveyed a recognizable and expressive message. The promontorial rock past which the natives rowed their canoes was occupied by a spirit. A tree or spring housed a nymph, and a certain individually characterized valley, or isle offshore was the homestead of a god or the playground of the devil.[33]

Neutra's science of "bio-realism"—based on Gestalt psychology, anthropology, and other life sciences—attempted to adapt advanced technologies to what he perceived as the biological reality of the individual. He wanted to devise a system of human settlement in which the arcadian pastoralism already enjoyed by the rich in summer homes and elsewhere could be made accessible to the majority. Neutra was not particularly comfortable working with wealthy clients, but he accepted their commissions as a way of furthering his cause. He believed that architecture was universal, but the landscape was always local. Thus, Neutra merged his acute sensitivity to the local landscape with the European modernist tradition of treating nature as mere backdrop to man-made architecture, both in cities and in rural settings, with the soft forms of nature providing a contrast to machine-age materials. But unlike Le Corbusier, who would lift his building masses into the air, Neutra invariably grounded his houses to achieve a physical and visual connection between interior and exterior.

The arcadian grace that Neutra sought for small gardens is exemplified by the Warren
Tremaine estate in Montecito (1948). Here, as in most of his houses, Neutra's early training
with the distinguished Swiss landscape architect Gustav Ammann is evident. From Ammann
he absorbed a deep love of plants, and Neutra's gardens usually incorporate both native and
exotic plants, forming what he called "an ensemble of plants that can keep natural company."[34]
Working with Lockwood de Forest, Neutra sited the Tremaines' elegant single-story house,
which contained a superb collection of modern paintings, on the edge of a grove of oak trees
at the top of a slight slope. The boulders from the excavation were retained and interplanted
with native and drought-tolerant shrubs. Their coarse textures and soft colors contrasted with
the bold geometry of the architecture.[35]

De Forest died before the garden was completed, and Ralph Stevens took over his
practice. Stevens converted the dry hillside garden into a superb succulent garden. Many of the
boulders were removed and replaced by a colorful, carpetlike planting created from numerous

❧

**Warren Tremaine garden, Montecito, 1948. Garden designed by Ralph Stevens; house
designed by Richard Neutra. Ice plant, aloes, and other succulents form a carpetlike
panel in front of the house. The garden survives, but the planting has been somewhat
altered.** Photo: David C. Streatfield, 1976

massed small succulents and hillocks of zoysia grass; the foliage of giant yuccas and aloes was echoed at a small scale by the rich forms of massed agaves. The plant palette was not unlike that in some of Kate O. Sessions's earlier gardens, but the spatial quality was quite different, setting up a continuous mass of color that acted as a counterpoint to the architecture.

The house has so many large sheets of butt-jointed glazing that it is almost like a diaphanous tent, and there are large sliding-glass panels that open from the house onto a heated concrete-paved terrace. This merging of interior and exterior is emphasized by the way the roof overhang was cut back around the trunks of one of the oak trees, recalling the Gamble house (chapter 3) and Val Verde (chapter 6).

JAMES MOORE
GARDEN

In the James Moore garden at Ojai (1950), Neutra carried the integration of structure and garden even further. The house, sited at the end of a long curving drive, overlooks a panoramic view of the orchards of the Ojai Valley. A winding staircase from the parking area approaches the house. At the top of the slope the stairs lead to a path that becomes a bridge across the narrow end of a small pond that wraps around one end of the house. The living room has large expanses of glass on two sides overlooking the moatlike pool, which serves as an irrigation pond and cools the house; its edges are lavishly planted with a riot of vibrantly hued plants. Thus the house, a diaphanous geometric frame construction of planes, seems to float in space above the brightly colored and textured foreground.

❧

James Moore garden, Ojai, 1950. Garden and house designed by Richard Neutra. The pond doubles as a source of irrigation water and as a visual focus for the living room and its terrace.

Photo: Norman J. Johnston, 1982

CHARLES EAMES
GARDEN

In the Moore garden, as in Church's gardens for El Novillero, the garden in the foreground is differentiated from the landscape beyond, which is treated as a form of borrowed scenery. By contrast, Charles Eames—the architect, filmmaker, and industrial designer—incorporated the natural landscape into his own garden at Pacific Palisades (1948). The superb site, atop a high cliff, faces the ocean. A shallow meadowlike valley rises on the north into a steep hillside, behind a row of tall eucalyptus trees. The house was part of the Case Study program, which was promoted by *California Arts and Architecture* as a forum for modernism. Each year from 1945 to 1966 the magazine commissioned and built a prefabricated light-steel-frame house in order to demonstrate the potential of mass-produced housing.[36] Even though the program was not a great success in raising developers' consciousness about the superiority of modernism or in establishing new building technologies, some very fine designs were produced for it, of which Eames's is undoubtedly the finest.

The initial design proposed a two-story pavilion on a bridge spanning the upper part of the little valley. But after the Eames family spent more time on site, frequently picnicking and camping there, they realized that the proposed house would destroy the meadow, the finest feature of the site. After the structural steel had been delivered, a new design was pre-

Below. **Charles Eames garden, Pacific Palisades, 1948. Designed by Eames for himself. This wildflower meadow, which was to have been the site of the house, became the principal visual focus of the garden.**

Photo: Eames Office, 1993

Right. **Charles Eames garden. The more intimate spaces around the house provide outdoor rooms that offer views of the meadow.**

Photo: Derry Moore, 1979

pared, intended to preserve the meadow. Behind the eucalyptus trees a 200-foot-long (61-meter) platform was excavated from the sloping ground, its upper side retained by a 9-foot-tall (2.7-meter) continuous concrete wall. The new house comprises two separate pavilions with a court between, placed so that the upper floor of each pavilion opens onto the hillside. This arrangement gives the structures secondary visual roles in the landscape. The visitor looks down the shallow valley, planted with wildflowers, to the waters of the Pacific. Large eucalyptus trees shelter the pavilions, casting shadows on the taut grid of the facades and shading the intimately scaled spaces around the pavilion. The house looks *into* the landscape of the meadow in a way that recalls Charles Fletcher Lummis's El Alisal (chapter 3). This garden survives in excellent condition.

Ernest Watson garden, Montecito, 1948–49. Garden and house designed by Lockwood de Forest; completed by Elizabeth de Forest and Richard Brimer. Except for a small paved terrace adjoining the little shacklike house, there is no distinguishable garden, although in fact the garden occupies several acres at the foot of the Santa Ynez Mountains. Existing boulders were retained, and the garden was designed as a completely natural-seeming collection of chaparral plants, visually indistinguishable from the chaparral higher up the mountain slope. This garden survives, but it has been substantially altered. Photo: David C. Streatfield, 1972

C. E. Davis garden, Pasadena, 1969. Designed by Florence Yoch. Terraces and pergolas draped with wisteria surround the swimming pool. Photo: David C. Streatfield, 1976

C. E. DAVIS
GARDEN

During the 1960s many designers turned to diverse traditions for inspiration. Florence Yoch's design for a Pasadena garden (1969) is modernist in its use of a restrained palette of materials, colors, and forms. These are combined with subtle and witty references to the past, and all the elements are unified by a pervasive use of white flowering plants. In spring white wisteria, *Myrtus communis albocarpa,* crape myrtle trees, evergreen magnolias (*magnolia grandiflora*), and Yulan magnolias (*Magnolia denudata Yulan*) provide delicate washes of white blossoms throughout the garden. The long, graceful racemes of wisteria thread through the pergolas and twist up against the plain forms of the villa. The simply articulated spaces and the carefully selected colors and textures of the plants provide a beautiful integration of built and natural forms. The garden, which survives in excellent condition, was created for the C. E. Davises, for whom Yoch had designed three previous gardens. The house was sited at the edge of a slope with a number of oak trees. The living rooms connect directly to terraces that feature a Moorish fountain and a small swimming pool treated as an ornamental pool. Outside these formal elements a series of paths and garden spaces provides a circuit walk around and below the house.

From the entry court a crape myrtle walk leads to a trapezoidal ramped walk planted on either side with magnolias and surfaced with red rock paving. The stark contrast between the trees' dark glossy leaves and the plain terrace and garden walls recalls some of the more

C. E. Davis garden. The rill and fountain on this terrace recall Spanish garden design,
but the setting is otherwise modernist in its simplicity. Photo: David C. Streatfield, 1976

experimental work by Thomas Church in the 1930s. The magnolia walk leads down to a retaining wall, from which cantilevered stairs descend to an oval terrace, where gracefully curving narrow concrete paving ribs radiate out from an oak tree. This elegant use of forms was drawn from the vocabulary of seventeenth-century Baroque garden design. A similar device was used at the other end of the woodland walk that runs across the slope below the house. These fanciful concrete curves were designed not on paper but on site, by flipping a hose until the desired form was achieved. An iris walk leads from the red granite terrace to the service area of the house and provides a contrasting green mood.

HENRY
McINTYRE
GARDEN

Lawrence Halprin also sought inspiration from garden traditions for a historical site in Northern California. His design for the Henry McIntyres (1961) was for a 2-acre (.8-hectare) site in Hillsborough, subdivided from the former New Place estate (chapter 4). Halprin used this as an opportunity to explore the potential of Hispanic garden forms for an architectonic garden. The site was a sloping meadow defined by flanking groves of eucalyptus trees, like the wings of a stage set. Halprin and Joseph Esherick worked very closely to integrate house and garden with this landscape for the McIntyres, a sophisticated couple with an important art collection. The house was placed at the base of the slope, its living rooms opening onto a series of small garden rooms enclosed by concrete walls. These in turn opened onto the main garden room, the inner end of which was excavated from the slope. Its retaining walls stepped down the hill at the sides to become the walls of the smaller gardens.

A fountain on a platform several feet above the main level was the source of all the water in the garden. The water flowed into a pool and along narrow runnels and down stair-

Left. C. E. Davis garden. A gracefully curving flight of stairs links the magnolia walk to a lower court, where the concrete ribs radiating out from a well around an oak tree add a note of baroque fancifulness. Photo: Shirley Kerins, 1990

Opposite. Henry McIntyre garden, Hillsborough, 1961. Garden designed by Lawrence Halprin; house designed by Joseph Esherick. The fountain on the upper terrace recalled the use of water in Spanish gardens and gave the illusion of being the source of all the water in the garden. The garden was remodeled by Thomas Church for another client in the late 1960s. Photo: Morley Baer, 1965.

Henry McIntyre garden. The center of the garden was originally occupied by an island planted with ivy and olive trees.

Photo: Morley Baer, 1965

cases into further rills, which debouched into a rectangular pool in the center of the lowest level. An island at the center of this pool was planted with ivy and two olive trees. These were the only plants in the garden, reflecting the client's desire for a garden with little greenery. This extremely austere design of concrete, water, and olive trees was entirely gray. Subtle contrasts of texture were provided by three kinds of poured concrete and by the water running in dark-painted channels. The relation of the garden to the landscape reaffirmed the idea that a garden should be a set of spaces distinct from the outer landscape. The slope above the garden was left as an unirrigated meadow, its eucalyptus trees complementing the grays inside the garden.

Like much of Halprin's work this design emphasized an inherently humane purpose. Halprin wrote in 1965: "I see space as a medium for motion. I see garden designers as choreographers of spaces in which organized movement takes place. . . . A garden to me is a spontaneous naturalistic phenomenon not in its form, but in its method of design. . . . A garden in this sense is not so much a designed object as an experience in time, change in season, variation in light, movement. Gardens, to me, are aesthetic events whose very nature is change."[37]

The antithesis of the color-filled Victorian garden, the McIntyre garden acknowledged the character of the local landscape, with its golden browns and subdued greens. The garden's sounds, smells, and textures captured the essence of nature without duplicating it. This process of abstraction led to Halprin's later public projects with waterfalls in Lovejoy Park and Forecourt Park in Portland, Oregon, and in Freeway Park in Seattle. The McIntyre garden was remodeled by Thomas Church for another client in the late 1960s.

ALCOA GARDEN

The modernist tradition that celebrated such abstraction and the exploratory use of new materials culminated in Eckbo's Alcoa garden in Hollywood. In 1950 Eckbo and his wife acquired a half-acre (.2-hectare) lot in Wonderland Park, a subdivision of sixty-five lots in the Hollywood Hills above Laurel Canyon. The steep topography had been graded into a series of

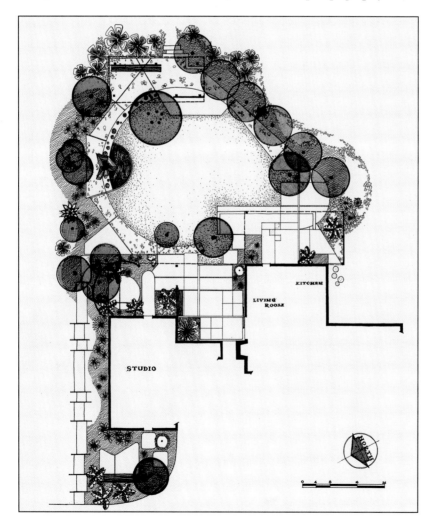

Plan of Alcoa garden, Hollywood, 1960. Designed by Garrett Eckbo, on commission from the Aluminum Company of America (Alcoa), for himself. The fountain is at the left of the curving path, and the pavilion is at the top.

Alcoa garden. Different colors and designs of perforated anodized-aluminum panels create striking effects of transparency and define the spaces opening off the house.

Photo: Julius Shulman, 1958

terraces that typified much of the development in the Los Angeles Basin and the San Fernando Valley during the 1950s, as flat sites became less available. About half the lots in this subdivision were purchased by a group of individuals, including the Eckbos, who had participated in an aborted cooperative-housing project, known as Community Homes, in the San Fernando Valley.[38] This innovative example of social planning had been blocked by the imposition of the Federal Housing Administration's highly discriminatory Regulation X, intended to prevent the integration of different races. An important part of the Community Homes plan had been the use of streetside tree planting to establish patterns of local identity and to provide visual connections with the regional landscape. Eckbo worked with property owners to establish similar connections in Wonderland Park by planting each block with a different species of tree on the perimeter of the terraced lots, thus establishing a visual continuity from the bottom to the top of the canyon walls.

In 1960 the local office of the Aluminum Company of America (Alcoa) asked Eckbo to produce a design promoting the use of aluminum in the garden. He created the Alcoa garden on his own Wonderland Park lot. A path from the house led around the oval back lawn to a small pavilion and a flowerlike fountain in olive green cast aluminum. The rectangular

Alcoa garden. One of Garrett Eckbo's
daughters reclines on a chair in one of the
small gardens opening from the house.
Photo: Garrett Eckbo, 1959

Alcoa garden. The flowerlike fountain made of sheet aluminum is contrasted with
pieces of volcanic rock and small beds of succulents. Photo: Julius Shulman, 1959

pavilion is a simple structure of wooden posts and beams to which were attached a corrugated roof and vertical panels of perforated brown and gold anodized aluminum. These elements provided delicate effects of transparency and color, in strong contrast to the bolder textures of yuccas, succulents, and flowering trees. Eight-foot-deep (2.4-meter) patios were created around the living room and the studio beneath a slender wooden structure; panels of perforated aluminum were attached to this structure to provide privacy. The small-scale shadows thrown by these panels complemented the intimate scale of the poured concrete paving, precast terrazzo tiles, and decorative ceramic tiles designed by Edith Heath, all of which further emphasize the smallness.

By the end of the 1960s modernism was a spent force in garden design. Private garden design had become unprofitable because the intense, highly personal relationship between client and designer and the supervision of construction and planting were so time-consuming. Most landscape-architecture practices were devoted to large-scale projects such as shopping centers, office parks, college and university campuses, housing projects, and public parks. In many ways this seemed appropriate, since issues of planning the urban and suburban landscape had been at the core of the modernist agenda. In fact, a strong connection linked this publicly oriented design and the earlier modernist private gardens. Garrett Eckbo and Robert Royston, in particular, regarded the private garden as a place for spatial and design experimentation aimed at the solution of larger design problems. For example, the treatment of space and the abstract forms used in Eckbo's Union Pacific Bank in Los Angeles were remarkably similar to those in his earlier garden designs. Thus, the minimal modernist gardens of California were prophetic of the new public landscapes of later decades.

8
OLD
REALITIES,
NEW
POSSIBILITIES

In the 1980s California's booming economy provided a new opportunity for younger landscape designers to take up the challenge of garden design as a fine art. In part this was a reaction against what was perceived as the failure of the environmental movement of the 1970s to produce a new, visually coherent aesthetic based on an understanding of landscape processes. The state's prosperity and soaring real-estate values coincided with an explosion of interest in gardens, which yielded new garden magazines, a garden book club (established in 1981), and numerous books on gardens and garden designers. Garden history emerged as an area of serious study, and some scholars began to examine twentieth-century designers and gardens.[1]

Gardens created since 1980 address a number of familiar themes in new ways. The designers in this chapter represent a different range of backgrounds from the architects, landscape architects, and nurserymen who created most of the gardens discussed earlier. Unconventional and often progressive, they make designs that are fresh and vital, and in some cases, intended to provoke discussion about their meaning. But their innovativeness does not mask their adherence to one of the two parallel approaches to garden design that have dominated this book. The first two gardens to be discussed represent the imposition of imported sources on the landscape. The latter two gardens feature aesthetic elements that, in different ways, grew out of the landscape.

Like many earlier garden designers in California, Topher Delaney responds to the California landscape through explicit references to time. "A garden is about history, a sense of permanence in impermanence."[2] She believes that gardens express the passage of time and communicate faith in human continuity. Whereas earlier garden designers would replicate particular periods or fabricate an illusion of rooted maturity, Delaney creates collages of selected times and places to express her clients' personalities and her own artistic preferences.[3] Trained as a landscape architect at the University of California at Berkeley, she has returned to the practices of the 1920s by forming her own construction company, which gives her complete control over the quality of the materials and craftsmanship in her gardens.

MARIN COUNTY GARDEN

In a Marin County hillside garden (1981), which has recently been remodeled, Delaney solved drainage problems and addressed the lack of usable outdoor space. She regraded the hillside into two terraces, each of which had drainage structures and provided paved areas. Their design united a free-form jazziness derived from West Coast 1950s coffee-shop architecture with abstract shapes inspired by Henri Matisse's paper cutouts. The palette of purple, pink, blue, sulfur yellow, and flashes of teal was selected to be both soothing and provocative. The planting against the terrace walls was basically restricted to a large mass of mixed perennials and another of penstemon and artemisia, low and muted in color. Two paved

~~~~

Marin County garden, 1981. Designed by Topher Delaney. The steps from the lower to the upper patio were originally framed by inclined posts, intended to support a canopy of lavender wisteria. This garden has been drastically remodeled.

Photo: Topher Delaney, 1989

patios—one on each terrace—as well as stepping stones on the upper terrace provided lively areas of color. Colored dye was added to the concrete mix, and the tinted paving was made even livelier by the incorporation of fragments of slate and ceramic tile.

Both terrace walls were colored. The upper one was pink mottled with blue. The lower was blue and was pierced at one end by a freestanding irregular form, reminiscent of a thunderbolt. The lower terrace also had a wrought-iron fence with rhythmic curves and zigzag shapes that enclosed the space and served as a trellis for vines. The shadows it threw on the ground reinforced the shapes of the topography.

❧──❧

Left. **Marin County garden. A cascade of sulfur-yellow concrete steps, inset with slate panels, zigzagged down a steep slope from the lower patio.**

Photo: Topher Delaney, 1989

❧──❧

Opposite. **Marin County garden. The wrought-iron fence on the lower terrace combined horizontal patterns derived from the landscape with jagged lines and a grid, creating a whimsical design.**

Photo: Topher Delaney, 1989

Frances Butler's Shadow Garden (1983) in Berkeley revives on a very small scale the traditions of the English eighteenth-century poets' "emblematic gardens" and *ferme ornée*.[4] Encompassing references to cultural themes and personal associations, the Shadow Garden is a palimpsest of continually evolving plants and other materials, expressing changes of mind, weather, and time. The original design for Butler, by the architect William Coburn, consisted of checkerboard paving and a series of trellis structures that were allowed to decay into ruins.

Shadow Garden, Berkeley, 1983. Designed by Frances Butler for herself. Plants and structures are arranged to provide a series of rich poetic references. Photo: Marc Treib, 1983

◦~◦~◦

Shadow Garden. In 1988 Butler revised her garden into a "Dictionary of Shadow Effects," in which tiles and towers are used to suggest different types of shadow symbolism. One tower addresses shadow in representation (such as architectural drafting) and in silhouettes. One tower indicates power (with a version of Giorgio de Chirico's painting *The Seer*) and weakness (with a reference to John Bude's sculpture *The Overshadower*). And another tower has a double-tiger image on a corner, with William Blake's "Tiger, Tiger Burning Bright" poem wrapped around both sides, in reference to the way a shadow "doubles" its source. Photo: Saxon Holt, 1993

Butler then reorganized Coburn's design into a composition of images and texts that were continually rearranged. Lines of tiles lead the eye along the ground to mazelike piles of frames resembling sleds, made of poles and mesh, which can be (and are) frequently moved. When the sun shines, these structures cast shadows, altering with the time of day and the season.

A poet, Butler inserts fragments of text inscribed on tiles. The texts and the shifting patterns of shadows cast by the various structures create a changing set of images and references to themes, places, and time that have deep personal meaning for the owner and that may or may not engage the visitor.

The new ecological awareness that evolved throughout California during the 1970s led to the imposition of water rationing by several communities. Santa Barbara County, for example, limited the use of water for irrigation and attempted to control growth by requiring developers to demonstrate that enough water was available to support any proposed development on a site. This led to a great reduction in the size and number of lawns, as well as to many other water-conserving practices, including drip irrigation and the use of native and other drought-tolerant plants.

The need to conserve water has sparked some designers to try innovative solutions. In Santa Barbara, Isabelle Greene (granddaughter of the architect Henry Greene, of Greene and Greene) has designed several gardens in which lush greenness has been replaced by lush color. On Mrs. Valentine's 4-acre (1.6-hectare) estate in the foothills of Montecito she surrounded an austere house, designed by Warner and Grey and inspired by pueblo design, with a series of wet and dry gardens. A dry river of cool gray granite chips winds around two sides of the house, terminating in a terrace that overlooks a vibrantly colored garden. A series of low, irregularly shaped terraces was inspired by the rice paddies of Indonesia. To suggest water, blue kleinia (*Senecio kleinia*) was planted in long flowing ribbons on the terraces, along with plants such as sedums, lavender, aloes, echeveria (*Echeveria elegans*), dusty miller (*Artemesia stellerana*), blue zoysia grass, a bronze pennisetum grass, and yuccas. In one section of the garden, grape standards are planted in a long, narrow bed enclosed by hedges of clipped santolina *(Santolina*

Valentine garden, Montecito, 1980. Designed
by Isabelle Greene. The long flowing beds,
inspired by Indonesian rice paddies, are
planted with dense ground cover contrasted
with the striking forms of yuccas.
Photo: Robert M. Fletcher & Associates, 1987

Valentine garden. The flowing shapes of the ribbonlike planting of succulents in the foreground provide a strong visual contrast to the angular walls and paved areas in the background. Photo: Robert M. Fletcher & Associates, 1987

chamaecyparissus). Beds of plants require varying degrees of irrigation, including new forms of drip irrigation, but the use of succulents greatly reduces the need for water. Rivulets of broken slate, which appear to spill over from the upper garden, and garden paths of decomposed granite further reduce water usage. The plant palette is not unlike those used earlier by Kate O. Sessions and Ralph Stevens, but its effect is more boldly abstract.

EL ALISAL

El Alisal, Charles Fletcher Lummis's garden in Highland Park (chapter 3), has been redesigned to demonstrate how vividly colorful gardens can be created using drought-tolerant plants. Lummis's wildflower meadow had disappeared by the 1920s; the garden was renovated by Theodore Payne in the 1930s but again fell into neglect. In 1986 the Historical Society of Southern California, whose headquarters is at El Alisal, obtained a grant from the Santa Monica Mountains Conservancy to redesign the garden. With additional funding from various sources a design was devised by Professor Robert Perry, of California State Polytechnic University at Pomona, to convert the garden into a demonstration of water-conservation practices. His restoration changed the rather institutional parklike character of Payne's renovation into a native-plant garden. Asphalt paths were repaved with decomposed granite, and the garden was divided into zones requiring different amounts of water.

At the end of the house is a citrus garden filled with bright yellow Meyer lemons (*Citrus limonia* 'Meyer'), kumquats (*Fortunella margarita*), and tangelos (*Citrus* x *tangelo*). Native plants are placed throughout the garden. In front of the house are colorful plants such as dwarf crape myrtles (*Lagerstroemia indica*), rockroses, Christmasberry or toyon (*Heteromeles arbutifolia*), hybrid Cali-

El Alisal. A decomposed granite path leads past a deep bed of verbena and California poppies beneath a palo verde tree (*Cercidium floridum*) in a composition that exemplifies the color range of native California plants. Photo: Tom Engler, 1987

fornia lilacs, and the Howard McMinn manzanita (*Arctostaphylos densiflora* 'Howard McMinn'). A small paved area in front of the house overlooks a relatively large open meadow, planted with *Achillea millefolium* 'Rosea.' This yarrow with rosy red flowers can be used as a substitute for turf with occasional mowing, or it can be allowed to flower in the summer months. Its lacy foliage has more textural diversity than a grass lawn, is much easier to maintain, and requires less water.

Annuals have been used to provide strong seasonal color. Wildflower seeds have been scattered in open places and around new plantings. In April such plants as California poppies (*Eschscholzia californica*), baby blue-eyes (*Nemophila menziesi*), desert bluebells (*Phacelia campanularia*), and spider lupine (*Lupinus benthamii*) provide a mosaic of color that Lummis would have enjoyed. On the west and north sides of the house, in cooler and shadier places beneath sycamores, are ferns, bush anemone, and flowering currants. In another section of the garden is a collection of plants from other parts of the world with similar climatic conditions, such as the Canary Islands, Chile, South Africa, and Australia.

Most of the gardens in this book are pleasure gardens that have satisfied a need for refuge, social status, or pleasure. Productive gardens sometimes accompanied these pleasure gardens but were invariably relegated to secondary and usually hidden places. In 1973 the Farallones Institute, a nonprofit Bay Area organization dedicated to the promotion of ecologically sound planning, created the experimental Integral Urban House in Berkeley. An attempt to treat the house and garden as a self-contained ecosystem, it demonstrated how a typical urban lot could support a family of four with a fish tank, orchard, vegetable plots, and an area for rabbits and chickens. It contained plants cultivated, without pesticides, not for their ornamental but for their productive value.[5]

JOHN LYLE
GARDEN

This conceptual approach has been taken further by John Lyle, a professor of landscape architecture at California State Polytechnic University, Pomona. His scholarship and his professional work proceed from his belief that any landscape manifests interdependent physical and biological processes and is never just a static phenomenon. The models developed by ecologists regarding such interdependency can be used as the basis for planning not only gardens but entire communities.

Lyle's own garden, on a two-thirds-acre (.2-hectare) lot in a subdivision in Sierra Madre, demonstrates how a garden can be both life sustaining and life enhancing by poetically referring to the physical and biological processes of the regional landscape.[6] His garden contains a fruit-tree orchard, an herb garden, a carp pond, and a planted corridor for wildlife. Most of the lot is planted with drought-tolerant species, but there are underground cisterns that store water for irrigation. Situated at the base of the San Gabriel Mountains (the same range that faced the garden at Cañon Crest; see chapter 2), the garden is in what John McPhee has called the "battle zone . . . where people meet the mountains."[7] Lyle's design alludes to this battle, though in a gentle fashion. Before this landscape was developed, the fast-moving water of the mountain streams would rush onto the valley floor of the Los Angeles Basin, where stony washes would slow the water down enough so that it could percolate into the ground. Such washes were dotted with small plants struggling to survive, and their struggle is evoked in Lyle's garden by a gravel-paved area crossed by stepping stones with a number of small plants. A similar reference to the landscape occurs in another part of the garden, where a winding flight of stairs simulates the roaring torrents of water bursting out of the mountains.

Gardens are exceptionally fragile creations, and in recent years garden restoration has become an important issue.[8] The gardens at Filoli, Lotusland, and Rancho Los Alamitos are being conserved and opened to the public by nonprofit organizations. But with the exception of Los Alamitos, their history is not determining their conservation. For example, the kitchen garden at Filoli (chapter 4) has been reworked into a series of ornamental display gardens, and the rare opportunity for visitors to see a traditional working kitchen garden has been lost. Some of the wacky qualities of Lotusland (chapter 5) are disappearing, as Ganna Walska's theater garden and swimming pool are being renovated and rejuvenated in ways that express the current designers' orderly values rather than Walska's flamboyant and disjointed eccentricities. Even relatively minor but ill-informed changes can irreparably ruin a garden. In my opinion, the William Dickenson garden in Hope Ranch (chapter 6) has been obliterated by vulgar intrusions that are completely at variance with the subtlety of de Forest's design. Inadequate maintenance can also greatly reduce the chances of a garden's survival, as seems to be happening at Casa del Herrero (chapter 5). The Rancho Los Alamitos Foundation, by contrast, has spent considerable time documenting the history of that garden (chapter 6), and the plans for restoring it and interpreting it to the public are being determined by the garden's own long history.

Unfortunately, there are no statewide or local programs designed to preserve important private gardens. The newly established Garden Conservancy is protecting a garden in Walnut Creek as well as Lotusland, but there are many neglected gardens throughout the state that deserve protection as significant examples of particular periods or of work by important designers. (Some of the historic garden trusts in England could serve as useful precedents for this.) At the heart of the problem is a lack of public understanding of the cultural value of older gardens and the unwillingness of private owners to relinquish their right to do as they please with their own property.

In summing up this survey of Californians' attempt to create a "perfected nature" in one of the most sublime landscapes in North America, an obvious question that must be raised

John Lyle garden, Sierra Madre, 1986.
Designed by Lyle for himself. This garden,
opening off the house, uses rocks
and gravel to evoke the landscape character of
the plain at the foot of the mountains above
Lyle's garden.

Photo: John Lyle, 1986

John Lyle garden. The design of the stair
represents the highly dynamic effect of a
stream coursing down the side of the
mountains.

Photo: John Lyle, 1986

is whether the two approaches I've outlined here—the imported and the regional—will continue indefinitely.

History cannot predict, but it can define broad patterns and continuing problems. There is every reason to anticipate that future shifts in economic and social policy will cause reverberations in the world of garden design, as they have in the past. The change from Mexican to American rule, the extensive immigration into the state around the turn of the century, and the onset of the Depression were all major turning points that resulted in changes in garden design. Also, since the time that California became part of the United States, gardens have been decreasing in size. The massive Mexican ranchos were divided into rural estates, which in turn were subdivided into smaller properties. The vast increase in population after World War II led to another wave of subdivision. This trend to miniaturization will no doubt go on as the population and land values continue to increase, but there are limits to how small a garden can be.

The changing patterns of design traditions documented in this book represent "invented traditions," in which a process of cultural recovery from one or several pasts occurs. The ransacking of the past that characterized nineteenth-century garden design in California reflects attempts to maintain connection with several pasts as a way of feeling grounded. These were often romantic rather than factual reconstructions. The ranch-house garden, for example, was an effort to fuse Hispanic and Yankee garden traditions that had only a faint basis in historical truth. Future uses of the past will again transform original meanings into new ones that express their own time.

Reactions to the sublime scale and kaleidoscopic colors of the California landscape have oscillated between pleasure and repugnance. Many eastern visitors have been appalled by the golden color of California's hills in the long, hot summer. The most dominant reaction has been to create the garden as a green space. Even Florence Yoch, one of the most sophisticated and sensitive designers to practice in California, felt that the English lawn tradition was the finest. The continuing influx of newcomers into California will almost certainly mean the continuation of such negative reactions to what is left of the sublime natural landscape.

The range of design evident in California gardens represents a clear exercise of choice that is cultural, reflecting both shared and individual values. Even the regionalist solutions favored by a small number of garden owners and designers have been determined as much by cultural factors as by the physical demands of a particular place. And all of California's gardens represent a tradition based on a visual rather than an ecological relationship to the landscape. This last tendency is intertwined with two factors: the heretofore unlimited supply of water, and the ease of growing just about any plant in California. The state's sophisticated irrigation technology and exceptionally long growing season have made it possible to create almost every kind of garden there.

That tradition may be coming to an end. A six-year drought that began in 1987 resulted in water rationing and a serious exploration of Xeriscaping—the use of drought-tolerant plants and new, more efficient forms of irrigation—especially since lawns have been identified as making the heaviest nonrural demand for water. In 1992 the state legislature passed legislation requiring all cities to develop water-conserving landscape ordinances by January 1, 1993.

Such measures are a sensible recognition of the fact that, as Mary Austin recognized long ago, California is a land of little rain.[9] But droughts have happened with unfailing regularity in the past and their long-term implications have invariably been ignored after the drought ended. In *East of Eden,* John Steinbeck poignantly described the reactions of farmers in the Salinas Valley: "And it never failed that during the dry years the people forgot the rich years, and during the wet years they lost all memory of the dry years. It was always that way."[10] Californians' attitudes about the availability of water and its use will determine the state's future.[11] Only a fundamental rethinking will make it possible, as several Californians had hoped at the turn of the last century, for California to develop a culture in which the scarcity of water is accepted and celebrated rather than flagrantly ignored. The acceptance of this inalterable reality will necessitate changes in individual gardens and in communities.

The garden has always been a metaphor for the landscape, embodying responses to nature. The oldest garden traditions in desert environments were based on religious beliefs in the sacredness of water as the very essence of life. The Islamic garden used little water but used it joyously, celebrating it both as a life-giving source and an element of beauty. Even such a secular society as modern California can look to the Islamic garden as a source of inspiration for new garden design. It can also look back to its own traditions, such as the rancho garden, the smaller gardens of the 1920s, and to the work of pioneering figures such as Kate O. Sessions, Theodore Payne, Lockwood de Forest, and Thomas Church. The integration of such precedents can counter the critique of modern gardens made in 1981 by Dame Sylvia Crowe, the distinguished English landscape architect: "The lack of peace in many gardens today is intensified because, although throughout history garden traditions have fertilized each other, never before have there been so many cross-currents and so little opportunity for the flood of ideas to evolve a tradition to local conditions."[12]

The prolonged drought of the past few years and the decline in California's prosperity are propitious conditions for the development of a California garden tradition that is a synthesis of local and analogous design traditions, that also incorporates the human necessity for places of repose, fantasy, and retreat. The challenge for garden designers will be to develop a new tradition based on sound ecological principles that can also refresh and uplift the spirit.

Notes

INTRODUCTION

1. Garci Ordóñez de Montalvo, in James D. Hart, *A Companion to California* (New York: Oxford University Press, 1978), p. 398.

2. Victoria Padilla, *Southern California Gardens: An Illustrated History* (Berkeley and Los Angeles: University of California Press, 1961). This is largely a history of horticulture in the southern counties of the state.

3. A. E. Hanson, *An Arcadian Landscape: The California Gardens of A. E. Hanson, 1920–1932,* ed. David Gebhard and Sheila Lynds (Los Angeles: Hennessey and Ingalls, 1985); James J. Yoch, *Landscaping the American Dream: The Gardens and Film Sets of Florence Yoch: 1890–1972* (New York: Harry N. Abrams; Millwood, N.Y.: Sagapress, 1989).

4. James R. Lowe to David Belden, February 8, 1864, Belden Papers, Bancroft Library, University of California, Berkeley.

5. William Hammond Hall to James Flood, February 1874, William Hammond Hall letter book, William Hammond Hall Papers, California Historical Society Library, San Francisco.

6. Thomas Moore, interview with author, February 1974. I am grateful to Thomas Moore for providing this information.

7. Jessie Murray, interview with author, February 1974.

8. Mrs. Charles Edwin Davies, interview with author, February 1979. See Yoch, *Landscaping the American Dream,* pp. 205–16, for an example of a maintenance report.

9. Ben C. Truman, *Semi-Tropical California: Its Climate, Healthfulness, Productivity and Scenery* (San Francisco: A. L. Bancroft and Co., 1874), p. 13.

1. HISPANIC GARDENS

1. Sir George Simpson, *Narrative of a Journey Round the World during the Years 1841 and 1842,* 2 vols. (London: H. Colburn, 1847), 1: 408.

2. Ibid.

3. Captain Duhaut-Cilly, "Duhaut-Cilly's Account of California in the Years 1827–8," *California Historical Society Quarterly* 8 (June 1929): 159.

4. Edwin Bryant, *What I Saw in California: Being the Journal of a Tour, in the Years 1846, 1847* (New York: D. Appleton and Co.; Philadelphia: George S. Appleton, 1849), p. 397.

5. Ibid., pp. 316, 405.

6. Tom Brown, "Gardens of the California Missions," *Pacific Horticulture* 49 (Spring 1988): 8.

7. George W. Hendry and Margaret P. Kelly, "The Plant Content of Adobe Bricks, with a Note on Adobe Brick Making," *California Historical Society Quarterly* 4 (December 1925): 361–73.

8. Bryant, *What I Saw in California,* p. 317.

9. Duhaut-Cilly, "Account of California" (June 1929), p. 150.

10. Ibid., p. 158.

11. Brown, "Gardens of the California Missions," p. 6.

12. Charles Gibbs Adams, "The Spanish Influence in California Gardening," in Elvenia Slosson, *Pioneer American Gardening* (New York: Coward-McCann, 1951), p. 273.

13. Ibid., p. 274.

14. Ibid.

15. Victoria Padilla, *Southern California Gardens: An Illustrated History* (Berkeley and Los Angeles: University of California Press, 1961), p. 21.

16. Vancouver, ibid., p. 22.

17. Reid, ibid., p. 24.

18. Bryant, *What I Saw in California,* p. 391.

19. Padilla, *Southern California Gardens,* p. 25.

20. Guadalupe Vallejo, "Ranch and Mission Days in Alta California," *Century Magazine* 41, n.s. 19 (December 1890): 188–89.

21. Captain Duhaut-Cilly, "Duhaut-Cilly's Account of California in the Years 1827–8," *California Historical Society Quarterly* 8 (September 1929): 228.

22. Bryant, *What I Saw in California,* p. 385.

23. Harold Kirker, *California's Architectural Frontier: Style and Tradition in the Nineteenth Century* (Salt Lake City: Peregrine Smith Books, 1960; reprint, 1986), p. 8.

24. Helen Hunt Jackson, *Ramona* (Boston: Roberts Brothers, 1884), p. 20.

25. Ibid., p. 21.

26. Ibid., pp. 21–22.

27. Kirker, *California's Architectural Frontier,* p. 16.

28. For Rancho Guajome, see Iris Wilson Engstrand and Thomas L. Scharf, "Rancho Guajome: A California Legacy Preserved," *Journal of San Diego History* 20 (Winter 1974): 1–14. For Rancho Los Cerritos, see William Montgomery, "Studies in Southern California Landscape History Applied to the Development of Rancho Los Cerritos" (Master of Landscape Architecture, California State Polytechnic University, Pomona, 1975).

29. Charles Dudley Warner, *Our Italy* (New York: Harper and Brothers, 1891), p. 18.

2. VICTORIAN EDEN

1. David C. Streatfield, "Paradise on the Frontier: Victorian Gardens on the San Francisco Peninsula," *Garden History* 12 (Spring 1984): 158–80.

2. Tom Turner, *English Garden Design: History and Styles since 1650* (Woodbridge, England: Antique Collectors' Club, 1986), pp. 124–31.

3. Brent Elliott, *Victorian Gardens* (London: B. T. Batsford, 1966), pp. 33–36.

4. See Andrew Jackson Downing, *A Treatise on the Theory and Practice of Landscape Gardening, Adapted to North America,* 6th ed. (New York: A. O. Moore and Co., 1859); Andrew Jackson Downing, *The Architecture of Country Houses* (New York: D. Appleton and Co., 1850); Andrew Jackson Downing, *Cottage Residences,* 4th ed. (New York: Wiley and Halsted, 1856).

5. Charles H. Shinn, *The Pacific Rural Handbook* (San Francisco: Dewey and Co., 1879).

6. Streatfield, "Paradise on the Frontier," pp. 71–72.

7. Downing, *Treatise,* p. 421.

8. Ibid., p. 424.

9. Florence Atherton Eyre, *Reminiscences of Peninsula Gardens from 1860–1890* (San Francisco: San Francisco Garden Club, 1933), p. 20.

10. Brent Elliott, "Mosaiculture: Its Origins and Significance," *Garden History* 9 (Spring 1983): 76–98.

11. Unidentified visitor, in Helen Weber Kennedy and Veronica K. Kriszie, *Vignettes of the Gardens of San José de Guadalupe* (San Francisco: Garden Club, 1938), p. 41.

12. Henry Winthrop Sargent, "Supplement to the Sixth Edition of Landscape Gardening: Containing Some Remarks about Country Places and the Best Method of Making Them; Also an Account of the Newer Deciduous and Evergreen Plants, Lately Introduced into Cultivation, Both Hardy and Half-Hardy," in Andrew Jackson Downing, *A Treatise on the Theory and Practice of Landscape Gardening, Adapted to North America* (New York: A. O. Moore and Co., 1859), p. 481.

13. W. B. West, in E. J. Wickson, *California Nurserymen and the Plant Industry, 1850–1910* (Los Angeles: California Association of Nurserymen, 1921), p. 28.

14. Hall's letters are on file at the California Historical Society Library, San Francisco.

15. The landscape architect William Sawrey Gilpin was the nephew of William Gilpin, an amateur artist and prolific writer. McLaren possessed a copy of William Sawrey Gilpin's *Practical Hints upon Landscape Gardening with Some Remarks on Domestic Architecture as Connected with Scenery* (London: T. Cadell, 1832).

16. See Charles Nordhoff, *California for Health, Pleasure and Residence: A Book for Travellers and Settlers* (New York: Harper and Brothers, 1882); Ben C. Truman, *Semi-Tropical California: Its Climate, Healthfulness, Productivity and Scenery* (San Francisco: A. L. Bancroft and Co., 1874).

17. *Pacific Rural Press,* March 1874; Truman, *Semi-Tropical California,* p. 13.

18. Victoria Padilla, *Southern California Gardens: An Illustrated History* (Berkeley and Los Angeles: University of California Press, 1961), pp. 54–55, pp. 142–45.

19. Shinn, *Pacific Rural Handbook,* p. 42.

20. John Brown, Jr., ed., *History of Riverside and San Bernardino Counties* (Madison, Wis.: Western Historical Association, 1922), p. 350.

21. For histories of the Huntington gardens, see William Hertrich, *The Huntington Botanical Gardens* (San Marino, Calif.: Huntington Library, 1949); and James Maher, *The Twilight of Splendor* (Boston: Little, Brown and Company, 1975), pp. 215–308.

22. See Sir Henry Steuart, *The Planter's Guide,* 2d ed. (Edinburgh: J. Murray, 1828); Hertrich, *Huntington Botanical Gardens,* pp. 26, 34–36.

23. Gary W. Lyons, "The Development of the Huntington Desert Garden: Past and Future," *Cactus and Succulent Journal* 41 (January–February 1969): 10–29; and "The Huntington Desert Garden Today," same issue, pp. 51–56; see also pp. 120–22; 151–54; 221–24.

24. William Hertrich to Henry E. Huntington, September 11, 1913, William Hertrich Papers, Huntington Library, San Marino, California.

25. John McLaren, "A Year-Round Garden," *Sunset* 64 (February 1930): 21.

26. A. T. Johnson, *California: An Englishman's Impressions of the Golden State* (London: Stanley Paul and Co., 1913), pp. 26–27.

27. Ibid., p. 27.

3. ARTS AND CRAFTS GARDENS

1. The Arts and Crafts gardens of California were entirely different from the regionalist gardens of the Midwest, such as those created by Jens Jensen, which rigorously adhered to the use of native plants and evoked the specific forms of the prairie. See Robert E. Grese, *Jens Jensen: Maker of Natural Parks and Gardens* (Baltimore: Johns Hopkins University Press, 1992).

2. Alfred D. Robinson, "The Fitness of Things," *California Garden* 4 (April 1913): 4.

3. David F. Myrick, *Montecito and Santa Barbara: The Days of the Great Estates* (Glendale, Calif.: Trans-Anglo Books, 1991).

4. Charles Fletcher Lummis, "The Carpet of God's Country," *Out West* 22 (1905): 306–17.

5. Mrs. Francis King, *Pages from a Garden Note-Book* (New York: Charles Scribner's Sons, 1921), pp. 195–203.

6. The C. M. Robertson house in the Ojai Valley, also designed by Hunt and Grey, demonstrates particularly well the relationship of the profile of the house to the profile of the distant mountain range. It is the frontispiece to Grace Tabor, *The Landscape Gardening Book* (New York: McBride, Winston and Co., 1911).

7. "What the Club Advocates," 1898, in the Hillside Club's *Yearbook, 1911–12,* pp. 6–7, Fred H. Dempster Papers, Bancroft Library, University of California, Berkeley.

8. Charles Augustus Keeler, *The Simple Home* (San Francisco: Paul Elder and Co., 1904), p. 12.

9. Diane Harris, "Maybeck's Landscapes," *Journal of Garden History* 10 (July–September 1990): 145–61.

10. Irving Gill, "The Home of the Future: The New Architecture of the West: Small Homes for a Great Country," *Craftsman* 30 (May 1916): 147.

11. Kate O. Sessions, "Bulbs for Rainless Winters," *California Garden* 3 (August 1911): 5.

12. Sessions, in Elizabeth C. MacPhail, *Kate Sessions, Pioneer Horticulturist* (San Diego: San Diego Horticultural Society, 1976), p. 84.

13. Henrietta P. Keith, "Swimming Pools That Share the Sun," *Craftsman* 29 (December 1915): 312–17.

14. *Irving Gill, 1870–1936* (Los Angeles: Los Angeles County Museum, 1958), p. 26.

15. David C. Streatfield, "Echoes of England and Italy 'On the Edge of the World': Green Gables and Charles Greene," *Journal of Garden History* 2 (October–December 1982): 377–98.

4. IMPORTED STYLES: NORTHERN CALIFORNIA

1. Bruce Porter, Introduction, in Porter Garnett, *Stately Homes of California* (Boston: Little, Brown and Company, 1915), p. xii.

2. Margaretta J. Darnall, "Garden Worthy of Contemplation," *Pacific Horticulture* 51 (Fall 1990): 47–51.

3. Ibid., p. 51.

4. Porter, in Garnett, *Stately Homes of California,* p. xii.

5. Herbert Croly, "The Country House in California," *Architectural Record* 34 (December 1913): 483–519.

6. Stephen Child, *Landscape Architecture: A Series of Letters* (Palo Alto, Calif.: Stanford University Press, 1927), pp. 13–14.

7. For Platt's Italianate gardens, see Keith Morgan, *Charles A. Platt: The Artist as Architect* (Cambridge, Mass., and London: MIT Press, 1986), pp. 24–62, 78–129.

8. Melville McPherson, "The Transplanted Italian Villa," *Architect and Engineer* 27 (November 1911): 45.

9. Marion Cran, *Gardens in America* (London: Herbert Jenkins, 1931), p. 101.

10. Chesley Bonestell, interview with author, February 1974.

11. For a discussion of Porter's background, see Patricia Nelson O'Brien, "Filoli" (Master of Landscape Architecture thesis, University of California, Berkeley, 1975).

12. Margaretta J. Darnall, "The Carolans: An Unfinished Garden," *Pacific Horticulture* 49 (Summer 1988): 7–11.

13. Michael Laird, *The Formal Garden: Traditions of Art and Nature* (London: Thames and Hudson, 1992), pp. 188–89, 211–12.

14. Darnall, "Carolans," p. 11.

15. For a discussion of Filoli during Mrs. Roth's ownership, see Mai K. Arbegast, "Shrubs of Filoli," *Pacific Horticulture* 37 (July 1976): 15–22.

16. Porter, in Garnett, *Stately Homes of California,* p. xii.

5. IMPORTED STYLES: SOUTHERN CALIFORNIA

1. William Paul Blair, "Francis Townsend Underhill," *Pacific Horticulture* 51 (Summer 1991): 7–12.

2. Helen S. Thorne, "When an Easterner Gardens in the Golden West," *Garden Magazine* 21 (April 1921): 178–80.

3. Elizabeth de Forest, "Old Santa Barbara Gardens and How They Came to Be," *Pacific Horticulture* 38 (Winter 1977–78): 34.

4. Claudia Lazzaro, *The Italian Renaissance Garden* (New Haven, Conn., and London: Yale University Press, 1990), pp. 100–108.

5. Frank A. Waugh, "A Personal View of California Gardens," *Garden and Home Builder* 40 (December 1924): 233.

6. Charles Gibbs Adams, "Our Architectural Tragedy," *California Southland* 10 (July 1928): 28–29.

7. Mrs. Francis King, "Chronicles of the Garden," *House Beautiful* 53 (February 1923): 142.

8. Marion Cran, *Gardens in America* (London: Herbert Jenkins, 1931), p. 121.

9. Gipsy Johnson, interview with author, July 1977.

10. Carleton M. Winslow, Jr., and Nicola L. Frye, *The Enchanted Hill: The Story of Hearst Castle at San Simeon* (Millbrae, Calif.: Celestial Arts, 1980), pp. 48–73; Woody Frey, "Making the Gardens at San Simeon," *Pacific Horticulture* 39 (Fall 1978): 39–44.

11. Charles Gibbs Adams, "Gardens of the Stars," *Saturday Evening Post,* March 2, 1940, p. 74.

12. Ibid.

13. Ibid.

14. Cran, *Gardens in America,* p. 137.

15. For La Toscana, see A. E. Hanson, *An Arcadian Landscape: The California Gardens of A. E. Hanson, 1920–1932,* ed. David Gebhard and Sheila Lynds (Los Angeles: Hennessey and Ingalls, 1985), pp. 69–84.

16. Edward Huntsman-Trout, in Susan Jane Gross, "The Gardens of Edward Huntsman-Trout" (Master of Landscape Architecture thesis, California State Polytechnic University, Pomona, 1976), p. 26.

17. David C. Streatfield, "Suburbia at the Zenith," *Landscape Architecture* 67 (September 1977): 424.

18. I am indebted to the late Vera Cornell for showing me these drawings prepared by her husband.

19. *Sunset* 107 (September 1951): 50.

20. George W. Waters, "Lotusland," *Pacific Horticulture* 44 (Spring 1983): 20–25.

21. Ruth Shellhorn, interview with author, February 1974.

22. I am grateful to Thomas Moore for allowing me to consult Yoch's notes for a proposed book.

23. For an extended discussion of these ideas see Rebecca Warren Davidson, "Past as Present: Villa Vizcaya and the 'Italian Garden' in the United States," *Journal of Garden History* 12 (January–March 1992): 1–28.

24. Mark Daniels, "Another Authority Occupies This Niche," *California Arts and Architecture* 39 (May 1931): 62.

6. REGIONAL GARDENS

1. Smith, in John Taylor Boyd, Jr., "Houses Showing a Distinguished Simplicity," *Arts and Decoration* 33 (October 1930): 60, 112.

2. For a detailed history of the garden at Rancho Los Alamitos, see "Historical Overview," by David C. Streatfield, in Russell Beatty, Renee Bradshaw, and David C. Streatfield, *Landscape Plan for the Rancho Los Alamitos Foundation* (Long Beach, Calif.: Rancho Los Alamitos Foundation, 1987).

3. Ibid., p. 36.

4. Ibid., pp. 44–45.

5. Katherine Bixby Hotchkis, *Trip with Father* (San Francisco: California Historical Society, 1971), p. 40.

6. Marion Cran, *Gardens in America* (London: Herbert Jenkins, 1931), p. 133.

7. Frank Lloyd Wright, *Autobiography* (New York: Duell, Sloan and Pearce, 1943), p. 251.

8. Schindler, in David Gebhard, *Schindler* (Santa Barbara, Calif.: Peregrine Smith, 1980), pp. 47–48.

9. Ibid., p. 48.

10. Ibid.

11. Theodore Payne, *Life on the Modjeska Ranch in the Gay Nineties* (Los Angeles: Kruckeberg Press, 1962), pp. 30–33.

12. Geraldine Knight Scott, interview with author, June 1970.

13. Prentice Bloedel, interview with author, July 1982. Bloedel was in de Forest's class at Thacher.

14. William F. Peters, "Lockwood de Forest, Land-

scape Architect, Santa Barbara, California, 1869–1949"
(Master of Landscape Architecture thesis, University of
California, Berkeley, 1971), pp. 34–39.

7. THE NEW GARDEN

1. For a survey of modernist landscape architecture, see
Marc Treib, ed., *Modern Landscape Architecture: A Critical Review* (Cambridge, Mass.: MIT Press, 1993).

2. Stephen Krog, "Whither the Garden," in *Dena-
tured Visions: Landscape and Culture in the Twentieth
Century,* ed. Stuart Wrede and William Howard Adams
(New York: Museum of Modern Art; Harry N.
Abrams, 1991), pp. 94–105; Stuart Wrede, "Landscape
and Architecture: The Work of Erik Gunnar
Asplund," *Perspecta* 20 (1983): 195–214.

3. Ruth Shellhorn, interview with author, February
1974.

4. George Cukor, interview with author, March
1976.

5. Thomas Church, "The Villa d'Este at Tivoli,"
California Arts and Architecture 44 (October 1933): 15.

6. Thomas Church, "The Small California Garden:
Chapter 1, A New Deal for the Small Lot," *California
Arts and Architecture* 43 (May 1933): 16.

7. In 1937 the museum had held the first exhibition
of landscape design in the country. See San Francisco
Museum of Art, *Contemporary Landscape Architecture and
Its Sources* (San Francisco: San Francisco Museum of
Art, 1937).

8. Diane Wilk Shirvani, "Eclecticism in Landscape
Architecture," *Avant-garde* 2 (Summer 1989): 62–77.

9. David C. Streatfield, "Thomas Church and the
California Garden, 1929–1950," in *Festschrift: A Collection of Essays on Architectural History* (Salem, Oreg.:
Northern Pacific Coast Chapter, Society of Architectural Historians, 1978), p. 68. Church had been greatly
impressed by Aalto's work when he visited Scandinavia
with William Wurster in 1937. The organic forms of
Aalto's glass vases and molded-plywood furniture so
attracted Church that he and his wife obtained the
franchise to sell Aalto's furniture in San Francisco.

10. Garrett Eckbo, "Small Gardens in the City, a
Study of Their Possibilities," *Pencil Points* 18 (September 1937): 573–86.

11. Christopher Tunnard, *Gardens in the Modern
Landscape* (London: Architectural Press, 1938). Tunnard advocated a modern landscape tradition that
embraced socially oriented programming of all open
space, a rhythmic use of plants, and the visual integration of structural features into the topography. He recommended modern art (especially painting and
sculpture) and Japanese design traditions as possible
sources for this new approach.

12. William Wilson Wurster, "The Unity of Architecture and Landscape Architecture," in *Landscape
Design* (San Francisco: San Francisco Museum of Art
and Association of Landscape Architects, 1948), p. 6.

13. Ibid., p. 7.

14. Claire Falkenstein, "Sculpture in Relation to
Landscape Architecture," ibid., p. 9.

15. Under the editorship of Walter Doty and
Proctor Mellquist, *Sunset* became a major organ of
populist taste. With the professional advice of Baylis
and his wife, Maggie Baylis, the book section of *Sunset*
was developed to provide how-to advice for home
owners who were unwilling or unable to hire professional help. The full impact of this magazine on residential taste in California has yet to be assessed, but it
was considerable. (Walter Doty, interview with author,
June 1970, and Proctor Mellquist, interview with
author, April 1986.)

16. Thomas Church, "The Entrance Garden of Mr.
and Mrs. G. M. Greenwood," *California Arts and Architecture* 51 (June 1937): 30.

17. Thomas D. Church, "Peace and Ease," *House
Beautiful* 94 (October 1952): 209.

18. George Rockrise, interview with author, September 1974.

19. Tom Turner, *English Garden Design: History and
Styles since 1650* (Woodbridge, England: Antique Collectors' Club, 1986), pp. 113–29.

20. Thomas Church, interview with author, February 1974.

21. Streatfield, "Thomas Church and the California
Garden," pp. 69–71.

22. Maggie Baylis, interview with author, March
1986. Royston had found Church's work to be unex-
citing for this very reason. (Robert Royston, interview
with author, March 1986.)

23. Halprin, in Herbert Weisskamp, *Beautiful Homes
and Gardens in California* (New York: Harry N.
Abrams, 1965), p. 72.

24. Ibid.

25. Lawrence Halprin, "Structure and Garden
Spaces Related in Sequence," *Progressive Architecture* 39
(May 1958): 96.

26. Ibid., pp. 95–97, 102–3.

27. Lawrence Halprin, interview with author, June 1975, and Joseph Esherick, interview with author, March 1986.

28. Ladd, in Weisskamp, *Beautiful Homes and Gardens in California,* pp. 154, 158.

29. Huntsman-Trout, in Susan Jane Gross, "The Gardens of Edward Huntsman-Trout" (Master of Landscape Architecture thesis, California State Polytechnic University, Pomona, 1976), pp. 26, 28.

30. Beatrice Huntsman-Trout, interview with author, August 1976.

31. Eckbo, "Small Gardens in the City," p. 573.

32. Eckbo, in J. William Thompson, "Standard Bearer of Modernism," *Landscape Architecture* 80 (February 1990): 90.

33. Richard Neutra, *Mysteries and Realities of the Site* (Scarsdale, N.Y.: Morgan and Morgan, 1951), pp. 10, 12.

34. Neutra, in Elizabeth B. Kassler, *Modern Gardens and the Landscape* (New York: Museum of Modern Art, 1964), p. 65.

35. Julius Schulman's photographs of de Forest's design are in ibid., pp. 18–22.

36. For more about this program, see Elizabeth A. T. Smith, ed., *Blueprints for Modern Living: History and Legacy of the Case Study Homes* (Los Angeles: Museum of Contemporary Art; Cambridge, Mass., and London: MIT Press, 1989).

37. Halprin, in Weisskamp, *Beautiful Homes and Gardens in California,* p. 74.

38. For more about Community Homes, see Garrett Eckbo, *Landscape for Living* (New York: Architectural Record with Duell, Sloan and Pearce, 1950), figs. 237–49.

8. OLD REALITIES, NEW POSSIBILITIES

1. See, for example: Morris R. Brownell, " 'Burning Project': British Garden History and Now," in Robert P. Maccubbin and Peter Martin, eds., *British and American Gardens in the Eighteenth Century* (Williamsburg,

Va.: Colonial Williamsburg Foundation, 1984), pp. 5–18; *A. E. Hanson, An Arcadian Landscape: The California Gardens of A. E. Hanson, 1920–1932,* ed. David Gebhard and Sheila Lynds (Los Angeles: Hennessey and Ingalls, 1985); and James J. Yoch, *Landscaping the American Dream: The Gardens and Film Sets of Florence Yoch, 1890–1972* (New York: Harry N. Abrams; Millwood, N.Y.: Sagapress, 1989).

2. Marcia Tanner, "Topher Delaney's Faith in the Future," *Garden Design* 10 (May–June 1991): 71.

3. Ibid., pp. 71–78.

4. The *ferme ornée* was a more modest and rustic version of the eighteenth-century circuit garden, which provided a walk along which a visitor encountered numerous symbolic references to the classical past, such as statues, urns, and temples. For example, at the poet William Shenstone's farm, The Leasowes, there was a circuit walk through the fields, with verses inscribed on vases and on plaques on trees.

5. See Farallones Institute, *The Integral Urban House: Self-Reliant Living in the City* (San Francisco: Sierra Club, 1978).

6. John Tillman Lyle, "Can Floating Seeds Make Deep Forms?" *Landscape Journal* 10 (Spring 1991): 37–47.

7. John McPhee, "The Control of Nature: Los Angeles Against the Mountains," *New Yorker,* September 26, 1988, p. 59.

8. Lisa M. Kunst and Patricia M. O'Donnell, "Historic Preservation Deserves a Broader Meaning," *Landscape Architecture* 71 (January 1981): 53–55.

9. Mary Austin, *Land of Little Rain* (1903; Garden City, New York: Anchor Books, 1961).

10. John Steinbeck, *East of Eden* (New York: Viking Press, 1952), pp. 5–6.

11. See Norris Hundley, Jr., *The Great Thirst: Californians and Water, 1770s–1990s* (Berkeley and Los Angeles: University of California Press, 1992), pp. 419–22.

12. Sylvia Crowe, *Garden Design* (London: Packard Publishing, 1981), p. 13.

Public Gardens

Most of the gardens discussed in this book are privately owned and are not open to the general public. Those that are regularly accessible are listed below. The times and prices of admission are subject to change, so call to confirm before visiting.

EL ALISAL, Highland Park, Los Angeles. 200 East Avenue Forty-three. House and garden open Friday–Sunday, noon–4:00 P.M. Phone: (213) 222-0546. Free admission.

FILOLI, Woodside. Cañada Road, near Edgehill. Take I-280 south, go west on Edgewood Road, and then north on Cañada Road for one mile; the entrance is on the left. Open mid-February to mid-November. Guided tours, Tuesday–Thursday, 10:00 A.M. and 1:00 P.M., and Saturday on the half-hour, 9:30 A.M.–1:30 P.M. (reservations required); tours without a guide can be taken on Friday and on the first Saturday and second Sunday of each month (except the second Sunday of October), 10:00 A.M.–2:00 P.M. Phone: (415) 364-2880. Admission. $8.00, adults; $4.00, children under 12.

GAMBLE HOUSE, Pasadena. 4 Westmoreland Place. Mandatory guided tours of the house, Thursday–Sunday, noon–3:00 P.M.; the grounds are open every day, 9:00 A.M.–4:30 P.M. Flat-heeled shoes are required. Phone: (818) 793-3334. Admission: $4.00.

HEARST CASTLE, San Simeon. East of San Simeon Village, just off Highway 1. Open daily. Mandatory guided tours, every day, 8:20 A.M.–3:00 P.M. (sometimes later). Advance reservations are essential. Phone: (800) 444-7275. Admission: $14.00, adults; $8.00, children.

HENRY HUNTINGTON LIBRARY AND BOTANIC GARDENS, San Marino. 1151 Oxford. Open Tuesday–Friday, 1:00–4:30 P.M.; Saturday and Sunday, 10:30 A.M.–4:30 P.M. Phone: (818) 405-2100. Admission: $5.00, adults; $3.00, children.

HOLLYHOCK HOUSE, BARNSDALL PARK, Los Angeles. 4800 Hollywood Boulevard. Mandatory guided tours of the house and garden court, every day but Monday, noon, 1:00, 2:00, and 3:00 P.M. Phone: (213) 662-7272. Admission: $1.50, adults; $1.00, seniors; children under 12, free.

LACHRYMA MONTIS, Sonoma. Third Street West. Open daily, 10:00 A.M.–5:00 P.M. Phone: (707) 938-9559. Admission: $2.00, adults; $1.00, children ages 6–12; children under 6, free.

LOTUSLAND, Santa Barbara. 695 Ashley Road. New entrance is off Cold Springs Road at Sycamore Canyon Road. Mandatory guided tours, Wednesday–Saturday, 10:00 A.M. and 1:30 P.M. Advance reservations required. Open to groups by appointment only. Phone: (805) 969-3767. Admission: $6.00 per person in a vehicle carrying three or more persons; $8.00 per person in a vehicle carrying two persons; $10.00 per person in a vehicle carrying one person; $5.00 per bicycle.

MISSION LA PURISIMA CONCEPCION, Lompoc. Located at the northwest junction of Route 246 and Lompoc-Casmalia Road. Open daily, 10:00 A.M. (sometimes earlier)–5:00 P.M. Phone: (805) 733-3713. Admission: $5.00 per vehicle (up to nine persons)

MISSION SAN LUIS REY, San Luis Rey. Four miles northeast of Oceanside. Take Mission Avenue exit from I-5, go four miles, then turn north on San Luis Rey Road (Route 76). Open Monday–Saturday, 10:00 A.M.–4:00 P.M.; Sunday, noon–4:00 P.M. Phone: (619) 757-3651. Admission: $3.00, adults; $1.00, children.

RANCHO LOS ALAMITOS, Long Beach. 6400 East Bixby Hills Road. Enter through residential guard gate at corner of Palo Verde and Anaheim. Open Wednesday–Sunday, 1:00–5:00 P.M. Tours every half hour; the last one starts at 4 P.M. Phone: (310) 431-3541. Free admission.

RANCHO SANTA ANITA, LOS ANGELES COUNTY ARBORETUM, Arcadia. 301 North Baldwin Avenue. Open daily, except Christmas, 9:00 A.M.–4:30 P.M. Phone: (818) 821-3222. Admission: $5.00, adults; $3.50, senior citizens, students, and children 13–17; $1.00, children 5–12; children under 5, free.

RUDOLPH SCHINDLER HOUSE, Los Angeles. 835 North Kings Road. Open Saturday and Sunday, 1:00–4:00 P.M., and by appointment. Phone: (213) 651-1510. Admission: $5.00.

Biographies of Designers

THOMAS CHURCH
Born 1902, Boston, Massachusetts
Died 1978, San Francisco, California

Landscape architect. Studied landscape architecture at University of California, Berkeley, 1918–22, and Harvard University, 1924–26. Traveled in Italy and Spain after graduation, 1926. Opened a small office in connection with the Pasatiempo Golf Course and Country Club, Santa Cruz County, California, 1929. Moved to San Francisco, 1932; practiced in the same office until his death. Practice was largely residential, although he was a consultant on several university campuses. Worked closely with leading Bay Area architects, including William Wurster, Gardner Dailey, and Joseph Esherick. Published numerous articles in *California Arts and Architecture* and *House Beautiful,* 1930–early 1950s.

LOCKWOOD DE FOREST
Born 1896, New York, New York
Died 1949, Santa Barbara, California

Landscape architect and architect. Son of Lockwood de Forest, a prominent New York painter and art collector. Educated at Thacher School, Ojai, California. Studied at Williams College, Williamstown, Massachusetts, 1917, and University of California, Berkeley, 1919–20. Worked for Ralph Stevens, Santa Barbara, 1920. Opened his own practice in Santa Barbara, 1920; practiced there until his death, except for a brief period in the Bay Area during the mid-1930s. Married Elizabeth Kellam, who assisted him as a plant consultant, 1925. Practice was almost entirely residential.

GARRETT ECKBO
Born 1916, Cooperstown, New York
Lives in Berkeley, California

Landscape architect. Grew up in Alameda, California. B.L.A., University of California, Berkeley, 1932–36; M.L.A., Harvard University, 1936–38. With fellow students James Rose and Dan Kiley, initiated the "Harvard Revolution," a challenge to the Beaux-Arts system of educating landscape architects. Worked for the Farm Security Administration in San Francisco, 1939–43. Partner in Eckbo Williams, San Francisco, 1942–45; in

Eckbo, Royston, and Williams, 1945–58, Los Angeles; in Eckbo, Dean, and Williams, Los Angeles, 1958–64; in Eckbo, Dean, Austin, and Williams, San Francisco, 1964–73; in EDAW, San Francisco, 1973–76. In independent practice, 1976 to present. Author of many articles and books, including *Landscape for Living* (1950) and *Urban Landscape Design* (1964). Up to the early 1950s his firm's emphasis was largely residential; it then spread into public, commercial, and institutional projects.

LAWRENCE HALPRIN
Born 1916, New York, New York
Lives in Kentfield, California

Landscape architect and planner. B.S., plant sciences, Cornell University, 1939; M.S., plant sciences, University of Wisconsin, 1941; B.L.A., Harvard University, 1943. Worked for Thomas Church, 1945–49. Ran Lawrence Halprin and Associates, 1949–75. Partner in Roundhouse, San Francisco, 1975 to present. After the mid-1950s his firm's work was largely nonresidential. Wrote several books: *Cities* (1963, 1972); *The Freeway in the City* (1968); *RSVP Cycles: Creative Processes in the Human Environment* (1970); *Taking Part—A Workshop Approach to Collective Creativity* (1974).

EDWARD HUNTSMAN-TROUT
Born 1889, Tintern, Canada
Died 1974, West Los Angeles, California

Landscape architect. Born Edward Trout Huntsman. Adopted by an aunt and uncle following his mother's death; changed his name to Edward Huntsman-Trout. In Florida, 1903–7; moved to Hollywood, 1907. A child prodigy, studied science at the University of California, Berkeley, 1909. Studied landscape architecture at Harvard University, 1913–15, but did not graduate. Worked for Fletcher Steele in Boston, 1915–16, and A. D. Taylor in Cleveland, 1916–17 and 1919–20. Moved to Los Angeles, 1920. Worked for the Beverly Hills Nursery designing gardens for movie stars, 1920–22. Opened his own office in Hollywood, 1923, and in Beverly Hills, 1936. Practice was almost entirely residential. Most important project was the design of Scripps College, Pomona, with the architect Gordon Kaufmann.

BRUCE PORTER
Born 1865, Martinez, California
Died 1955, San Francisco, California

Painter, garden designer. Received no formal education; traveled in Europe at least six times. A member of Les Jeunes, a group of San Francisco artists greatly influenced by the Pre-Raphaelites, 1895–97. Primarily a painter, respected as arbiter of taste by many Bay Area architects—including Willis Polk and Arthur Brown—who employed him as a garden designer.

ROBERT ROYSTON
Born 1918, San Francisco, California
Lives in Mill Valley

Landscape architect. B.L.A., University of California, Berkeley, 1940. Worked for Thomas Church, San Francisco, 1940–41 and 1945–46. Partner in Eckbo, Royston, and Williams, San Francisco, 1946–58. In partnership variously with Asa Hanamoto, Eldon Beck, Edward Abey, and Kazno Alley, Mill Valley, 1958 to present. From 1945 until mid-1950s, practice was almost entirely residential; since then has been largely nonresidential, concentrating on public, commercial, and institutional projects. Taught at University of California, Berkeley, late 1940s and early 1960s.

PAUL THIENE
Born Germany
Died 1971, Pasadena, California

Landscape architect. Trained as a horticulturist in Germany; emigrated to the United States, 1898. Worked for Olmsted Brothers in Brookline, Massachusetts, 1898–1911. Sent by the firm with Lloyd Wright to establish nursery for the Panama-California Exposition, San Diego, 1910. When the Olmsted firm withdrew, he became consulting landscape architect. In partnership with Wright, Los Angeles, 1914–16; in practice in his own firm, 1916–29—responsible for planting and office management. Practice was entirely residential.

RUDOLF ULRICH
Born 1841, Weimar, Germany
Died 1906, New York, New York

Landscape gardener. Trained as gardener in Saxony, Italy, and England. Worked on Henry Probasco estate, near Cincinnati, 1867–72. Hired by Darius Ogden

Mills to design California estate, Millbrae, 1873. Worked on the Milton Lathom estate, 1874, and James Flood estate, 1876, both Menlo Park. In the 1880s designed the grounds of the three largest resort hotels in California: the Rafael Hotel in San Rafael, the Hotel del Monte in Monterey, and the Raymond Hotel in South Pasadena. Originated the concept of the "Arizona garden," a collection of desert plants. At the Columbia World's Exposition in Chicago, 1893, supervised the planting of the grounds.

LLOYD WRIGHT
Born 1890, Oak Park, Illinois
Died 1976, Los Angeles

Architect and landscape architect, eldest son of Frank Lloyd Wright. Attended University of Wisconsin, 1907–9. Traveled with his father in Europe, 1909–10. Apprenticed to Olmsted Brothers in Brookline, Massachusetts, 1910–11. Sent by Olmsted brothers with Paul Thiene to establish nursery for the Panama-California Exposition, San Diego, 1910. Worked for Irving Gill, San Diego, 1912–15. In partnership with Thiene, Los Angeles, 1914–16. Worked for the architect William Dodd, Los Angeles, 1916. Worked for Paramount Studios, Hollywood, 1916–17. Landscape architect for his father's California projects, 1920–27. In independent practice, 1927 until his death. Designed several visionary and unexecuted civic schemes.

FLORENCE YOCH
Born 1890, Santa Ana, California
Died 1972, Carmel, California

Landscape architect. Studied at University of California, Berkeley, 1910; Cornell University, 1912; and University of Illinois, where she graduated in 1915. In private practice, 1915 until her death; in partnership with Lucille Council, 1925–64. Yoch was the principal designer; Council ran the office and did much of the planting design. Practice was entirely residential, for clients in the affluent suburbs of the Los Angeles Basin and in Santa Barbara and Montecito—with the notable exception of their work on the California Institute of Technology campus in Pasadena and a garden at Bullocks, Beverly Hills. Until mid-1930s their work was noted for its historicist character; by late 1940s Yoch was designing more modernist work.

Selected Bibliography

BOOKS AND EXHIBITION CATALOGS

Andree, Herb, and Noel Young. *Santa Barbara Architecture*. Santa Barbara, Calif.: Capra Press, 1980.

Angier, Belle Sumner. *The Garden Book of California*. San Francisco: Paul Elder and Co., 1906.

Baer, Kurt J. *Architecture of the California Missions*. Berkeley: University of California Press, 1950.

Bakker, Elna. *An Island Called California: An Ecological Introduction to Its Natural Communities*. Berkeley, Calif.: University of California Press, 1971.

Bissell, Ervanna Bowen. *Glimpses of Santa Barbara and Montecito Gardens*. Santa Barbara, Calif.: Schauer Printing, 1926.

Braunton, Ernest. *The Garden Beautiful in California*. Los Angeles: Times-Mirror Press, 1946.

Butterfield, H. M. *Home Floriculture in California*. California Agricultural Extension Circular No. 53. Berkeley: University of California, The College of Agriculture, 1931, 1937.

Byne, Arthur, and Mildred Stapley Byne. *Spanish Gardens and Patios*. Philadelphia: J. B. Lippincott, 1928.

Church, Thomas D. *Gardens Are for People*. New York: Reinhold Publishing Corp., 1955.

————. *Your Private World: A Study of Intimate Gardens*. San Francisco: Chronicle Books, 1969.

Clark, Alson, ed. *Myron Hunt, 1868–1952: The Search for a Regional Architecture*. Los Angeles: Hennessey and Ingalls, 1984.

Cran, Marion. *Gardens in America*. London: Herbert Jenkins, 1931.

Dobyns, Winifred Starr. *California Gardens*. New York: Macmillan, 1931.

Duffield, Mary Rose, and Warren D. Jones. *Plants for Dry Climates: How to Select, Grow and Enjoy*. Tucson, Ariz.: H. P. Books, 1981.

Eckbo, Garrett. *Landscape for Living*. New York: Architectural Record with Duell, Sloan and Pearce, 1950.

Eyre, Florence Atherton. *Reminiscences of Peninsula Gardens from 1860–1890*. San Francisco: San Francisco Garden Club, 1933.

Farallones Institute. *The Integral Urban House: Self-Reliant Living in the City*. San Francisco: Sierra Club, 1978.

Freudenheim, Leslie Mandelson, and Elizabeth Sacks Sussman. *Building with Nature: Roots of the San Francisco Bay Region Tradition*. Santa Barbara, Calif., and Salt Lake City: Peregrine Smith, 1974.

Garnett, Porter. *Stately Homes of California*. Boston: Little, Brown and Company, 1915.

Garrett Eckbo: Philosophy of Landscape. Process Architecture 90. Tokyo: Process Architecture Publishing Co., 1990.

Gebhard, David. *George Washington Smith, 1876–1930*. Santa Barbara: University of California, 1964.

————. *Lloyd Wright, Architect: 20th-Century Architecture in an Organic Exhibition*. Santa Barbara: University of California, Art Galleries, 1971.

————. "The Design of the Landscape in the Work of Reginald D. Johnson, Gordon B. Kaufmann, and Roland F. Coate." In *Johnson, Kaufmann, Coate: Partners in the California Style*. Edited by Jay Belloli et al. Santa Barbara, Calif.: Capra Press, 1992.

Griswold, Mac, and Eleanor Weller. *The Golden Age of American Gardens: Proud Owners, Private Estates, 1890–1940*. New York: Harry N. Abrams, 1991.

Halprin, Lawrence. *Lawrence Halprin: Changing Places*. San Francisco: San Francisco Museum of Modern Art, 1986.

Hanson, A. E. *An Arcadian Landscape: The California Gardens of A. E. Hanson, 1920–1932*. Edited by David Gebhard and Sheila Lynds. Los Angeles: Hennessey and Ingalls, 1985.

Hertrich, William. *The Huntington Botanical Gardens, 1905–1949*. San Marino, Calif.: Huntington Library, 1949.

Hines, Thomas S. *Richard Neutra and the Search for Modern Architecture*. New York and Oxford: Oxford University Press, 1982.

Hockaday, Joan. *The Gardens of San Francisco*. Portland, Oreg.: Timber Press, 1988.

Jackson, Helen Hunt. *Ramona*. Boston: Roberts Brothers, 1884.

Lawrence Halprin. Process Architecture 4. Tokyo: Process Architecture Publishing Co., 1978.

Lockwood, Charles. *The Estates of Beverly Hills*. Beverly Hills, Calif.: Margrant Publishing Co., 1984.

Longstreth, Richard. *On the Edge of the World: Four Architects in San Francisco at the Turn of the Century*. New York and Boston: Architectural History Foundation and MIT Press, 1983.

McLaren, John. *Gardening in California*. San Francisco: A. M. Robertson, 1908, 2d ed. 1927.

MacPhail, Elizabeth C. *Kate Sessions, Pioneer Horticulturist*. San Diego: San Diego Horticultural Society, 1976.

McWilliams, Carey. *Southern California Country: An Island on the Land*. Salt Lake City: Peregrine Smith Books, 1946; reprint 1983.

Mathias, Mildred E., ed. *Flowering Plants in the Landscape*. Berkeley and Los Angeles: University of California Press, 1982.

Mitchell, Sydney B. *Your California Garden and Mine*. New York: M. Barrows and Company, 1947.

Moulin, Gabriel. *Gabriel Moulin's San Francisco Peninsula: Town and Country Houses, 1910–1930*. Compiled by Donald DeNevis and Thomas Moulin. Sausalito, Calif.: Windgate Press, 1985.

Myrick, David F. *Montecito and Santa Barbara*. Vol. I: *From Farms to Estates*. Vol. II: *The Days of the Great Estates*. Glendale, Calif.: Trans-Anglo Books, 1988 and 1991.

Newcomb, Rexford. *Old Mission Churches and Historic Houses of California*. London: J. B. Lippincott Co., 1925.

———. *The Spanish House for America*. Philadelphia: J. B. Lippincott Co., 1927.

Nordhoff, Charles. *California for Health, Pleasure and Residence: A Book for Travellers and Settlers*. New York: Harper and Brothers, 1882.

Padilla, Victoria. *Southern California Gardens: An Illustrated History*. Berkeley and Los Angeles: University of California Press, 1961.

Perry, Bob. *Trees and Shrubs for Dry California Landscapes: Plants for Water Conservation*. San Dimas, Calif.: Land Design Publishing, 1981.

Rowntree, Lester. *Hardy Californians*. New York: Macmillan Co., 1936.

Saunders, Charles Francis. *With the Flowers and Trees in California*. New York: McBride, Nast and Company, 1914.

———. *Trees and Shrubs of California Gardens*. New York: Robert M. McBride and Company, 1926.

Schmidt, Marjorie. *Growing California Plants*. Berkeley, Los Angeles, and London: University of California Press, 1980.

Shinn, Charles H. *The Pacific Rural Handbook*. San Francisco: Dewey and Co., 1879.

Smith, Elizabeth A. T., ed. *Blueprints for Modern Living: History and Legacy of the Case Study Homes*. Los Angeles: Museum of Contemporary Art; Cambridge, Mass., and London: MIT Press, 1989.

Smith, Kathryn. *Frank Lloyd Wright, Hollyhock House and Olive Hill: Buildings and Projects for Aline Barnsdall*. New York: Rizzoli, 1992.

Starr, Kevin. *Americans and the California Dream, 1850–1915*. New York: Oxford University Press, 1973.

————. *Inventing the Dream: California Through the Progressive Era*. New York: Oxford University Press, 1985.

————. *Material Dreams: Southern California Through the 1920s*. New York: Oxford University Press, 1990.

Streatfield, David C. "Thomas Church and the California Garden, 1929–1950." In *Festschrift: A Collection of Essays on Architectural History Prepared by the Northern Pacific Coast Chapter, Society of Architectural Historians: Dedicated to Professor Marion Dean Ross, Chapter Founder, on the Occasion of His Sixty-fifth Birthday*. Salem, Oreg.: Northern Pacific Coast Chapter, Society of Architectural Historians, 1978.

Truman, Ben C. *Semi-Tropical California: Its Climate, Healthfulness, Productivity and Scenery*. San Francisco: A. L. Bancroft and Co., 1874.

Weisskamp, Herbert. *Beautiful Homes and Gardens in California*. New York: Harry N. Abrams, 1965.

Wickson, Edward J. *California Garden Flowers*. San Francisco: Pacific Rural Press, 1926.

Winslow, Carleton M., Jr., and Nicola L. Frye. *The Enchanted Hill: The Story of Hearst Castle at San Simeon*. Millbrae, Calif.: Celestial Arts, 1980.

Yoch, James J. *Landscaping the American Dream: The Gardens and Film Sets of Florence Yoch: 1890–1972*. New York: Harry N. Abrams; Millwood, N.Y.: Sagapress, 1989.

ARTICLES AND MASTER'S THESES

Adams, Charles Gibbs. "Gardens of the Spanish Days." *Annual Publications* (Historical Society of Southern California) 15 (1932): 347–55.

Arbegast, Mai K. "Shrubs of Filoli." *Pacific Horticulture* 37 (July 1976): 15–22.

Bakker, Elna. "No Gazanias." *Pacific Horticulture* 51 (Spring 1990): 3–6.

Beatty, Russell A. "An Island in Time." *Pacific Horticulture* 50 (Summer 1989): 61–70.

Blair, William Paul. "Francis Townsend Underhill." *Pacific Horticulture* 51 (Summer 1991): 7–12.

Boyd, John Taylor, Jr. "Houses Showing a Distinguished Simplicity." *Arts and Decoration* 33 (October 1930): 57–60, 112.

Brown, Tom. "Gardens of the California Missions." *Pacific Horticulture* 49 (Spring 1988): 3–11.

Butler, Frances. "Two Poetry Gardens: Giving Voice to the Genius Loci." *Places* 1 (Summer 1984): 68–75.

Croly, Herbert. "Houses by Myron Hunt and Elmer Grey." *Architectural Record* 25 (April 1909): 531–55.

Darnall, Margaretta J. "The Carolans: An Unfinished Garden." *Pacific Horticulture* 49 (Summer 1988): 7–11.

————. "Garden Worthy of Contemplation." *Pacific Horticulture* 51 (Fall 1990): 47–51.

de Forest, Elizabeth. "Old Santa Barbara Gardens and How They Came to Be." *Pacific Horticulture* 38 (Winter 1977–78): 31–36.

Duhaut-Cilly, Captain. "Duhaut-Cilly's Account of California in the Years 1827–8." *California Historical Society Quarterly* 8 (June, September 1929): 131–66, 215–50, 306–36.

Eckbo, Garrett. "Sculpture and Landscape Design." *Magazine of Art* 31 (April 1938): 202–8, 250.

Engstrand, Iris Wilson, and Thomas L. Scharf. "Rancho Guajome: A California Legacy Preserved." *Journal of San Diego History* 20 (Winter 1974): 1–14.

Frey, Woody. "Making the Gardens at San Simeon." *Pacific Horticulture* 39 (Fall 1978): 39–44.

Gebhard, David. "The Spanish Colonial Revival in Southern California, 1895–1930." *Journal of the Society of Architectural Historians* 26 (May 1967): 131–47.

Gill, Irving. "An Architecture in a New Land." *Craftsman* 22 (August 1912): 465–73.

Goodhue, Bertram G. "'El Fureidis' at Montecito, California: The Villa of James Waldron Gillespie." *House and Garden* (September 1903): 97–100.

Gross, Susan Jane. "The Gardens of Edward Huntsman-Trout." Master of Landscape Architecture thesis, California State Polytechnic University, Pomona, 1976.

Hall, George D. "The Estate of W. L. Dodge, Hollywood." *Architect and Engineer* 61 (April 1920): 87–90.

Hawley, Henry. "An Italianate Garden by Greene and Greene." *Journal of Decorative and Propaganda Arts* 2 (Summer–Fall 1986): 32–45.

Howard, John Galen. "Country House Architecture on the Pacific Coast." *Architectural Record* 40 (October 1916): 322–55.

Lyle, John Tillman. "Can Floating Seeds Make Deep Forms?" *Landscape Journal* 10 (Spring 1991): 37–47.

Messenger, Pam-Anela. "El Novillero Revisited." *Pacific Horticulture* 43 (Summer 1982): 23–29.

Montgomery, William. "Studies in Southern California Landscape History Applied to the Development of Rancho Los Cerritos." Master of Landscape Architec-ture thesis, California State Polytechnic University, Pomona, 1975.

Peters, William F. "Lockwood de Forest, Landscape Architect, Santa Barbara, California, 1869–1949." Master of Landscape Architecture thesis, University of California, Berkeley, 1971.

Robinson, Alfred D. "The Fitness of Things." *California Garden* 4 (April 1913): 4.

Simo, Melanie. "The Education of a Modern Landscape Designer." *Pacific Horticulture* 49 (Summer 1988): 19–30.

Streatfield, David C. "The Evolution of the California Landscape," parts 1–4, *Landscape Architecture* 130: "Settling into Arcadia," January 1976, pp. 39–46; "Arcadia Compromised," March 1976, pp. 117–26; "The Great Promotions," May 1977, pp. 229–49; "Suburbia at the Zenith," September 1977, pp. 417–24.

———. "Echoes of England and Italy 'On the Edge of the World': Green Gables and Charles Greene." *Journal of Garden History* 2 (October–December 1982): 377–98.

———. "Paradise on the Frontier: Victorian Gardens on the San Francisco Peninsula." *Garden History* 12 (Spring 1984): 158–80.

———. "Where Pine and Palm Meet: The California Garden as a Regional Expression." *Landscape Journal* 4 (Fall 1985): 61–72.

———. "The Garden at Casa del Herrero." *Antiques* 130 (August 1986): 287–88.

Thorne, Helen. "When an Easterner Gardens in the Golden West." *Garden Magazine* 21 (April 1921): 178–80.

Waters, George. "Lotusland." *Pacific Horticulture* 44 (Spring 1983): 20–25.

Acknowledgments

The research on which this book is based has been conducted over several years and owes much to the generosity of many institutions and individuals.

I have enjoyed the resources and professional services of the Huntington Library, San Marino; the Bancroft Library and the Documents Collection of the College of Environmental Design of the University of California, Berkeley; the San Francisco Public Library; the libraries of the California Historical Society, in San Francisco and Los Angeles; the library of the San Mateo County Historical Association; the library of the Santa Barbara Historical Society; the Architectural Drawings Collection of the University of California, Santa Barbara; the Special Collections Library of the University of California, Los Angeles; the Smiley Library, Redlands; the Los Angeles Public Library; and the library of the San Diego Historical Society. In each of these institutions I have benefited from the highest levels of librarianship.

My research was partially funded by a number of institutions. I wish to thank the Beatrix Farrand Fellowship program of the Department of Landscape Architecture, University of California, Berkeley; the National Endowment for the Arts; and the Department of Landscape Architecture, University of Washington. In recent years I have received generous encouragement from Sally Schauman by her reducing my teaching load.

Many landscape architects agreed to be interviewed and shared with me recollections of their own practices and of colleagues. I wish to acknowledge the generous help given by the late Thomas D. Church, the late Ralph D. Cornell, Francis Dean, the late Elizabeth de Forest, Garrett Eckbo, the late A. E. Hanson, the late Edward Huntsman-Trout, the late A. E. Kuehl, Thornton Ladd, the late Lutah Maria Riggs, Robert Royston, the late Geraldine Knight Scott, and Ruth Shellhorn.

Several owners provided valuable information and insights that otherwise would have vanished. Mrs. John Bacon, Sr.; the late Ruth, Lady Crocker; the late George Cukor; Mr. and Mrs. C. E. Davis; Harriet Doerr; the late Janet Fleishhacker; the late Katherine Bixby Hotchkis; the late Beatrice Huntsman-Trout; Daniel James; Gipsy Johnson; and Mrs. Russell Keil, Sr.

Many friends generously shared research or steered me toward new sources and ideas. I am much indebted to Russell Beatty, Janet Brown Becker, Robert M. Fletcher, Carol Greentree, David Gebhard, Mac Griswold, Vincent Healy, Jr., Michael Laurie, Richard Longstreth, Randall M. Mackinson, Vonn-Marie May, Pamela Seager, Eleanor Weller, Sally Woodbridge, and Pamela Young. Several friends also cheerfully provided a comfortable place to stay: Sydney Baumgartner, Robert M. Fletcher, John Furtado, the late Beatrice Huntsman-Trout, Edward and the late Anne Janelli, Vonn-Marie May, Thomas J. Ingmire, Bobbi and Tito Patri, Priscilla Thomas, and Bruce and Nola Sharky.

Linda Gorremans, Sandra Strieby, Vicky Witherspoon, and Maria Morris struggled valiantly with my indecipherable scrawls and typed numerous versions of the manuscript. Nancy Grubb provided impeccable editing, Margot Clark-Junkins was a resourceful picture editor, and Joel Avirom created a handsome design.

My greatest indebtedness is to Madeleine Wilde, who always provided support and encouragement when it was most needed.

Index

Photography Credits

The photographers and the sources of photographic material other than those indicated in the captions are as follows (numerals refer to pages):

In memory of my mother and father,
who fostered my interest in gardens.

෩──෨

Front cover: Lockwood de Forest garden, Santa Barbara, 1926.
Designed by de Forest for himself. Photo: Saxon Holt, 1988
Back cover: Willis Ward garden, Montecito, 1916. Designed by
Francis T. Underhill. Photo: Saxon Holt, 1993
Frontispiece: La Toscana, Montecito, 1929. Garden designed by
A. E. Hanson for Kirk Johnson. Photo: David C. Streatfield, 1969

EDITOR: NANCY GRUBB
DESIGNER: JOEL AVIROM
PRODUCTION EDITOR: OWEN DUGAN
PICTURE EDITOR: MARGOT CLARK-JUNKINS
PRODUCTION MANAGER: SIMONE RENÉ

First edition

Library of Congress Cataloging-in-Publication Data

Streatfield, David C.
    California Gardens: Creating a New Eden / David C.
Streatfield.
        p.   cm.
    Includes bibliographical references (p.   ) and index.
    ISBN 1-55859-453-1
    1. Gardens—California—History. 2. Gardens—
California—Pictorial works. I. Title.
SB466.U65C295   1994
712'.09794—dc20   93-37162